Futureproof City

The *Futureproof City* creates adaptability and resiliency in the face of the unknown challenges resulting from technological change, population explosion, global pandemic, and environmental crisis. A paradigm shift is urgently required in the means of conceiving, delivering, and managing city development to create better places to live. This book brings to the fore many new solutions currently being proposed and piloted globally, identifying ten key areas affecting the physical fabric of our cities where governments, planners, investors, and the individuals responsible for shaping lives can refocus their understanding, priorities, and funding in order to more effectively utilise the limited financial, natural, and time resources available. It will be key reading for every policy maker and professional working in sustainability, development, technology, health and welfare, investment, and risk issues in cities today.

Barry D. Wilson was born in London and has lived and worked across four continents in a career spanning over 30 years as a multi-skilled, design and construction professional and mediator. He received award from the China International Urbanization Development Strategy Research Committee for his contribution to China's urbanisation transformation in 2012 and was awarded the Reed Mallik Medal from the Institution of Civil Engineers in 2019. He is a Fellow of both the Hong Kong Institutes of Urban Design and Landscape Architecture and is Adjunct Assistant Professor at the Faculty of Architecture, University of Hong Kong.

Futureproof City

Ten Immediate Paths to Urban Resilience

BARRY D. WILSON

NEW YORK AND LONDON

First published 2022
by Routledge
605 Third Avenue, New York, NY 10158

and by Routledge
2 Park Square, Milton Park, Abingdon, Oxon, OX14 4RN

Routledge is an imprint of the Taylor & Francis Group, an informa business

© 2022 Barry D. Wilson

The right of Barry D. Wilson to be identified as author of this work has been asserted by him in accordance with sections 77 and 78 of the Copyright, Designs and Patents Act 1988.

All rights reserved. No part of this book may be reprinted or reproduced or utilised in any form or by any electronic, mechanical, or other means, now known or hereafter invented, including photocopying and recording, or in any information storage or retrieval system, without permission in writing from the publishers.

Trademark notice: Product or corporate names may be trademarks or registered trademarks, and are used only for identification and explanation without intent to infringe.

Library of Congress Cataloging-in-Publication Data
Names: Wilson, Barry D., author.
Title: Futureproof city : ten immediate paths to urban resilience / Barry D. Wilson.
Description: New York, NY : Routledge, 2022. | Includes bibliographical references and index.
Identifiers: LCCN 2021012254 (print) | LCCN 2021012255 (ebook) | ISBN 9780367631963 (hardback) | ISBN 9780367631956 (paperback) | ISBN 9781003112488 (ebook)
Subjects: LCSH: Sustainable urban development. | City planning—Environmental aspects. | Urban policy.
Classification: LCC HT241 .W55 2022 (print) | LCC HT241 (ebook) | DDC 307.1/416—dc23
LC record available at https://lccn.loc.gov/2021012254
LC ebook record available at https://lccn.loc.gov/2021012255

ISBN: 978-0-367-63196-3 (hbk)
ISBN: 978-0-367-63195-6 (pbk)
ISBN: 978-1-003-11248-8 (ebk)

DOI: 10.4324/9781003112488

Typeset in Dente and Avenir
by Apex CoVantage, LLC

Contents

Preface vii

Introduction: A Clarion Call: The Urgent Case for Doing Things Differently 1

1 Putting Wellness First: Re-evaluating Human Priorities in the Context of Health and Happiness 13

2 Reconsider, Rethink, Redirect: Envisioning and Collaborating to Plan Resilient Living Places 29

3 Right Development in the Right Place: Mitigating the Challenges of Climate Impact through Land Management 49

4 Frames of Blue and Green: Adopting Green and Blue Infrastructure as the Fundamental Network to Plan Cities 65

5 Placing for Age: Adapting Urban Development for Diversity and Inclusivity 83

6 Think Fast, Think Smart: Incorporating Opportunities in the Digital Revolution 101

7 Empowering the Future: Transitioning to the Stored Energy Economy 121

Contents

8 Unleashing Urban Potential: Repurposing Streets to People's Needs — 139

9 Prosperity through Density: Accommodating Burgeoning Urban Populations — 163

10 Both Safe and Dependable: Providing New Means to Quality Shelter for All — 183

Conclusion: Towards a New Mindset: Meeting the Needs of the Coming Urban Revolution — 205

Index — 231

Preface

Our cities and lifestyles have been shaped by what's gone before. In the midst of what is now a climate emergency, as the impossible must become possible, we urgently need to relinquish outdated "planning-as-usual models", envision the world in which we want to live, and then urgently take step to change it and shape it for the better. Time is against us.

> *I am looking out of the window of my home. What do I see? Not so much in the distance since the air is thick with smog. Down on the street someone has thrown their trash into the small stream. It smells a bit and there are no fish, it's a dead river, so people continue dumping their waste. I can see a rusty old shopping trolley just emerging from the blackness. Some of my neighbours grow vegetables on the river bank, but I wonder whether they are safe to eat. I don't trust the tap water.*

This is a memory I have. It's of growing up in the UK in the 1970s. Frequently I get asked to say what it is like overseas, is it better there, how do they solve things? How can we make our cities in China like those overseas? I remember that we had dirty streets, polluted rivers, acid rain and choking chimneys, accidents were common. We had all the same problems 40 years ago as we have today in China. I remember all the old, industrial buildings where we used to play, being demolished, whole city centres being torn up under the planner's hand, those tight, twisting streets of ancient memories disappearing forever and being replaced with huge, modern, impersonal, blocks of car parking, barriers and highways. Longstanding, friendly communities were torn apart and scattered far out of town; all in the name of supposed progress.

We all want to live in a greener, cleaner, safer world. I think this is a common vision. It's a vision shared in the United Nations Sustainable Development goals. It's a vision generally held by your governments, by your colleagues, by you. We want to live and work in cities that puts health and wellness first. In lively, safe environments, in caring communities, where stress is minimised. What might those cities look like? Would they have cars clogging the streets? Could you walk your kids safely? Are you able to see into the distance from your window? Do you know your neighbours? Can you drink clean water straight from the tap? Might the buildings create energy rather than consuming it? Are there green streets, clean streets, clean air, soil, and water?

Back in 1973 I remember planting a tree with all my school friends. There was a national promotion "plant a tree in '73". Then we got to "plant one more in '74". It was the start of a new awareness for me. I remember litter bins arriving everywhere, plus the signs reminding us of fines for littering. I remember school education programmes telling us:

> *Don't dump rubbish in rivers and streams.*
> *Don't throw garbage on the streets for someone else to pick up.*
> *Don't smoke cigarettes which foul the air and harm others.*

Education was the key to a new generation of thinking about the environment we wanted to live in. Change in behaviour was essential. Slowly the rivers cleaned up; the fish came back. Slowly the trees were planted; the birds and wildlife came back. Slowly buildings smelt clean and old industry was replaced; the sky came back. Slowly old buildings were saved and transformed to new uses, communities reinvigorated, and new jobs created. Lots of these problems seemed insurmountable at the time, but they were surmounted. Today we have new and bigger problems than ever in maintaining the huge and ageing populations moving into cities through urbanisation. We have the ever-increasing risk of major and repeated catastrophes caused by climate change. We have the loss of cultural heritage and diversity from globalisation. We have environmental degradation from developing in the wrong place.

On top of all this, the rapid pace of change in our lives makes us busier than ever and it becomes overwhelming just trying to keep up. Technology, business, and social structures are rapidly evolving to meet new challenges. But people generally don't like change, it upsets them and they resist it. Typically, we have used past examples, regardless of good or bad to plan future development. In China, we have repeatedly looked overseas for ideas and blindly replicated them. Today this appears to be an unacceptable solution for a rapidly changing world. We are already at the very forefront of change right here, today, in China and we need to plan and design by anticipating tomorrow's world. By expecting the unexpected. By envisioning our own futures. A few years ago, I had no idea I was going to be regularly collecting a shared bike from the street to go to work, or calling a car share on my mobile phone, or even owning a mobile phone. I can now, however, manage to foresee soon that when I call a vehicle it will arrive without a driver. But will it be a car or will it be a drone that arrives? Will I need to travel by road or can I fly? Will I have to use my cellphone to call or could I just "think it" to arrive?

Most of the material for this book originally developed as a part of just having to try to keep informed with the myriad of changes affecting my professional work during these momentous times. I have been collecting the information and sharing it as regular essays and columns over the last few years; however, in putting it together for this book, which is a much more detailed update of the award-winning article published by the Institution of Civil Engineers in 2018, I found that the world had changed even faster than even I had predicted, in part through COVID-19, so that it needed completely new, up-to-the-moment research. In doing so, I have tried to keep it as accessible as possible to all and sundry; it is not intended to go deep into any one area, and as a result I hope that a little understanding of many complex things will aid many of those who need a better overview and perspective in order to make more informed work and life decisions, enable better communication and collaboration, and ultimately assist those who shape our lives in one form or another each day. The examples shared are global and are benchmarks in their setting, yet they all set out to include new ways of thinking and require behavioural change. They also include suspending existing costly and wasteful planning and development practices, and anticipating new lifestyles based on three key areas close to my heart: future transport and technology needs; minimised environmental, social, and cultural impact; and reducing disaster risk.

Thanks go to all those who helped shape the ideas fomenting over the years and to those directly mentioned in these pages. Especial gratitude to my young daughter for the inspiring graphics introducing the Ten Immediate Paths to Urban Resilience.

Barry Wilson
December 2020

I'm Looking out of the I'm looking out of the window of my home. It used to be an old factory but has been charmingly converted into a mixed use development, including affordable housing, elderly accommodation and primary healthcare facilities where the staff check on the residents both remotely, using IT, as well as with personal visits. The kindergarden, primary school and converted "loft space" attract lots of young couples and it's very friendly with lots of community managed activities where I meet others living and working here in the business incubator where I run my new "city planning" start up, so I don't have to travel to work every day. Outside of the window I am surrounded by trees and see a stream with ducks flapping happily. I can see far into the distance and the sky is bright blue. There are no roads and I see people arriving to their work at the rooftop aerial taxi station and others on the ground in electric pods, slowly mingling with bikes and pedestrians on their way from the metro station. There is a "ring ring" and an image of my daughter pops up as a hologram in front of me. She tells me it's a beautiful day outside and suggests I join her at our local community farm on the roof, where we can do some gardening and then eat our own-grown vegetables together at the canteen for lunch.

What kind of future do you want to build for your children?

This article was first printed in the
South China Morning Post on 14 July 2017.

Introduction: A Clarion Call
The Urgent Case for Doing Things Differently

There is both scientific basis and social expediency in making urgent and wholesale global changes in the way humanity conducts itself. Having entered the Anthropocene epoch and experienced the immediate impacts of the Fourth Industrial Revolution, population explosion, mass urbanisation, global pandemic, uncontrollable pollution, ecosystem collapse and climate emergency, the world is at a tipping point and yet national governments are seemingly unable to adequately address the difficult challenges and make collective decisions at the scales and speeds required. A "great reset" is, however, necessarily arriving, yet it will be led by the cities rather than nation states, through their ability to react faster, adapt more efficiently, and communicate more closely with their citizens to address their changing needs. Cities that take urgent and radical action, embracing significant adaptation as essential in addressing their longer-term future through building more balanced, resilient, and human-centric environments, will become global leaders in a near and different future, whilst others will delay at their peril.

2 Introduction: A Clarion Call

> *"Consequences are unpitying. Our deeds carry their terrible consequences, quite apart from any fluctuations that went before – consequences that are hardly ever confined to ourselves."*
>
> George Eliot, *Adam Bede*, 1859

A Normal World?

It's easy to consider life before the global COVID-19 pandemic of 2020 as being "normal". It was not normal, it was already seriously changed, and so completely changed that scientists had already given it a new name. We were now living in a new "Epoch", a new geological time period: the Anthropocene. There is no agreed date for the start of this "new normal"; some scholars, like William Ruddiman, mark it as change over several thousands of years since humans first started settling the earth and cultivating land and animals (Ruddiman, 2003). Another widely held view relates to a threshold of the "Great Acceleration" brought about from the mid-twentieth century onwards with the onset of the atomic age, the widespread use of industrial and agricultural chemicals, and rapid population growth. Whatever the date, the coming of the Anthropocene is marked by the substantial human impact on land use, ecosystems, biodiversity, and species extinction. Since 1950 alone, algal biomass decreased by around 40%, probably in response to ocean warming (Boyce et al., 2010), whilst since the dawn of human civilisation, 83% of wild mammals have disappeared (Bar-On et al., 2018). Of course, one of the main indicators of physical change has been the increase of atmospheric carbon dioxide, leading in turn to greater heat absorption and the current climate emergency. The global average atmospheric carbon dioxide levels in 2019 were higher than at any point in at least the past 800,000 years whilst average temperatures have increased 1.4°F since just the early twentieth century, with the 20 warmest years all occurring since 1981 and the ten warmest of those all since 2008 (Lindsey, 2020). Mean sea level has been rapidly rising over the past 100 years, yet the rate has doubled since 1993, due to thermal expansion caused by increased heating. The sudden melting of glaciers and ice sheets has not even started to impact those levels yet, but is about to make a significant contribution, whilst the number and intensity of extreme climate events have been rising over the last four decades (US, NCDC, 2020).

Not only has the physical environment been rapidly changing, but the last century also saw the coming of the age of digital innovation, which has hurtled us into the Fourth Industrial Revolution, involving "a convergence of technologies and disciplines, nonlinearity, and a re-emergence of digital into material and physical domains", according to Thomas Philbeck, Global Leadership Fellow at the World Economic Forum (NASEM, 2017). There is, however, no historical precedent for the speed of current breakthroughs. Less than 1% of the world's technologically stored information was digital in the late 1980s, but that figure surpassed 99% by 2012 and at the current rate, humanity is able to double the information storage capacity of civilisation every two to three years (*Encyclopedia Britannica*, 2019). Technological evolution is therefore currently at an exponential rather than a linear pace and is disrupting almost every industry in every country around the world, where the breadth and depth of these changes is heralding the transformation of entire systems of production, management, and governance. It's important to stress that "almost" every industry is being disrupted. The construction industry has been notoriously poor at modernising, slow to introduce new technology in both construction and management processes, and demonstrates some of the lowest productivity rates globally. Since 1995, the global average value-added per hour has grown at around a quarter of the rate of manufacturing. France and Italy have seen a reduction in productivity by 17%, Germany and Japan are flat, while the US has experienced a 50% plunge since the late 1960s. The construction industry employs about 7% of the world's working-age population and represents about 13% of global gross domestic product (GDP), making it one of the global economy's largest sectors. No sector has performed worse economically (Barbosa et al., 2017). According to MGI's Digitization Index, construction is among the least-digitised sectors in the world, where the US comes second to last and Europe is in last position (Manyika et al., 2015). In the UK, the independent "Farmer Review of the UK Construction Model – Modernise or Die" highlighted that "well understood, long standing and deep-seated problems" have existed for many years in the construction industry, and yet even in this age of global transformation, the industry continued to avoid taking measures to address the issues and modernise by using more efficient and faster ways of building (Farmer, 2016). The Review points out a long list of reasons why the industry has not upgraded; however, the overall diagnosis reports a reactionary culture trying to survive with low capital reserves, non-aligned interests, a deep-seated resistance to change, and no incentives to try to do so. Director Percy Chang of the leading Asian contractor Gammon Construction suggests the industry is held back by the inefficiencies of scale thwarting a common vision, where clear leadership and a lack of standardisation and integration is missing across the board (Chang, 2020). If the construction industry has not been able to modernise through the past "slow" years, how will it possibly cope in the new age of innovation?

The Inevitability of Change

The way in which our cities have been planned, shaped, and constructed has continued to remain based upon longstanding and outmoded principles. Cities, and those that envision them, have in the past been reticent to respond to the massive shifts required because the way in which the built environment takes shape requires time to plan, finance, and construct, whilst humanity itself is in general resistant to change. Yet history tells us that change is inevitable and it's how we react to change that defines events, leaders, and nations. We see this currently with climate change, population explosion, and urbanisation. We are witnessing one of the most dramatic periods of change in world history and are facing some of the most important decisions ever to be taken. Scientists and reputable advisory bodies have long identified the problems, most appropriate solutions, and ways to move forward as being quite clear-cut, and yet they are rarely followed, particularly in the short term. Changes seem only acceptable in small incremental steps that allow time for people and markets to adjust. Why should that be?

Rosabeth Moss Kanter of the Harvard Business School suggests ten reasons why people resist change, which include loss of control, uncertainty about possible surprises, insecurity through change, and the potential for unknown ripple effects (Kanter, 2012). So change takes time, and gaining consensus to make changes holds us back from progress. As the traditional African proverb goes: "He who wants to go quickly goes alone. He who wants to go far goes together."

Without extensive and accessible digital databases, research, mapping, and surveying remain lengthy processes, as is the planning process itself, building community consensus, and undertaking mandates for action. These processes all require complete transformation in the way they are undertaken, using the opportunities of the digital revolution to utterly transform the industry. The standard models of development remain linear, using case studies and past metrics to anticipate and reproduce future expectations. Plan-making is particularly slow, cumbersome, bureaucratic, and expensive (HM Government, 2017). In today's fast-changing world, by the time a project is initiated, it can already be out of date.

It's increasingly clear that with the massive disruption and exponential changes now manifest, planning by numbers is a redundant model that is applying vast public resources in the wrong places. The sustainable economy is fundamentally changing the ways of life, work, and interrelations, but requires iterative rather than linear systems of change based on vision, communication, adaptability, and integration. Akin to businesses, city shapers need to be placing far more emphasis on anticipating the potentials of a future marketplace and working out how to get there rather than extrapolating past results as indicative of accommodating growth. Adjusting the planning dimension of cities to meet the needs of an unknown but somewhat foreseeable future is necessary, whilst also starting to make changes in preparedness by providing shock absorbers against surprising eventualities that will always arise. Planning processes need to rapidly adapt to allow more flexibility and continually re-align development thinking to meet this unknown future.

The world's best ever ice hockey player, Wayne Gretzky, is said by Steve Jobs to have come up with the famous quote of "Skate to where the puck is going, not where it has been" (Jobs, 2007). This has been taken as standard business consultant advice for 15 years in how to achieve success. It's important today that cities first decide where the puck should arrive and then to make sure that it arrives there, otherwise it will be a matter of forever playing catch up. It's also important that a new vision acts as a guide, a vision of living in places much better than presently exist, and that this vision rejects the business-as-usual planning approaches that have brought urban living to this rather desperate point.

Towards a Great Reset

The World Sustainable Built Environment Conference 2017 in Hong Kong provided a chance for development experts to gather together at the most influential meeting of its kind, bringing together green building advocates, policy-makers, academics, and industry practitioners from all over the world to exchange and inform. This was on the back of Donald Trump's decision to pull the US out of the "COP21" Paris Climate Agreement and yet, somewhat surprisingly, there was still a strong sentiment of bullishness regarding the development sector's ability to meet the urgent and overwhelming level of change needed to redress the balance of a world in socio-economic and political meltdown. The knowledge, technology, and aspiration appeared to exist in droves to change the current pattern of development. Following the close of the twenty-third annual Conference of the Parties (COP23) in Bonn later that year, further green shoots appeared to suggest that the world's nations were, just about, moving forward to make the wholesale changes that are required to be in place post-2020 as the commitments of the Paris

Agreement come into effect. Whilst talk is no longer focused on whether it is possible to meet targets, but rather on the setting of new, more challenging ambitions, the ability to make change is not in doubt, merely the political will. But the tide of rapid change is gathering momentum, from the "European Green Deal" to the Biden presidency's Building Back Better" and the World Economic Forum's proposal for a "Great Reset". Policy-makers and global financers are reassessing their positions and tipping points are finally being reached due to the impacts of COVID-19 that will result in more rapid and dramatic changes to traditional means of energy and transportation than many anticipate, leading to paradigm shifts in policy, commerce, and lifestyle. A period of massive transformation, innovation, and integration has arrived.

The 17 Sustainable Development Goals generated by the United Nations (UN) General Assembly in 2015 are intended to be achieved by the year 2030 and are part of a UN Resolution called the "2030 Agenda" (UN General Assembly, 2015). They establish the global roadmap towards achieving better development outcomes based on resiliency and sustainability. Whilst being so broad, they have come in for some degree of criticism, yet they form a landmark achievement with 169 ambitious targets that are able to focus global development priorities and, regardless of that criticism, are the best guide that exists to date. They act as "a call for action by all countries – poor, rich and middle-income – to promote prosperity while protecting the planet. They recognize that ending poverty must go hand-in-hand with strategies that build economic growth and address a range of social needs including education, health, social protection, and job opportunities, while tackling climate change and environmental protection. More important than ever, the goals provide a critical framework for COVID-19 recovery" (UN SDG, 2020a). The UN calls the pandemic "an unprecedented wake-up call" and suggests "leveraging this moment of crisis, when usual policies and social norms have been disrupted, bold steps can steer the world back on track towards the Sustainable Development Goals. This is the time for change, for a profound systemic shift to a more sustainable economy that works for both people and the planet" (UN SDG, 2020b) and in his Lecture, "Tackling the Inequality Pandemic: A New Social Contract for a New Era", the Secretary-General António Guterres noted that: "The COVID-19 pandemic has brought home the tragic disconnect between self-interest and the common interest; and the huge gaps in governance structures and ethical frameworks. To close those gaps, and to make the New Social Contract possible, we need a New Global Deal to ensure that power, wealth and opportunities are shared more broadly and fairly at the international level" (UN Secretary-General, 2015).

Out with the Old, in with the New

So a return to "normal" would not seem possible. In actual fact, there exists no "normal" to go back to, little desire to return to ways of the past, and an urgent necessity for manifest change. With 100 million more people set to be pushed into extreme poverty by 2030 and millions of people in coastal cities to be driven from their homes by 2050, urgent action is needed to build the resilience of vulnerable communities in the face of climate shocks (UN Climate Change, 2020). The 2030 Agenda is the vision to development and the Goals form the 2030 targets that cannot be ignored. Looking at details of how radical new approaches to urban development might be implemented, reference can be taken from the "New Urban Agenda", an outcome document agreed upon from the Habitat III, the United Nations Conference on Housing and Sustainable Urban Development held in Quito in 2016. It is intended to guide how the world changes over the next 20 years through the urbanisation efforts of nations, cities, and regional leaders, as well as international development funders, UN programmes, and civil society (UN-Habitat, 2016). The Agenda lays the groundwork for policies and approaches that need to extend and impact far into the future, and seeks to create a mutually reinforcing relationship between urbanisation and development, whereby they work in tandem towards what is deemed more sustainable development. Its guidelines offer new approaches in reaching better outcomes for patterns of land use, how a city is formed, and how resources are managed. Core issues of adequate housing and sustainable human settlement are the focus, but there are seven key factors that will shape the future of cities: the relationship between the environment and urbanisation; risk reduction; urban resilience; ensuring the safety and security of all urban residents, equity in the face of globalisation; democratic development; and respect for human rights. An area of immediate importance has been figuring out how to set up global monitoring mechanisms to track these issues. UN-Habitat, the agency that focuses on urbanisation, is responsible for overseeing the implementation of the New Urban Agenda and its draft "Action Framework for Implementation of the New Urban Agenda" (AFINUA), which aims to set out the essential ingredients for implementation, leadership, measurement, and provisions. The "City Prosperity Initiative" has been established as both a metric and policy dialogue to offer decision-makers the conditions to formulate adequate policies based on solid data, information, and knowledge, and through the Initiative, UN-Habitat is offering support to local and national governments in establishing customised monitoring mechanisms, which should allow for better-informed decision-making on policies and regulations, city planning, and finance management for implementation. So far, 400 cities are signed up.

Meanwhile, it has become evident that many cities have themselves been changing the very concept of what a city is, rapidly morphing into mega-regions, urban corridors, and city-regions whose metropolitan areas are now becoming the major drivers of national economies. Their economic, social, and political geographies defy traditional conceptions of the "city", and those that transform better and faster are going to lead not only national economies but also global economies, benefiting from attracting visionary businesses and hosting a smarter, highly qualified workforce that wants to live and work in the best-quality environments. As happens after all revolutionary events, a new, often younger order will emerge and those cities traditionally seen as global leaders may no longer be able to claim the same accolades a decade later if they delay their transition towards new economies and value sets. Some governments, companies, and associations are procrastinating, delaying actions, and defending entrenched positions with the real belief that they are protecting jobs, supply chains, and social systems, particularly those with heavy reliance on fossil fuel resources. Yet they are merely delaying the inevitable, and every day of inaction is in fact a step backwards, requiring more extensive changes to be made at a later time when the costs will be more substantial, while in the meantime allowing others to get ahead and reap the benefits of the new opportunities being created. The medicine needs to be taken now, regardless of the bitter taste, as delay will only makes things worse: whether it's transitioning away from fossil fuel sources; acknowledging stranded asset necessity; adopting shared use and ownership models; regulating for polluter pays production; protecting land from development; prioritising ecosystems; overhauling food production and supply chains; or simply providing adequate mass housing solutions.

Who Is Responsible?

What then should cities be doing immediately to equip themselves sufficiently to meet the overwhelming demands of climate change, technological revolution, destabilised populations, and unprecedented urban expansion? How should they drag the lengthy and archaic processes of planning and shaping infrastructure and development into flexible, informed, and inclusive modern practices? Where should today's investments be made so that they are futureproofed to be relevant not just for today, but in a decade or even a century? This book lays out ten straightforward and formative "Paths to Urban Resilience" that can be actionable immediately by the stakeholder collective including policy-makers, planners, business managers, and community leaders in order to shift cities towards the real needs of tomorrow and beyond. Everybody has a part to play in adapting to a changing world over the next decade, yet the interrelationships are complex and retaining a view of the forest beyond the trees themselves is taxing for all. Compromises are going to have to be made and to do that, it's essential to be able to see the big picture, understand the overall direction, the intertwined narratives, the conflicting perspectives, and the cross-sector opportunities beyond the expertise of the individual or the sector.

The Ten Immediate Paths to Urban Resilience can provide a necessary overview and understanding of the background of the changing world from different narrative viewpoints in order to provide a firm foundation for decision-making. The Paths are not comprehensive and little is discussed in terms of urban waste handling and the pressing need to focus on the 3 Rs of "reduction", "re-use", and "recycling". Not one of these issues is close to being undertaken satisfactorily anywhere in the world, particularly in terms of the most important – "reduction" – since consumerism is primarily used to drive growth in most global economies and growth has come to be used as the measurement of human progress over and above more valuable indexes such as happiness, equity, or well-being. According to the Waste Atlas, municipal solid waste (MSW) generation is estimated at 1.9 billion tonnes annually, with almost 30% of it remaining uncollected. The waste that is collected is primary dumped into landfill, with just 19% being recycled or recovered, and 11% taken to energy recovery facilities. At least 3.5 billion people – roughly half of the global population – lack access to the most elementary waste management and with the continuation of existing practices, forecasts estimate that this will increase to around 5.6 billion people in 2050 or about 68% of the global population if unchecked (Waste Atlas, 2015). Potential social and environmental impacts, already at breaking point, are unimaginable. The main reason waste and the critical pollution and land impacts that go with it are not discussed specifically as one of the Immediate Paths to Urban Resilience is primarily that this is a wider global and societal issue, above that of the city alone, and one that particularly impacts rural and peri-urban societies. Nor is the role of food and its production and supply addressed for similar reasons. Two additional Paths could then, and indeed perhaps should, have been addressed around these two critical issues, along with their need to combine and fast-track breakthroughs in technology and scientific knowledge with the adoption of more collaborative and shared models of responsibility, equity, and

10 Introduction: A Clarion Call

adaptation. These are common themes demonstrated by the Ten Paths and are repeatedly outlined in the following chapters, on the premise of first accepting that urgent change is necessary, desirable, and inevitable, and then plotting a means of delivering on that necessity.

Whilst the Ten Immediate Paths to Urban Resilience have been sequenced in a layered manner in order to assist in building complimentary knowledge step by step, it is perfectly possible to read and assimilate the Paths in a different order from those provided herein and to jump around and select those of most relevance or resonance. Each chapter can act as an introduction to deeper research or broadened reading and in no way tries to address all issues in such a short space. What is provided is a one-stop shop that covers the major issues of the New Urban Agenda in the context of current data and thinking by experts in their fields, whilst outlining the trends of unprecedented change that highlight future directions and the opportunities that lie within. From these, it may also be possible to draw a clearer vision of the Futureproof City.

References

Barbosa, F. et al. (2017). *Reinventing construction: A route of higher productivity (executive summary)*. https://www.mckinsey.com/~/media/McKinsey/Business%20Functions/Operations/Our%20Insights/Reinventing%20construction%20through%20a%20productivity%20revolution/MGI-Reinventing-Construction-Executive-summary.pdf.

Bar-On, Y. M., Ron, M., & Phillips, R. (2018). The biomass distribution on Earth. *National Academy of Sciences, 115*(25), 6506–6511.

Boyce, D., Lewis, M., & Worm, B. (2010). Global phytoplankton decline over the past century. *Nature, 466*, 591–596.

Chang, P. (2020). How to bridge the last 100m? Presented at *Digitalisation: 2020 CITAC Anniversary Conference on Construction*. 11 November, Hong Kong.

Encyclopedia Britannica. (2019). Moore's law. https://www.britannica.com/technology/Moores-law.

Farmer, M. (2016). *The Farmer review of the UK construction labour model: Modernise or die*. Construction Leadership Council, London. https://www.constructionleadershipcouncil.co.uk/wp-content/uploads/2016/10/Farmer-Review.pdf.

HM Government. (2017). *Fixing our broken housing market*. White Paper. Ministry of Housing, Communities & Local Government.

Jobs, S. (2007). *Macworld Conference and Expo Keynote 2007*. San Francisco, CA.

Kanter, R. M. (2012). Ten reasons people resist change. *Harvard Business Review, 74*. https://hbr.org/2012/09/ten-reasons-people-resist-chang.

Lindsey, R. (2020). *Climate change: Atmospheric carbon dioxide.* https://www.climate.gov/news-features/understanding-climate/climate-change-atmospheric-carbon-dioxide.

Manyika, J. et al. (2015). *Digital America: A tale of the haves and have-mores.* New York: McKinsey Global Institute.

NASEM. (2017). The Fourth Industrial Revolution: Proceedings of a workshop – in brief. In *National Academies of Sciences, Engineering, Medicine* (p. 1). National Academies Press.

Ruddiman, W. F. (2003). The anthropogenic greenhouse era began thousands of years ago. *Climatic Change, 61*, 261–293.

UN Climate Change. (2020). *Update from Climate Champions on Occasion of Climate Ambition Summit.* United Nations Framework Convention on Climate Change: New York.

UN General Assembly. (2015). *Resolution adopted by the General Assembly on 25 September 2015, Transforming our world: The 2030 Agenda for Sustainable Development (A/RES/70/1).* United Nations General Assembly.

UN-Habitat. (2016). The new urban agenda. In *Habitat 3: United Nations Conference on Housing and Sustainable Urban Development* (pp. 1–66). United Nations Human Settlements Programme.

UN SDG. (2020a). *Sustainablity Development Goals.* https://www.un.org/sustainable development.

———. (2020b). *Covid-19 response.* https://www.un.org/sustainabledevelopment/sdgs-framework-for-covid-19-recovery.

UN Secretary-General. (2015). *Secretary-General's Nelson Mandela Lecture: "Tackling the inequality pandemic: A new social Contract for a new era".* United Nations.

US, NCDC. (2020). *Global Climate Change Indicators.* https://www.ncdc.noaa.gov/monitoring-references/faq/indicators.php#warming-climate.

Waste Atlas. (2015). *Global waste clock.* http://www.atlas.d-waste.com.

Putting Wellness First

Re-evaluating Human Priorities in the Context of Health and Happiness

Urbanisation has always perhaps occurred as a result of the human desire to improve life opportunities, primarily through wealth accumulation. But evaluating those improvements in financial terms alone has led to imbalanced allocations of space, access, and activities in cities. The COVID-19 epidemic has brought into close focus the need for a change in priorities and alternative modes of behaviour and urban living that are necessary to create cleaner, safer, and healthier places for all; places that make people's lives better and happier. Finding new ways of evaluating human progress and measuring how well our cities then meet people's true needs becomes an essential step towards their improvement in both acting as a first step in preventative care provision and in efficiently allocating limited funding under the weight of burgeoning urban population growth.

DOI: 10.4324/9781003112488-2

14 Putting Wellness First

Crumbling Values

"Nine-tenths of our happiness depends on health alone. With it everything becomes a source of pleasure, whereas without it nothing, whatever it may be, can be enjoyed."

Arthur Schopenhauer, *The Wisdom of Life*, 1851

What Is Progress?

It has been a longstanding and well-understood fact that healthy, happy populations are more productive and reduce the massive costs of healthcare and social services (Bloom and Canning, 2008; Oswald et al., 2015). Yet, dirty, polluted, inefficient cities have been created globally in the name of progress, prioritising economics above health and creating wealth rather than happiness. Measurements of progress have been universally structured around Gross Domestic Product (GDP) (Oswald et al., 2015), but what in fact is progress and how should it be measured? Unsurprisingly, it is not easy to find a clear definition because it is not an entirely objective concept (Schepelmann et al., 2009). It cannot be addressed solely by data-driven economic indicators since the subjective comes into play when considering the likes of health, well-being, happiness, quality of life, civilisation, and cultural perception. A country's GDP is the most commonly used national accounting indicator today. It forms the basic framework for the System of National Accounts (SNA), the internationally agreed standard set of recommendations on how to compile measures of economic activity as first published by the UN in 1953, with a standardised methodology that enables international comparison anywhere in the world (Wesselink et al., 2007). However, it is designed to measure just the value of production, not wider economics, so how is it that such a narrow measurement of progress has come to dominate the direction and aspirations of the world today?

The concept of GDP first arose during the Second World War as an assessment tool based on the needs of maximised war production; a means by which to gauge economic activity, investment, and employment during that time. First published in the US in 1942, its emergence was a significant and important measure, and subsequently became adopted as a simple indicator of national achievement in the post-war years, where its usefulness was perhaps particularly to be trumpeted in the Cold War against the threat of communism in which the US was entrenched. Promoted to stress the benefits of capitalist economics through that era, its legacy has been to shape the global value system into the twenty-first century at the particular disregard of wider considerations of human progress associated with socialist values. The current climate and environmental emergency, resource depletion, wealth disparity, and social disorder have all been driven through the myopic goal of GDP growth. The National Accounts of Well-Being published by the New Economics Foundation in 2009 pointed out that GDP 'obscured other vital parts of the economy: the core economy of family, neighbourhood, community and society, and the natural economy of the biosphere, our oceans, forests and fields' (Michaelson et al., 2009). More tellingly, way back in 1968, Robert Kennedy gave his famous speech at the University of Kansas, in which he stated that:

> Gross National Product counts air pollution and cigarette advertising, and ambulances to clear our highways of carnage. It counts special locks for our doors and the jails for the people who break them. It counts the destruction of the redwood and the loss of our natural wonder in chaotic sprawl. It counts napalm and counts nuclear warheads and armoured cars for the police to fight the riots in our cities … and the television programs which glorify violence in order to sell toys to our children. Yet [it] does not allow for the health of our children, the quality of their education or the joy of their play. It does not include the beauty of our poetry or the strength of our marriages, the intelligence of our public debate or the integrity of our public officials … it measures everything, in short, except that which makes life worthwhile.
> (Kennedy, 1968)

It has for some time been the case, even before the COVID-19 pandemic brought health issues to the forefront of everyday living, that a reconsideration of what is used to define progress and how that is measured has been urgently needed across global societies. Financial systems have their place, and especially GDP, but that should be within a broader range of principles and metrics that prioritise wellness and social prosperity over and above individual and economic factors in reshaping living places. Affordable housing, safer streets, cleaner air, and less stress within a fairer society model are what people really want and what they really need. The first Path to Resiliency is therefore a shift in appreciated values of what is really important in life, and must highlight the true worth of long-term security, health, and happiness above all other matters (Wilson, 2018). It must focus on "Putting Wellness First".

So how could measuring societal progress be done better? How can "Putting Wellness First" be measured instead of GDP? There have been a large number of advocates proposing alternatives that incorporate environmental and social aspects into the mix, with many also warning of the dangers of using one tool alone. One such tool is the Genuine Progress Indicator (GPI), which is predominantly used in measuring sustainability through more inclusive types of economics. It considers environmental and carbon footprints, impacts to existing resources, and the long-term impacts of pollution and environmental loss (Bagstad et al., 2014). Interestingly, whilst global GDP has increased more than threefold since 1950, economic welfare has actually decreased since 1978 according to GPI estimates, which extrapolated datasets from 17 countries containing 53% of the global population and 59% of global GDP (Kubiszewski et al., 2013). A further statistical composite is the Human Development Index (HDI), which is used by the United Nations Human Development Report (UNHDR) and utilises life expectancy, education metrics, and per capita income indicators to measure a country's development. Other useful indicators frequently referenced include Ecological Footprint, Biocapacity, the Gini coefficient, the Index of Economic Freedom, the Global Peace Index, the Global Competitiveness Index, the Environmental Protection Index, and the Life Satisfaction Index, the last of which comes out of the area of subjective well-being (SWB) and measures self-esteem, well-being, and overall happiness with life, and is utilised by the United Nations Educational, Scientific and Cultural Organization (UNESCO), the UNHDR, the World Health Organization (WHO), and the New Economics Foundation (NEF), to name but a few.

Over the past few years, many countries and organisations have started to launch their own initiatives to measure well-being. For instance, the Organisation for Economic Co-operation and Development (OECD), a club of the world's wealthiest countries, has developed a "better life index" as part of its Better Life initiative of 2011 (OECD, n.d.). An interactive Web-based tool, it underlines how prosperity is determined through the 11 topics of civic engagement, community, education, the environment, health, housing, income, jobs, life satisfaction, safety, and work-life balance. In fact, the organisation has already gone on record as having identified that per capita GDP is not even a good means of assessment of productivity progress, since important aspects of economic activity, such as household production, constitute between one-third and one-half of all valuable economic activity and are not accounted for (Veerle, 2011). Meanwhile, the World Bank understands that the value and importance of societal trust in market function as a component of wealth and well-being is not assessed through conventional means and could be over 20% of the value of all goods and services produced by businesses (Hamilton et al., 2016). There seems to be strong consensus that GDP just won't do.

The expression "Gross National Happiness" (GNH) (European GNH Institute, 2018) was coined as far back as 1972 by Sicco Mansholt, one of the founding fathers of the European Union (EU) and the fourth President of the European Commission (European GNH Institute, 2018). GNH includes an index which is used to measure the collective happiness and well-being of a population, and even forms the philosophical basis that guides the government of Bhutan, whose GNH Index is instituted as the very goal of government in the Constitution enacted in 2008 (Royal Government of Bhutan, 2008). The Bhutanese government established four pillars of GNH measuring sustainable and equitable socio-economic development; environmental conservation; preservation and promotion of culture; and good governance (Royal Government of Bhutan, 2009). Following up on the moves taken by Bhutan, a World Happiness Report has been published annually by the United Nations since 2012 in order to rank countries based on a wide variety of data, the most important being the life evaluations taken from the Gallup World Poll (Gallup, n.d.). As such, it predominantly utilises the aforementioned "subjective well-being" to evaluate progress. Gallup suggest that its poll is the most comprehensive and far-reaching survey in the world, connecting with over 99% of the world's adult population (Gallup, n.d.). Interestingly, Bhutan has not topped the list to date. So what makes us happy?

Even those not familiar with Abraham Maslow and his 1943 paper "A Theory of Human Motivation" will still be able to inform us of what they consider to be their basic physical needs: the ability to breathe clean air, maintain reasonable health, eat and drink, find shelter, and clothe themselves. After that, our basic needs according to Maslow then focus on finding safety and security (McLeod, 2007). And yet even in the developed world, despite its GDP riches, providing those simple basic needs to the population has become challenging, where breathing polluted air and eating contaminated food and water have passed largely unnoticed for decades. A 2020 analysis of 12 US cities showed that millions of US citizens are facing rising and unaffordable bills for running water, with the combined price of water and sewage having increased by an average of 80% between 2010 and 2018. More than two-fifths of residents in some cities are living in neighbourhoods with unaffordable bills and risk being disconnected or losing their homes if they cannot pay (Lakhani, 2020). A global housing crisis is once more upon us, featuring homelessness, repossession, and unaffordable costs to large sectors of societies that are struggling to come to terms with a sense of their own values as to what is important. Are they happy?

Subjective well-being is being seen increasingly as the important tool in assessing progress in welfare and happiness terms, and governments now have more data and tools to systematically collect and analyse the considerations that make up Life Satisfaction. The most recent World Happiness Report focused on the aspects affecting life satisfaction from social trust and environmental factors. Having someone to count on, a sense of freedom to make key life decisions, generosity, and trust are all key issues and demonstrate that a good social environment operates to reduce inequality. The Report identifies that inequality of well-being is more important than income inequality in explaining average levels of happiness. Furthermore, life evaluation scores are generally higher for those living in cities than those in rural areas, and increasingly so for less developed economies. However, in the most well-developed countries, rural dwellers become increasingly happier than those in the cities, where belonging to a sense of local community becomes a key factor. Accumulated 'positive mood experiences' experienced in cities are related to being outdoors, in good weather, and within green space or the natural environment, and these are accentuated when undertaken as an activity with a friend or partner (Burger et al., 2020).

The United Nations Sustainable Development Goals (SDGs) ratified in 2015 currently form the benchmark for achieving holistic progress by the year 2030. They are assessed against 169 clear targets spread across 17 aspirational goals aimed at tackling nearly every facet of life under economic, social, and environmental development. Progress towards achieving the SDGs is published in the form of reports and accessed online via the 'SDG-Tracker' launched in June 2018, which presents data across 232 indicators from the UN and other international organizations (Ritchie et al., 2018). Meanwhile, the Sustainable Development Report assesses the progress of implementation across all 17 Goals through six *SDG Transformations* and publishes the *SDG Index and Dashboards*. Such a broad initiative has its detractors; however, since the SDGs are supposedly driving human well-being, how well do they actually reflect life satisfaction and wellness, and align with civic and environmental interests? There does in fact appear to be a significant correlation between the SDG Index and SWB scores assessed in the World Happiness Report, which appears to indicate that economic growth is an important early driver of well-being, but economic factors become increasing less important as development proceeds and that a more nuanced approach to civic development is required when trying to improve citizen well-being. Simply put, as countries get richer, their population's sense of well-being stagnates unless continued economic growth is driven by sustainable concepts that can address improving environmental quality, reduced inequality, and improved welfare outcomes.

Environment and Well-Being

"The best predictor of how healthy you are and how long you are likely to live is how wealthy you are" states Professor Catharine Ward Thompson, the founder and Director of internationally recognised research centre OPENspace, whilst discussing the vital importance and value to people of all ages and capabilities of having access to quality landscape spaces, wherever they are living. "This has been true for centuries and continues to be so, even in advanced and sophisticated societies, where those with the poorest health remain typically the least well off." There is increasing evidence that access to good-quality environments, particularly access to natural environments, is one of the easiest and most cost-effective ways of reducing social inequality. "The greatest benefits can be seen to those most disadvantaged" (Ward Thompson, 2018). Understanding that there have been links between the provision of green space and personal health is not new, but the scientific data to substantiate the positive benefits has long been in short supply. Let us recall the last great period of urbanisation in the second half of the nineteenth century. The new technologies of that time led to a massive leap in industrialisation, requiring a huge number of workers to come to the cities, where relentless shifts required them to live close to the factories. In the US, the population in cities such as Philadelphia, Boston, and New York exploded and congestion, pollution, crime, and disease were prevalent problems. Theorists at this time began developing planning models to mitigate the problems caused by rapid urban growth and the government quickly grew to understand the need and benefits of providing healthy environments for the working populations within the cities in order to balance out the poor urban conditions. Central Park in Manhattan, Prospect Park in Brooklyn, and the Emerald Necklace of parks in Boston were at the centre of engineering solutions to control water and demonstrated Frederick Law Olmsted's brilliant work as a 'Landscape Architect' in integrating engineered green space at the heart of cities as a means to manage crippling environmental and social issues. Meanwhile, in the UK, similar conditions pushed philanthropic organisations to press town and city governments to provide public parks and pleasure grounds for the burgeoning urban populations, and increasingly people looked towards 'rational recreation' as a solution in providing social, educational, and moral improvement (Cunningham, 2016). Victorian Britain was wholly caught up in concerns about economics, society, and morality. Reports into worker conditions in many manufacturing towns in the mid-nineteenth century led to statistical research being conducted to guide new laws, educate, and achieve social, cultural, and economic progress (Briggs, 1968). The 1833 Select Committee on Public Walks had a remit to "consider the best means of securing open spaces in the immediate vicinity of populous towns, as public walks calculated to promote the health and comfort of the inhabitants", following demonstrated links between data, rational recreation, and social reform and progress. The report's conclusions surmised that industrial expansion, increases in property prices, and urban enclosures had not allowed for the needs of the masses for space to walk, exercise, or entertain themselves; providing such spaces would augment the "comfort, health and content" of the "humbler classes" (Parliament, 1833). Nick Piercy suggests that the 1833 Slaney Report was the epitome of the mid-nineteenth-century need to collect data and propose changes for the public good (Piercy, 2020). The Report was to see the later emergence of the "people's parks", yet these did not emerge directly from the public purse; it was ultimately the ruling elite who provided the majority of land and finance, with astute landowners presumably anticipating the financial benefits green spaces would provide to property prices, along with the one-upmanship of providing better facilities than others and fostering elements of civic pride (O'Reilly, 2013). London and the great European cities had large amounts of land in the hands of the aristocracy and the Royal Parks initiated grants of access to the public to meet these expectations, along with other aristocratic and wealthy landowners over the following decades. Derby Arboretum is generally understood to be the first publicly owned, landscaped, urban recreational park in Britain, having been opened in 1840 following the donation of the land by local philanthropist Joseph Strutt, and to designs by "Landscape Architect" John Claudius Loudon. Strutt did not provide an endowment for the upkeep of the Arboretum, believing that while it should be open to the general public free of charge on a Sunday as well as on a Wednesday afternoon, on other days "a small sum should be required from persons entering the garden" (Loudon and Strutt, 1840).

The connection between landscape and personal heath seems to have separated during the latter half of the twentieth century with the growth of modern medicine obscuring some longstanding basic understandings. In fact, a 1999 Environment, Transport and Regional Affairs Committee held a new inquiry into the neglect of town parks in order to reconsider the benefits and the condition of parks, their funding, and the roles and responsibilities of the government in their protection and maintenance (Parliament, 1999). Unsurprisingly, many of the issues arising from the inquiry remained similar to those highlighted by the very first committee of 1833 mentioned above – for example, the need to recognise the many benefits which parks provide to communities, as well as the risk of decline without sufficient investment. It seems that although the connections between green space and parks were established, they were often poorly understood and unsustainable without robust scientific evidence. When Ward Thomson established OPENspace in 2001, she found there was little or no research available on how access to outdoor environments affected health. But as advanced economies have become more aware of the prevalence of non-communicable diseases such as heart and lung disease, obesity and diabetes, an urgency for more understanding has developed. Newly completed research in these areas has been able to employ new and sophisticated techniques that have been able to re-establish those intuitive links and satisfy the rigorous scientific standards necessary for acceptability. Public health is something that needs to work across all sectors and all environments, and investment in landscape as a public health tool is extremely low in cost and high in benefit compared to intensive corrective public medical costs. However, it takes a long time – perhaps even decades – to fully measure and witness the return on investment to society at large of quality landscape provision and of its recurrent maintenance cost. How can funding bodies be convinced of the real and valuable benefits that can be accrued? Ward Thomson suggests that obtaining data to demonstrate these facts and therefore to emphasise the need for funding has been difficult. The medical profession has rigorous standards of research and requires strong evidentiary procedures (Ward Thompson, 2018).

The UK Landscape Institute has been focusing on 'liveable cities' as one of its main platforms for some time, and in 2013 published its five principles and ten recommendations for the creation of healthy places as part of its work on public health. The principles outline that creating healthy places can help to overcome health inequalities and can promote healthy lifestyles; increase social interaction and reduce anti-social behaviour, isolation and stress; optimise opportunities for working, learning, and development; and also be restorative, uplifting, and healing for both physical and mental health conditions (Bull et al., 2013). The Institute recommends using healthy place-making to deliver real public health and well-being benefits at all levels of government and at all spatial scales, and suggests that the public health sector needs to be much more closely involved in guiding the planning, design, and management of new and existing development and, critically, to be involved at every stage of the process, from policy and strategy to engagement in the framing of specific proposals. Improved collaboration between health professionals, planning professionals, and key community stakeholders should help identify the multifunctional nature of landscape and its potential to offer positive public health outcomes. Unsurprisingly, more financial resources therefore need to be re-allocated to public space as a low-cost primary healthcare investment, allied with the same long-term budgetary commitment that primary care, transport, and other public services receive. Such funding needs to be enshrined in planning and development policy from the national level right through to the local level, with health performance indicators developed to ensure better-planned, designed, and managed places in order to secure further funding for continued research and knowledge development.

The Costs of Neglect

Living in cities means living with urban pollution, and this remains one of the biggest issues in relation to health, particularly in developing countries. Typically, such pollution is primarily considered in terms of air quality, where outdoor air pollution in both cities and rural areas was estimated to cause 4.2 million premature deaths worldwide in 2016 (World Health Organization, 2018). However, water, waste, light, and noise pollution all have serious compound impacts on the health of urban populations (Martínez-Bravo & Martínez-del-Río, 2019). India and China in particular have been struggling massively with toxic air as they rapidly industrialise. The issue finally raised its head in China in 2015, when former China Central Television anchor and investigative reporter Chai Jing raised mass public awareness of the health problems from smog when her online video documentary went "viral". Citing former Minister of Health Chen Zhu, the video claimed that an estimated half a million people died prematurely in China every year because of air pollution, yet critics at the time claimed there was no scientific evidence to support the video's link between the rising number of cases of heart disease and air pollution. However, a recently peer-reviewed study determined that an incredible 1.31 million premature deaths were attributable to ambient PM2.5 across mainland China in 2016 relating to stroke, heart disease, pulmonary disease, and lung cancer (Li et al., 2020). Meanwhile, four different studies from Sweden, the US, the UK, and China now link air pollution with cognitive impairment, dementia, and Alzheimer's disease (Grande et al., 2020; Younan et al., 2020; Carey et al., 2018; Zhang et al., 2018).

The main sources of urban water pollution are chemicals in surface and ground water that can result in human cell mutagenesis or the emergence of antibiotic resistant bacteria (UN Environment Programme, 2017). Exposure to chemical contamination is not only through water, but also through polluted food, workplaces, sprays, detergents, textiles, cosmetics, construction materials, and furniture (Ke et al., 2015); meanwhile, heat, light, and noise pollution have been shown to affect the abundance, behaviour, and distribution of many species (Hölker et al., 2010; Gomes et al.,

2016). The Committee on the Environment, Agriculture and Local and Regional Affairs to the European Parliament has reported that noise and light pollution is a major environmental and public health challenge leading to mental health disorders, depression, sleep disorders, hypertension, and anxiety, as well as the faster development of certain cancers, diabetes, and ulcers, and increased heart rate and blood pressure, with a weakening of the immune system, and can only be addressed comprehensively at the national, regional, and local levels (Parliamentary Assembly, 2010a). The Assembly's Recommendation 1947 of 2010 stresses the significant harmful effects of noise and light pollution on the environment in general and on biodiversity and human health in particular, and recommended a review of existing legislation and the drafting of a framework convention on the measures to be taken at a pan-European level (Parliamentary Assembly, 2010b). However, the European Parliament did not adopt these recommendations, feeling that with "its limited resources on promoting its core objectives … it does not consider that this recommendation falls within those priorities" (Parliamentary Assembly, 2011). At the time of writing, little further progress has been achieved.

Yet in 2020, the importance of healthy environments finally rose right to the top of worldwide issues as a result of the COVID-19 outbreak. Overnight, the crisis pushed healthcare to the very front of the global agenda, with economics a necessary casualty. The long-term impacts of the pandemic on shattered economies and individual mental well-being look significant, meaning that how cities respond and adapt in order to cope with further outbreaks and then mutate and replan will be a critical, continuous, and long-term issue. The WHO Healthy Cities Network has identified that cities will be at the forefront of change, having been the epicentres of the COVID-19 pandemic in terms of community transmission, as entry points for such transmission, and as focal points for necessary healthcare inputs. Municipal governments are essential providers of services and work most closely with the populace, including vulnerable groups. They are well placed to reach out and engage as part of the solution, acting as a interface with national governments in forming preparedness and response plans (World Health Organization, 2020).

The Index of Priority

In needing to address health and wellness as a major issue above even that of economics, whilst at the same time needing to meet the significant challenges presented by the climate emergency, an opportunity to radically rebuild values and approaches has emerged, in much the same way that the UK National Health Service (NHS) developed as a key social reform following the Second World War. A tipping point appears to have been reached whereby creating more 'liveable cities' will be essential for all rather than desirable for the few; this should finally consign the concept of continued growth through limitless production and consumption to the waste bin of history. The key component in reinforcing this change will be the mainstream adoption of "Putting Wellness First" indexes and the jettisoning of the use of GDP as a standard and important measurement. All and any of the alternative value indexes outlined above are a significant improvement on GDP in terms of gauging human progress and need to be adopted widely and consistently across national governments rather than siloed in organisational reporting, as is currently the case. Further and more sophisticated iterations can also be expected to be continually developed as access to wider datasets is extended through the rapid extension in availability of Big Data that is currently emerging. So even adopting a single new value index today will potentially not be as sophisticated, accurate, or useful as that of one adopted tomorrow, and therein lies the rub. In measuring anything, both scientific and social communities alike prefer to compare 'like against like' rather than apples against oranges, so in continuing to measure GDP, 'like' comparisons can continue to be drawn to show clear evidence across the long timeframes of the later twentieth century and beyond. Despite its lack of fitness for purpose, the consistent data reporting and wealth of accumulated data provided by GDP has been the foundation for extrapolation and forward planning for decades, and makes it doubly hard to now reject out of hand. Yet continuing to utilise past data as an indicator of the future is not only meaningless in the current world of disruption, but in fact exacerbates the problem with continuing business-as-usual approaches in a changed environment. Projections based on extrapolated past metrics, which were always unreliable in the past, are now completely obsolete and new lines need to be drawn, "Putting Wellness First" in meeting the target-driven objectives of the coming decade.

References

Bagstad, K. et al. (2014). Methodological developments in US state-level genuine progress indicators: Toward GPI 2.0. *Ecological Indicators, 45,* 474–485.

Bloom, D. E., & Canning, D. (2008). *Population health and economic growth.* World Bank Publications.

Briggs, A. (1968). The Victorian city: Quantity and quality. *Victorian Studies, 11,* 711–730.

Bull, G. et al., 2013. *Public health and landscape: Creating healthy places.* https://landscapewpstorage01.blob.core.windows.net/www-landscapeinstitute-org/migrated-legacy/PublicHealthandLandscape_CreatingHealthyPlaces_FINAL.pdf.

Burger, M. J., Morrison, P. S., & Hendriks, M. (2020). Urban-rural happiness differentials across the world. *World Happiness Report 2020.* New York: Sustainable Development Solutions Network.

Carey, I. M. et al. (2018). Are noise and air pollution related to the incidence of dementia? A cohort study in London, England. *BMJ Open, 8*(9), e022404.

Cunningham, H. (2016). *Leisure in the Industrial Revolution: c. 1780–c. 1880.* Routledge.

European GNH Institute. (2018). *The Origin of GNH.* http://gnh.institute/gross-national-happiness-gnh-origin.htm (accessed 13 October 2020).

Gallup. (n.d.) *Gallup World Poll.* https://www.gallup.com/analytics/318875/global-research.aspx.

Gomes, D. G. et al. (2016). Bats perceptually weight prey cues across sensory systems when hunting in noise. *Science, 353*(6305), 1277–1280.

Grande, G. et al. (2020). Association between cardiovascular disease and long-term exposure to air pollution with the risk of dementia. *JAMA Neurology, 77*(7), 801–809.

Hamilton, K., Helliwell, J., & Woolcock, M. (2016). *Social capital, trust, and well-being in the evaluation of wealth.* World Bank.

Helliwell, J. F. et al. (2020). *World Happiness Report 2020.* Sustainable Development Solutions Network.

Hölker, F. et al. (2010). Light pollution as a biodiversity threat. *Trends in Ecology & Evolution, 25*(12), 681–682.

Ke, S., et al. (2015). Cadmium contamination of rice from various polluted areas of China and its potential risks to human health. *Environmental Monitoring and Assessment, 187*(7), 1–11.

Kennedy, R. F. (1968). *Remarks at the University of Kansas.* JFK Library, University of Kansas.

Kubiszewski, I. et al. (2013). Beyond GDP: Measuring and achieving global genuine progress. *Ecological Economics, 93,* 57–68.

Lakhani, N. (2020). Revealed: Millions of Americans can't afford water as bills rise 80% in a decade. *The Guardian,* 23 June. https://www.theguardian.com/us-news/2020/jun/23/millions-of-americans-cant-afford-water-bills-rise (accessed 4 May 2021).

Li, Y. et al. (2020). Specific differences and responses to reductions for premature mortality attributable to ambient PM2.5 in China. *Science of the Total Environment, 742,* 140643. https://doi.org/10.1016/j.scitotenv.2020.140643.

Loudon, J. C., and Strutt, J. (1840). *The Derby Arboretum: Containing a Catalogue of the Trees and Shrubs Included in It; a Description of the Grounds and Directions for Their Management; a Copy of the Address Delivered when it was Presented to the Town of Derby; by Its Founder, Joseph Strutt, Esq. And an Account of the Ceremonies which Took*

Place when it was Opened to the Public, on Sept. 16, 1840. Longman, Orme, Brown, Green & Longmans.

Martínez-Bravo, M. D. M., & Martínez-del-Río, J. (2019). Urban pollution and emission reduction. In W. Leal Filho, A. Azul, L. Brandli, P. Özuyar, & T. Wall (Eds.), *Sustainable cities and communities: Encyclopedia of the UN Sustainable Development Goals* (pp. 1–11). Springer.

McLeod, S. (2007). *Maslow's hierarchy of needs*. Simply Psychology.

Michaelson, J. et al. (2009). *National accounts of well-being: Bringing real wealth onto the balance sheet.* New Economics Foundation, London. http://www.nationalaccountsofwellbeing.org/learn/download-report.html.

Miranda, V. (2011). Cooking, caring and volunteering: Unpaid work around the world. In *OECD Social, Employment and Migration Working Papers, No. 116*. OECD Publishing. https://doi.org/10.1787/5kghrjm8s142-en.

O'Reilly, C. (2013). From "the people" to "the citizen": The emergence of the Edwardian municipal park in Manchester, 1902–1912. *Urban History, 40*(1), 136–155.

OECD. (n.d.). *Better Life Index.* Paris: Organisation for Economic Co-operation and Development.

Oswald, A. J., Proto, E., & Sgroi, D. (2015). Happiness and productivity. *Journal of Labor Economics, 33*(4), 789–822.

Parliament. (1833). *Public Health – Hansard.* House of Commons.

Parliament. (1999). *Environment, Transport and Regional Affairs – Twentieth report.* House of Commons.

Parliamentary Assembly. (2010a). *Noise and light pollution – Report.* Council of Europe.

Parliamentary Assembly. (2010b). *Noise and light pollution – Recomendation.* Council of Europe.

Parliamentary Assembly. 2011. *Noise and light pollution – Reply to recommendation.* Council of Europe.

Piercy, N. (2020). *A brief history of British public parks before 1870.* Playing Pasts.

Ritchie H. et al. (2018). *Measuring progress towards the Sustainable Development Goals.* https://sdg-tracker.org.

Royal Government of Bhutan. (2008). *The Constitution of the Kingdom of Bhutan.*

Royal Government of Bhutan. (2009). *Tenth five-year plan: 2008–2013.*

Schepelmann, P., Goossens, Y., & Makipaa, A. (2009). *Towards sustainable development: Alternatives to GDP for measuring progress.* Wuppertal Spezial.

UN Environment Programme. (2017). *Towards a pollution-free planet background report.* UN Environment Programme.

Ward Thompson, C. (2018). *An ecology of urban spaces.* http://www.initiatives.com.hk/180926-an-ecology-of-urban-spaces.html.

Wesselink, B., et al. (2007). Measurement beyond GDP. *Beyond GDP, 304.*

Wilson, B. D. (2018). An outline to futureproofing cities with ten immediate steps. *Proceedings of the Institution of Civil Engineers – Urban Design and Planning, 171*(5), 202–216.

World Health Organization. (2018). *Ambient (outdoor) air pollution.* https://www.who.int/news-room/fact-sheets/detail/ambient-(outdoor)-air-quality-and-health.

World Health Organization. (2020). *The WHO European Healthy Cities Network: A response to the COVID-19 pandemic close to the people.* https://www.euro.who.int/en/health-topics/environment-and-health/urban-health/who-european-healthy-cities-network/the-who-european-healthy-cities-network-a-response-to-the-covid-19-pandemic-close-to-the-people.

Younan, D. et al. (2020). Particulate matter and episodic memory decline mediated by early neuroanatomic biomarkers of Alzheimer's disease. *Brain, 143*(1), 289–302.

Zhang, X., Chen, X., & Zhang, X. (2018). The impact of exposure to air pollution on cognitive performance. *Proceedings of the National Academy of Sciences, 115*(37), 9193–9197.

2

Reconsider, Rethink, Redirect

Envisioning and Collaborating to Plan Resilient Living Places

The urgent press to meet 2030 climate goals will see an increasingly accelerated rejection of business-as-usual investment and development choices, with a continual series of disruptors emerging to create economic tipping points. Predicting even the near future is becoming an impossibility, and yet finding ways to drive progress whilst having to abandon traditional planning and management processes is imperative. In an age of immediately accessible information, where society has moved away from the "command and control", top-down decision-making methods of the past towards "suggest and select", citizen-led processes, a race is on. Those cities that transition their approaches fastest, most flexibly, and holistically will not only become the most resilient to the coming turmoil, but will also be able to provide globally desirable living opportunities that attract the best talent, the highest-quality labour supply, and generate more investment, thereby re-inventing themselves atop of a new global order characterised by the "city" rather than the "nation'. Can cities direct the transformation process by adopting flexible and adaptable bottom-up techniques, driven through stakeholder engagement and participation around a solid vision?

30 Reconsider, Rethink, Redirect

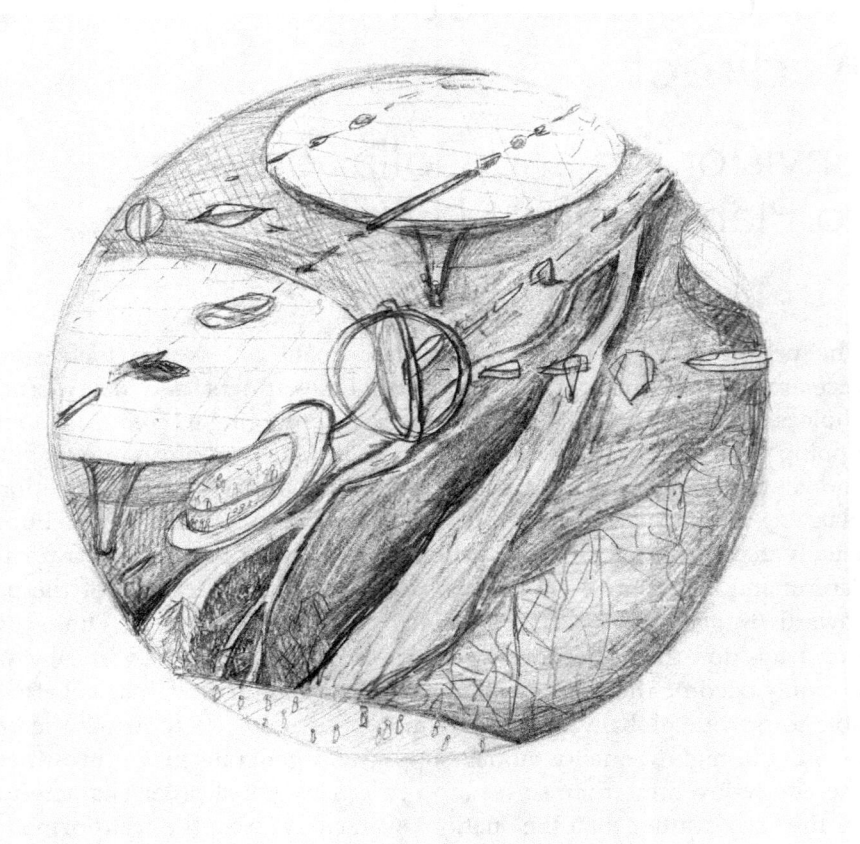

The Nature of Change

> *"Malum est consilium, quod mutari non potest."*
> [*It's a bad plan that cannot be changed.*]
>
> Publilius Syrus,
> Sententiae: Maxim 469, c. 43 BCE

Reconsidering the Considered

Much of the extent of the coming decade of radical global change will be dependent upon how cites approach their transformations to zero-carbon economies. Through its European Green Deal, the 27 EU Member States have committed to becoming net carbon neutral by 2050 and are launching a mission to reach 100 climate-neutral cities by 2030 (Gronkiewicz-Waltz et al., 2020). Fifty-four global cities under the C40 Cities group, representing more than 200 million residents, are on track to meet their 2030 climate goal objectives (C40 Cities, 2020). As reported, 23 regions, 524 cities, 1,397 companies, 569 universities, 74 investors, and 30 asset managers, responsible for a combined US$9.1 trillion, have joined the UN Race to Zero campaign, an international campaign for a healthy, resilient zero-carbon recovery led by the United Nations Framework Convention on Climate Change (UNFCCC) Champions for Climate Action. Collectively these actors now cover nearly 25% of global CO_2 emissions and over 50% of GDP (UN, Climate Change, 2020). This being the case, planned or expanded urban centres with primary investments in traditional infrastructure and institutions are going to find it increasingly hard to avoid the well-established, GDP-led development paths that will soon result in resource redundancy and stranded assets. However, promoting low-carbon transitions at the inception of the expansion of industrialisation implies a futureproofed fit, where economies will be designed to develop at the outset along a balanced path between productivity and consumption, and the environmental and societal cost that comes with this. Whilst initially transitions may be painful, delaying climate change action will only necessitate an even more rapid, costly, and difficult transition in the near future, whilst risk exposure to destabilising shocks will rise continually (Semieniuk et al., 2021).

The last few years have seen the green business market change fundamentally and it is the market that shall ultimately shape decision-making most quickly. Sean Kidney, CEO of the Climate Bonds Initiative, suggests how use of the term "green" is most likely just temporary and that soon requirements for "green" will be business as usual. A "green building" will just be a "building", in the same way as a "colour TV" is now just a "TV". Green will become the new standard (Kidney, 2015). Costs of production are falling rapidly as green product use is scaled up. Solar and wind power prices have become established to be cheaper than conventional goal/gas, even without subsidies, and this disparity is expected to widen so that soon renewables will be the energy of choice on a purely cost basis (Marcacci, 2020). Up until now, certification products and green awards have been essential in promoting both the business case and wellness benefits of sustainable development in the face of perceived higher costs. Such tools are potentially likely to become unnecessary as real-time evaluation now starts to take hold in the market and the consumer will be taking control of monitoring the actual quality performance of their environments. It is already possible to continually measure the outside air pollution in cities through phone apps, and this will increasingly expand to monitor the energy and health aspects of the buildings we occupy in order to measure optimum light, carbon dioxide (CO_2), particulates and volatile organic compound (VOC) levels. It is unfathomable that so much time is spent indoors, yet so little has been done to improve the health and wellness aspects of the places in which people stay. Specific conditions integrated into the architecture and design of both internal and exterior spaces can achieve improved human learning and productivity, whilst healthy environments can lead to improved employee attraction and retention, and can directly affect overall achievement in schools. Healthy places don't cost more to build, they just need more availability of information and monitoring, and that data will be increasingly available in the public domain in simple-to-understand formats and on free-to-use platforms as both public and private institutions understand the value of common data sharing. Such technology is not a future dream and is already in the marketplace. The market will react accordingly and places will become more healthy, whilst reducing energy use and promoting sustainable behaviour as part of "Putting Wellness First".

The past experience of market change is used as a gauge to inform what to expect when new technologies arrive. How quickly that disruptive technology took over and consumers adapted their behaviour is seen as key to understanding the changing world today. However, what is being witnessed currently is technological change on an unprecedented scale. Smarter technologies including automation, robotics, cleantech, 3D printing, and 5G are being adopted in homes, businesses and industry worldwide, connected through social media and smart devices (including wearables) and are changing the way we live and interact much faster than anyone could have imagined. Professor Ray Wills, Managing Director of Future Smart Strategies, suggests that recent market forecasts have continued to assume business-as-usual or traditional usage patterns, without anticipating shifts to be as fast or disruptive as they continue to be. Through his statistical analysis, he also anticipates the acceleration of change to increase exponentially (Wills, 2015). This implies that the planning of our cities, something generally carried out over several years based on accumulated past data, is hugely out of sync with current and future aspirations of our society, and that governments in particular are failing to react, regulate, and adapt at anywhere near the speed necessary to accommodate change. Tomorrow's population is expecting to be instantly informed about all and any matters, and to be able to independently evaluate through social media and ultimately mandate an action or product with transparent and real-time reaction. This raises the question of whether government in its various guises, based on outmoded management types, forms, roles, and structures, needs to be similarly re-assessed in order to be able to evaluate how it will be able to adequately serve the people through the twenty-first century.

Rethinking the Future

The much-heralded, 55 km-long Hong Kong-Zhuhai-Macau Bridge (HZMB) opened to the public two years behind schedule in October 2018. The bridge was the vision of Hopewell Holdings Gordon Wu and was identified back in 1998 as being a key part of the future of Hong Kong by linking the city with the bonanza of cheap land and labour resources lying in wait on the western side of the Pearl River. Justification for the HZMB came from being able to bring the area within a driveable three-hour commuting radius of Hong Kong, enhancing the attractiveness of the area to external investment for the upgrading of its industrial structure. Hong Kong appeared all set to benefit from this new economic hinterland by providing opportunities for local business to expand operation in the Mainland, particularly in the sectors of tourism, finance, and commerce. The Hong Kong government in particular stressed its ability to enhance Hong Kong's position as a trade and logistics hub as goods from the Western Pearl River Delta and Western Guangdong, Guangxi, could make better make use of the airport and container ports in Hong Kong (HKSAR, LegCo, 2009). Project co-ordination started in 2003 and construction started at the end of 2009, ten years after the conception of the project and importantly without following the repeated advice for building in the flexibility of provision for rail to be added if necessary. During that time, the surrounding economic landscape changed dramatically however.

Enter the adjacent city of Shenzhen, which was denied a connection with the proposed bridge back in 2004. As a result it then started planning for its own adjacent, 43 km-long northern connection across the Pearl River

Estuary (Shenzhen-Zhongshan Link) and was finally given the go ahead in 2011. Meanwhile, the China economic boom saw infrastructure projects across the Delta independently move on apace, particularly high-speed rail and express road links, and the development of the western region became focused directly towards Guangzhou and Shenzhen. Hong Kong had missed the proverbial boat! When the HMZB, by then Hong Kong's most expensive ever construction project at almost US$19 billion, opened in 2018, there was almost nobody needing to travel on it; just 2,200 daily vehicle crossings on average occurred during the month after it was opened, and in the interval since and at its busiest, that figure has never surpassed 4,800 (HKSAR, Transport Department, n.d.). To put this into perspective, that's fewer than two vehicles heading out each way every minute and so few that you could barely see another vehicle in front of you even on a six-lane highway. So what went so astoundingly, astronomically, and disastrously wrong?

According to the traffic projections from the original Feasibility Study, 9,200–14,000 vehicles would use the bridge per day following its opening in 2016 and this figure would be seen to gradually rise to between 35,700 and 49,200 by 2035 (Blackledge, 2016). The HK2030 Planning Study by the HKSAR Planning Department of 2007 cited the figure of 13,200 vehicle trips per day for year 2020 or just over 9% of the total vehicle crossings anticipated for all of Hong Kong – a whopping 142,800 average daily crossings (HKSAR, Planning Department, 2007). The average daily cross-boundary vehicle trips between Hong Kong and the Mainland did in fact rise from 35,800 in 2003 to 43,000 in 2010, but after that capacity remained relatively stable and by 2019, after the HZMB opened, the cross-boundary traffic between Hong Kong and Guangdong was at a daily average of just 46,000, less than a third of the massive volumes projected ten years earlier (HKSAR, Transport Department, 2020). Clearly the planning forecasts generated were frighteningly inaccurate, and clearly they also took no account of the fact that growth is not without capacity and that economic contexts change continually.

Whilst the speed of change in the Chinese development sector during the run-up period may have exceeded expectations, it is unclear how 142,800 crossings could ever have been anticipated across the border. Growth seems to have been seen in terms of some abstract mathematical concept, generated without the understanding of any human or physical context, without considering any potential for change, and without allowing for flexibility to reconsider options and build in contingency planning. Not adding the potential for rail in a soon to be rail-driven local transport environment seems negligent in the extreme. Times had evidently already changed well before construction started and yet the government planning juggernaut was unable to steer away from a mindset of inexorable sector growth and the massive outlay of underutilised infrastructure that was to follow, developing further underused road links, long-span bridges, reclamation, and airport development that continue to this day.

In fact, the previous bridge connection built to China from Hong Kong, a shorter, more direct link to the metropolis of Shenzhen, provides a further relevant case study. Opened in 2007, two years before construction even started on the HZMB, vehicle volumes on the Shenzhen Bay Bridge following its opening were well below its planned 80,000 vehicles-a-day capacity (HKSAR, Planning Department, 2007). "We expect Shenzhen Bay Bridge's two-way daily traffic will be 29,800 vehicles during its initial period of opening, and will rise to 60,300 vehicles a day in 2016" asserted Highways Department Chief Engineer Ma Ming-yiu confidently at the time (HKSAR, News, 2007). The average daily number of vehicle trips recorded at Shenzhen Bay crossing during the opening period in 2014 was quickly identified at just over 3,000 and for 2016 was 11,504 (HKSAR, Transport Department, n.d.). Specifically built for cross-border logistics transfer, the vast customs facilities lie empty still, with fields of bald tarmac and endless rows of closed inspection gates. The future was already boldly written on the wall.

Despite these lessons, more of the same are being added to the development pipeline, and an institutional inability to change the way in which planning is undertaken exists. In a business scenario, such manifest planning incompetence would see heads role and companies fail, but there has been no accountability for this shambles. Everyone in their daily lives prepares to expect the unexpected and make contingency plans, be it against train delays, weather events, or changes of mind, and so of course should leaders, decision-makers, and governments. More flexible approaches are essential in a world of uncertainty. The COVID-19 pandemic has been an example of unexpected change on a global scale, but many countries live with the continual threats of earthquakes, hurricanes, volcanic eruptions, floods, drought, war, pestilence, famine, terrorism, or bankruptcy, and the majority of leaders understand that climate change will come to destabilise the fabric of their cities more than ever. Resilience against the "expected unexpected" must become the most important facet of urban planning in the coming decade. In accepting that a change to current processes is essential, first there should be the decision to *reconsider* the commitments made and the way in which things are being done already. Is continuing with business as usual not throwing good money after bad; investing in yesterday and not tomorrow? Subsequently, *rethinking* some of the previous solutions is not weak leadership; it's responsible and adaptable governance based on the awareness of a changed context with new possibilities. It's a normal part of everyday existence, but one that struggles to be undertaken due to the time and scale of development decision-making processes and funding commitments. New working practices should allow for the continual *redirection* of priorities away from the fixed masterplan and towards the adaptable vision, allowing for optimal utilisation of the limited funds available and with the new focus on "Putting Wellness First".

In his 2014 book *Bringing Strategy Back: How Strategic Shock Absorbers Make Planning Relevant in a World of Constant Change*, Jeffrey Sampler started discussing how to plan for business resiliency in the face of rapid change and a unpredictable environment. His prescriptive model outlined the four "strategic shock absorbers" of Accuracy, Agility, Momentum, and Foresight aimed at helping leaders and decision-makers with the difficulties of medium- and longer-term planning (Sampler, 2014). Whilst primarily considered as a tool for businesses, there are lots of parallels that can be transferred to the urban planning context, especially since the case studies from India and Dubai demonstrate high-growth regions facing a rapid succession of "turbulence and turmoil", "expansion and contraction", with "growth and decline", which have now become pretty much the norm everywhere. The premise that decision-makers act cautiously when there are unpredictabilities ahead, yielding to the temptation to slow down and tread lightly, is an interesting one that resonates in the context of climate emergency, where leadership at all levels have been guilty of failing to act either quickly or resolutely enough. Kicking the can down the road has been a natural human response to unpredictability, but it's one that is clearly no longer viable in today's ultra-competitive environment, where if you snooze, you lose, both at a business level and even at a city management level. Utilising Sampler's four-point management strategy as an urban planning tool can be an effective way to rethink city resiliency approaches and many already well-developed cities have been increasingly moving towards using these tools as a means to effect more pertinent and effective leadership.

"Accuracy: Creating Order and Transparency"

According to Sampler, adopting "Accuracy" delivers fine-tuned and specific forecasting by understanding one's capabilities and performance. This allows for precision awareness of the competitive environment. In this case, a "one size fits all" approach to global urban development just won't cut it and the relevance of alternative development case studies needs to be far more critically evaluated. Each and every project, town, and city will need to have much more specific "self-realisation" by undertaking deeper positioning analysis and risk assessment in order to understand what is really relevant to it. Sampler suggests that there are three factors in this: Decision Triggers; Majlis System; and the Strategic Wedge. These could be re-applied to urban strategy planning theory and reconsidered as the "planning playbook", the "open town hall", and "rapid pilots":

Planning Playbook: Being able to react quickly and appropriately when the time comes, without a lot of discussion, either to difficulties or opportunities, requires clarity of purpose and limited option consideration. This requires advanced assessment of potentialities and a documented and approved procedure of if and when responses should be applied. A single masterplan is no longer apposite. Multiple potential-choice scenarios need to be played out in a "planning playbook" of potential urban eventualities and continually updated.

Open Town Hall: Dubai's "Management by Majlis" system is a type of decision-making process outlined by Sampler, rather like a town hall meeting. Leaders have weekly exchanges where anyone can attend on an equal footing, thus creating transparency and efficient fluidity of information exchange across multiple societal sectors, where options are restricted because qualitative core values are widely recognised by everyone. Town hall meetings have been a key part of the US democratic process for centuries, but with the technological advances of the Fourth Industrial Revolution, such meetings can be far more expansive and inclusive. Grassroots dialogue and consultation are recognised as being essential to successful outcomes, but they can be lengthy and frequently opaque. New methods need experimentation.

Rapid Pilots: Taking a small and low-risk, fact-finding step allows trials of new ideas to be implemented fast and lessons to be learnt quickly rather than strategising at length and then applying high-cost, high-risk interventions that may no longer be appropriate to changes in circumstances. Whilst already frequently adopted in urban realm design and management, the pilots should be used to create optionality and look for intelligence feedback rather than a confirmation of the adopted approach. As such, they need to be applied more quickly, less formally, and without expectation of certainty. The COVID-19 pandemic allowed this approach to come to the fore, with the rapid deployment of urban realm trials relating to bicycle lanes, road closures, and alternate working arrangements being implemented with wait-and-see results.

"Agility: Seizing and Repeating Opportunities"

Agility delivers speed and flexibility in terms of strategic options. Sampler describes two scenarios for Agility: Constant Adaptation and Making Strategy a Bottom-up Process. Constant Adaption recognises that planning for mid- and long-term scenarios is redundant, and that agility and flexibility require the continual re-appraisal of the current situation on short-term cycles. By further making strategy a bottom-up rather than a top-down process, mind and market reading as well as future prognosis testing act to originate strategy, and many more people are empowered to get involved in creation itself, opening up new and unconsidered options. These iterative-type applications are already being applied in sustainable urban design methodologies and could further be expanded and mainstreamed as the "playbook iteration", "urban concierge" and "city sandbox":

> **Playbook Iteration**: Urban development masterplans are typically framed in five-year, ten-year, or even longer-term concepts. By replacing masterplans with a "planning playbook", continual iterations can be developed as some options become obsolete, new hurdles emerge, or potential opportunities arise. The playbook is continually and organically developed, shared, tested, and augmented through "urban town hall" and "rapid pilot" methods.
>
> **Urban Concierge**: The amount of multisource data and information passing around on new trends and directions, developed research, and potential impacts is ever increasing, and is both easy to overlook and complex to disseminate. Concentrating information into a single point allows for the channelling of important or relevant information to the right places and the strengthening of opportunities for collaboration and cross-pollination.
>
> **City Sandbox**: Stakeholders at the urban realm level are multitudinous and informed. The complexities of interrelated systems and activities require the widest possible strategy base to consider conflicting requirements and unforeseen circumstances. Resolving differences and reporting preferences and solutions up the chain to urban facilitators and shapers sharply reduces the time for strategy development and public endorsement.

"Momentum: Speeding Past Shocks and Surprises"

According to Sampler, momentum delivers continuity and minimises disruption. Weathering difficulties requires the ability to absorb shocks and retain momentum. Focusing on the ends rather than the means allows for outcome-driven rather than method-driven approaches to be adopted in reaching goals, which is a compression capability tool common in technology space that encourages adaptation to overcome challenge. By further investing in intellectual and technical resources over and above physical resources, intellectual buffers can prove resilient and advantageous in terms of jumping hurdles and getting ahead:

> **Common Lens**: Urban envisioning is becoming an increasingly important tool for cities to achieve both a common public objective and generate shared stakeholder ownership and investment in simple terms that resonate and can be measurable as well as flexible to address changed circumstances.
>
> **Smart Cushion**: Investing in human and technological capital over and above physical infrastructure and job expansion allows cities to grow in real terms and invest in future assets. Intangible advantages that lead to a more resilient future can be developed, including innovation, creativity, problem solving, and effective communication.
>
> **Realm Trust**: Together with the "Open Town Hall" and "Urban Concierge" factors, cities should continually maintain an active "Realm Trust" of knowledgeable urban thinkers who can informally consider the implications and responses to potential changing scenarios before they come to pass. Such a trust is able to proactively rather than reactively engage in the changing world.

"Foresight"

Foresight delivers capability for sense-making and scanning the external environment, and Sampler offers both the need for Strategic Assumptions, which focus on the context of archival information that indicates whether a plan can succeed, and Alternate Strategies, which offer multiple adjacencies in terms of emerging potentialities:

> **Contextualised Case Studies**: Case studies form a cornerstone of urban design and planning; however, they are frequently applied without a thorough understanding of the situation they were required to meet, how they were shaped to address that specific situation, and whether that context can still be said to apply at the intended time, place, and system. A more critical analysis can supply missing depth that is essential in understanding the relevance of the study, its potential failings, and adaptations that might be suitable for consideration.

Formative Position Studies: Planning for change is all about the future and yet so many case studies only look to the past. Endless emerging research studies are ignored, trials are overlooked, and predictive trend analyses focus on the immediate, linear, and existing standards rather than the longer-term, disrupted, and improved standards. Anticipation and futureproofing against potential disruptors is of the essence.

Redirecting the Focus

Older cities and their streets were originally shaped organically around the geography of a place with access provided by horse and cart. Only more recently have they then had to deal with the difficulties of adapting and reshaping to conform to the needs of the motor vehicle, with the resultant impacts on existing urban communities. Modern planners have been quick to turn around these difficulties by using road and other grey infrastructure alignments as the primary urban development guide, creating regulated urban morphologies where the limited cultural and environmental resources would take more of a backseat. Rivers were marshalled, activities corralled, and inhabitants shackled. But it's now time to stop implementing development based on the principles of building costly "grey" infrastructural frameworks of roads, sewers, and drains, and then filling in the left-over gaps with zoned development. This is backwards planning, since the near future holds limited scope in cities for the continued prevalence of motor vehicles as we know them or for the building of engineered, stormwater systems unable to accommodate the pressures of climate change. Governments need to take a huge step back and rethink how they really want cities to work, positively planning where things should be and then working out how to best connect them through new and future communications technology. It is clear that whilst national policy and meeting stringent climate emergency targets for 2030 will be fundamental to development change; it is the cities themselves that are going to be at the rock face of implementation and they must prepare for continual adaption as new targets are released and new tipping points create unexpected opportunities. Their formative efforts have been and will continue to be critical in paving the way towards faster change.

Change can in fact be brought about rapidly; inspiration perhaps comes from Vancouver. In 2009, under Mayor Gregor Robertson's leadership, the city launched an ambitious programme to become the Greenest City on Earth by 2020. At the World Green Building Council (WGBC) Congress 2015, Deputy Mayor Andrea Reimer shared an impassioned outline of how the city has subsequently posted impressive results across ten broad environmental policy areas and detailing how greenhouse gas emissions, water use, and waste have been cut significantly, whilst comprehensive new strategies for urban food, urban forest management, green buildings, and green transportation were being implemented. Most interestingly, Reimer suggested that success has primarily been as a result of citizen engagement. More than 35,000 residents and 180 local organisations had been involved in actually writing the plan and overseeing the progress on targets and goals. It is the citizens who have driven the process of implementing the kind of life choices and trade-offs that they wished to make for the future, and these have been of far greater reach and deeper impact than anything that government could have achieved alone (Reimer, 2015). After achieving 80% of the high-priority actions named in the plan, the city set new targets in 2015 in collaboration with over 300 internal and external advisors. The public again provided their input, with over 46,000 people included in the process, of whom over 13,000 were considered to be highly engaged. The targets were refined with written input from over 850 community members (City of Vancouver, 2015). This kind of meaningful community involvement will be essential for all city policy-makers going forward in terms of ensuring buy-in to the process of change. A quick check on the current progress at 2020 shows that Vancouver now has the smallest carbon footprint per person in North America, but whilst community-driven targets on local food provision and bike and walking trips met the targets established, the majority, although improved, still seem a long way off and air quality has actually deteriorated compared to the 2008 baseline (City of Vancouver, 2020).

Edinburgh initiated a 2050 City Vision campaign back in 2016 which sparked public discussion about the future of the city and its residents" aspirations and concerns. Almost 65,000 voices played a part in creating "The Vision" of their city in being: Thriving; Welcoming; Fair; and Pioneering (City of Edinburgh, 2018). Key themes expressed were that people want to live in a city where the air is clean, that is litter-free, and where there are plenty of green spaces for them to enjoy. Whilst 65% of residents expressed satisfaction in the way in which the council manages the city (City of Edinburgh, 2019), liveability concerns featured safety, happiness, being welcoming, accessible as well as having good employment, education, and public transport in an inclusive, affordable, diverse, and connected city.

Singapore can point to its 1967 "garden city" vision as the original quality driver of its transformation into Asia's most liveable city according to Mercer (Andersen, 2019). The five focus initiatives of its Sustainable Singapore Blueprint really highlight the city's emphasis on quality of life:

"an active and gracious community"; "towards a zero waste nation"; "'eco smart" endearing towns"; "a leading green economy"; and "a 'car-lite" Singapore" (SG, Development, 2015). The city has always given people the impression of being progressive, modern, and efficient; however, it seems to be currently developing well beyond that and forging an increased reputation for being at the forefront of promoting innovative, forward-thinking approaches to sustainable urban living. Where once it was seen as a city learning from others and "walking amongst giants", the city now ranks second, behind only South Korea, in the 2020 Bloomberg Innovation Index (Jamrisko et al., 2021) and was chosen as the Smart City of 2018 at the Smart City Expo World Congress (Tan, 2018). This has required self-innovation in the city to generate solutions specifically tailored to Singapore's unique urban context. It has now become a global beacon of how to implement smart urban solutions in a meaningful manner that not only enhances the city's functioning, but also improves the services provided to its citizens and through them their quality of life, with a focus on building housing districts, such as Punggol Northshore, Kampong Bugis, and Marina South, using innovative design and technology, whilst old estates are being rejuvenated by introducing sustainability features through programmes such as Remaking Our Heartland that build on the distinct personality of each estate (Singapore Housing & Development Board, n.d. a), and HDB Greenprint, which encourages the public to propose ideas to further enhance green living (Singapore Housing & Development Board, n.d. b).

China may be driving change faster than anywhere. In 2015 the National Development and Reform Commission (NDRC) issued a notice on "Accelerating National Low-Carbon City (Town) Pilots" and eight national schemes were selected in a first batch to study and draft pilot implementation plans, guiding them to explore their own development modes featuring regional characteristics (China National Development and Reform Commission, 2016). The aims of these pilots were to focus on the integration of industrial development and urban construction, rational space distribution, intensive and comprehensive use of resources, low-carbon and environmentally friendly infrastructure, low-carbon and high-efficiency production, and creating a low-carbon and comfortable lifestyle (Yang et al., 2019). Meanwhile, the Central Government Policy Document "China's New Urbanisation Plan 2014–2020" had also asserted a focus and approach towards adopting low-carbon growth in cities so that urbanisation and economic growth may be integrated together in national policy. The emphasis on low carbon is highlighted and at the WGBC Congress 2015, Dr Stanley Yip of the Centre of Urban Planning & Design at Peking University outlined how China had already identified that new urbanisation needs would to be decarbonised with statutory goals of low or zero emissions as soon as possible, and outlined that individual cities would be required to adopt and enforce their own mandatory targets (Yip, 2015). The NDRC together with the National Energy Board had released an "Energy Innovation Action Plan (2016–2030)", which sharpened China's focus on innovation and highlighted how the country intended to use an energy technology revolution to become a global development leader and champion of sustainable growth. Driven to establish an "energy technology innovation system" by 2020, the plan is formed around 15 key innovative missions and the accompanying "Energy Technology Revolution Key Innovation Action Roadmap" clarifies the specific innovation goals, operational measures, and strategic direction of the action plan (China Energy Management Conservation Association, 2016). Dr Qiu Baoxing, former Vice Minister of Housing and Urban-Rural Development (MOHURD), outlined how China had been focusing both on raising public awareness about sustainability and clarifying how people could benefit both financially and in health terms from changes in behaviour conditioning. He suggests the developing vision of the future is very much focused on the use of big data analysis to allow citizens to independently start to shape and adapt their environments through the use of app-based software. Rapid technology solutions are being singularly embraced with the understanding that small improvements on a massive scale will make a significant difference, especially with a view to empowering citizens in reducing water and energy use themselves using a smartphone. Support for such technology, allowing flexible and individual choice, remains at the forefront of the Chinese government's energy policy (Qiu, 2015).

The moment for new envisioning firmly arrived as global city authorities used the various COVID-19 lockdowns to instantly transform their urban centres by closing miles of roads to car traffic, promoting cycling and walking, and making plans for more permanent interventions. European mayors such as Ada Colau in Barcelona and Anne Hidalgo in Paris have clear visions for the futures of their cities. Barcelona intends to close one in three streets in the Eixample District, creating public squares at junctions and ensuring citizens are no further than 200 metres from green space, whilst Hidalgo's plans include opening seven new "coronapistes", the dedicated bike paths on major boulevards, adding another 10 km to the 50 km of paths that were already created in May 2020, and extending the operation of "ephemeral terraces" where restaurants have spilled over into streets, occupying streets and parking places (Morrow, 2020). These kinds of "urban guerrilla tactics" may well just start the change in mindset required for long-term change, whereby the joy of using streets for community use rather than simply traffic flow is manifest. Hidalgo had been pushing environmental agendas during her first term in office and was preparing a plan to make the city's public transport entirely free, which will transform the French capital into one of the least car-centric major cities in Europe (Sullivan, 2018). Hidalgo further announced that petrol cars will be banished by 2030 (Love, 2017) and after a landslide second election victory in the summer of 2020, she immediately announced the concept of the "15 Minute City" for central Paris, grabbing global attention with the idea of enabling access to the six main urban activities related to living, working, supply, education, health, and enjoyment at a distance of no more than 15 minutes by foot or by bike. In May 2020, London's mayor, Sadiq Khan, announced a "Streetspace" plan that included a range of policies aimed towards rapidly accommodating a tenfold increase in cycling and a fivefold increase in walking, as well as promoting forms of electric micro-transport such as scooters (Mayor of London, 2020). The plan was implemented so quickly that it was subsequently deemed "unlawful" by the High Court in a case brought by taxi drivers (Ames, 2021). Khan sought his 2021 re-election on the platform of a carbon-neutral London by 2030. Meanwhile an experimental expansion of cycling lanes and pedestrianised zones right across the city of Milan under a plan called "Strade Aperte" (Open Streets) aims at adapting infrastructure to find space for social distancing as urban life is opened back up and includes reducing the majority of roads to a 30 km/hr speed limit (down from 50 km/hr) and adding 35 km to its existing bike network before the end of the year. Other cities that have implemented ambitious schemes include Auckland, Mexico City and Bogotá. Whilst the overall direction of urban travel has for some time been about rethinking local streets, in particular regarding open public spaces for people and local micro-mobility, rather than letting private ownership dominate the commons, the COVID-19 pandemic has rocketed forward transformations from urban planning theory into a global serious of real-time trials and pilots on an extensive scale. *Reconsidering, rethinking, and redirecting* are the activities of the decade. There will be no going back.

References

Ames, C. (2021). Judge throws out Khan's Streetspace scheme. *Highways Magazine UK*. https://www.highwaysmagazine.co.uk/Judge-throws-out-Khans-Streetspace-scheme/8811.

Andersen, M. (2019). Vienna tops Mercer's 21st Quality of Living ranking. *Quality of Livng Ranking*. https://www.mercer.com/newsroom/2019-quality-of-living-survey.html.

Blackledge, B. (2016, 6 December). *The HK-Zhuhai-Macau bridge: An economic excuse for a political gamble? Hong Kong Free Press.* https://hongkongfp.com/2016/12/06/the-hk-zhuhai-macau-bridge-an-economic-excuse-for-a-political-gamble.

C40 Cities. (2020, 11 December). *New analysis shows world's major cities on track to keep global heating to 1.5 °C.* https://www.c40.org/press_releases/new-analysis-world-cities-on-track.

City of Edinburgh. (2018). *2050 Edinburgh City Vision.* https://www.edinburgh2050.com.

City of Edinburgh Council. (2019). *2018 Edinburgh People Survey headline results – Referral from the Corporate Policy and Strategy Committee.* https://democracy.edinburgh.gov.uk/Data/City%20of%20Edinburgh%20Council/20190530/Agenda/item_85_-_2018_edinburgh_people_survey_headline_results.pdf.

City of Vancouver. (2015). *Greenest City 2020 Action Plan – part two: 2015–2020.* https://vancouver.ca/files/cov/greenest-city-2020-action-plan-2015-2020.pdf.

City of Vancouver. (2020). *Greenest City Action Plan 2020.* https://vancouver.ca/green-vancouver/greenest-city-action-plan.aspx.

China Energy Management Conservation Association. (2016). *Energy Technology Revolution Innovation Action Plan (2016–2030).* http://news.emca.cn/n/2016050 6100750.html

China National Development and Reform Commission. (2016). *China's policies and actions for addressing climate change.* China National Development and Reform Commission. https://www.ndrc.gov.cn/gzdt/201611/t20161102_825493.html.

Gronkiewicz-Waltz, H., Larsson, A., Boni, A. L., Andersen, K. K, Ferrao, P., Forest, E., Jordan, R., Lenz, B., Lumbreras J., Nicolaides, C., Reiter, J., Russ, M., Sulling, A., Termont, D., & Vassilakou, M. (2020). *100 climate-neutral cities by 2030 – by and for the citizens.* Publications Office of the EU, Directorate-General for Research and Innovation. https://doi.org/10.2777/347806.

HKSAR, LegCo. (2009). *Legislative Council Panel on Transport Hong Kong – Zhuhai – Macao Bridge: Main bridge and Hong Kong boundary crossing facilities* (LC Paper No. CB(1)1337/08–09(03)). Planning Department – Government of the Hong Kong Special Administrative Region. https://www.legco.gov.hk/yr08-09/english/panels/tp/papers/tp0424cb1-1337-3-e.pdf.

HKSAR, News. (2007, 30 June). *New link cuts journey time to Shenzhen.* https://www.news.gov.hk/isd/ebulletin/en/category/infrastructureandlogistics/070628/features/html/070628en06001.htm.

HKSAR, Planning Department. (2007). *HK 2030: Planning vision and strategy, final report.* Planning Department – Government of the Hong Kong Special Administrative Region. https://www.pland.gov.hk/pland_en/p_study/comp_s/hk2030/eng/finalreport/pdf/E_FR.pdf.

HKSAR, Transport Department. (2020). *Hong Kong: the facts – transport.* Transport Department – Government of the Hong Kong Special Administrative Region. https://www.gov.hk/en/about/abouthk/factsheets/docs/transport.pdf.

HKSAR, Transport Department. (n.d.). *Monthly traffic and transport digest* https://www.td.gov.hk/en/transport_in_hong_kong/transport_figures/monthly_traffic_and_transport_digest/index.html.

Jamrisko, M., Lu, W., & Tanzi, A. (2021). South Korea leads world in innovation as U.S. exits top ten. https://www.bloomberg.com/news/articles/2021-02-03/south-korea-leads-world-in-innovation-u-s-drops-out-of-top-10.

Kidney, S. (2015, 30 October). *Opportunities with Green Bonds for property, for cities, for the planet*. World GBC Congress 2015, Hong Kong. https://worldgbc2015.hkgbc.org.hk/upload/presentationfiles/Day2/Session7/Opportunities-in-the-Growing-Green-Bonds-including-China-Market-for-Low-carbon-Property_Mr-Sean-KIDNEY.pdf.

Love, B. (2017). Paris plans to banish all but electric cars by 2030, Paris, France. https://www.reuters.com/article/us-france-paris-autos/paris-plans-to-banish-all-but-electric-cars-by-2030-idUSKBN1CH0SI.

Marcacci, S. (2020). Renewable energy prices hit record lows: How can utilities benefit from unstoppable solar and wind? https://www.forbes.com/sites/energyinnovation/2020/01/21/renewable-energy-prices-hit-record-lows-how-can-utilities-benefit-from-unstoppable-solar-and-wind/?sh=3bb3eeb82c84.

Mayor of London. (2020, 6 May). *Mayor's bold new Streetspace plan will overhaul London's streets*. https://www.london.gov.uk/press-releases/mayoral/mayors-bold-plan-will-overhaul-capitals-streets.

Morrow, A. (2020). "Forget crossing Paris by car": Hidalgo lays out urban vision ahead of Olympics. https://www.rfi.fr/en/france/20201003-forget-crossing-paris-by-car-hidalgo-lays-out-urban-vision-ahead-of-olympics-2024-coronavirus.

Qiu, B. (2015, 29 October). *New normal, new green building*. World GBC Congress 2015, Hong Kong. https://worldgbc2015.hkgbc.org.hk/upload/presentationfiles/Day1/PlenarySession/New-Norm-of-China-Green-Building-Development_Dr-QIU-Baoxing.pdf.

Reimer, A. (2015, 29 October). *Improving quality of life in sustainable communities*. World GBC Congress 2015, Hong Kong. https://worldgbc2015.hkgbc.org.hk/upload/presentationfiles/Day1/PlenarySession/Improving-Quality-of-Life-in-Sustainable-Communities_Ms-Andrea-REIMER.pdf.

Sampler, J. L. (2014). *Bringing strategy back: How strategic shock absorbers make planning relevant in a world of constant change*. John Wiley & Sons.

Semieniuk, G., Campiglio, E., Mercure, J.-F., Volz, U., & Edwards, N. R. (2021). Low-carbon transition risks for finance. *Wiley Interdisciplinary Reviews: Climate Change*, 12(1), e678.

SG Development. (2015). *Sustainable Singapore Blueprint 2015: Our home, our environment, our future*. Ministry of the Environment and Water Resources, Ministry of National Development. https://sustainabledevelopment.un.org/content/documents/1537Sustainable_Singapore_Blueprint_2015.pdf.

Singapore Housing & Development Board. (n.d. a) *HDB greenprint.* https://www.hdb.gov.sg/about-us/our-role/smart-and-sustainable-living/hdb-greenprint.

Singapore Housing & Development Board. (n.d. b). *About the Remaking Our Heartland programme.* https://www20.hdb.gov.sg/fi10/fi10349p.nsf/hdbroh/index.html.

Sullivan, F. (2018). Paris gets serious about free transit. *CityLab.* https://www.citylab.com/transportation/2018/05/paris-ponders-an-audacious-idea-free-transit-for-all/560522/?utm_source=citylab-daily&silverid=MzI5ODU0MDkyNzUwSC.

Tan, H. H. (2018, 15 November). Singapore gets top accolade at Smart City Expo World Congress. *The Business Times.* https://www.businesstimes.com.sg/government-economy/singapore-gets-top-accolade-at-smart-city-expo-world-congress.

UN Climate Change. (2020). *Race to Zero Campaign.* United Nations Framework Convention on Climate Change. https://unfccc.int/climate-action/race-to-zero-campaign.

Wills, R. (2015, 30 October). *Distributed tech will bring regeneration of cities.* World GBC Congress 2015, Hong Kong. https://worldgbc2015.hkgbc.org.hk/upload/presentationfiles/Day2/Session7/Distributed-Ideas-and-Tech-Bringing-about-Regeneration-of-Cities_Prof.-Ray-WILLS.pdf.

Yang, W., Zhao, R., Chuai, X., Xiao, L., Cao, L., & Zhang, Z. (2019). China's pathway to a low carbon economy. *Carbon Balance and Management, 14*(1), 1–12.

Yip, S. (2015, 29 October). *Low carbon urbanization in China: Challenges and Reponses.* World GBC Congress 2015, Hong Kong. https://worldgbc2015.hkgbc.org.hk/upload/presentationfiles/Day1/Session1/Low-Carbon-Urbanisation-in-China-Challenges-and-Responses_StanleyYIP.pdf.

Right Development in the Right Place

Mitigating the Challenges of Climate Impact through Land Management

Rapid urbanisation in the twentieth century, coupled with the opportunities of technological innovation, has put unprecedented pressure on land resources, whereby financial and social expedients have risen above concerns of imbalance and risk. Expanding cities have sought to grow by creating or building on land that is particularly vulnerable to flood and climate impact, believing water can be tamed with new technology and the use of cleverly engineered systems of dykes, pipes, and gates. Such systems have been used effectively for centuries; however, they are expensive, inflexible, limited, and cannot replace the efficiency and adaptability of naturally evolved waterways and flood systems. Can the balance be redressed and developing cities learn from the lessons of the past by adapting key planning and design processes to prioritise low-impact development, and what integrated mitigation techniques can urgently be applied to modify existing urban areas?

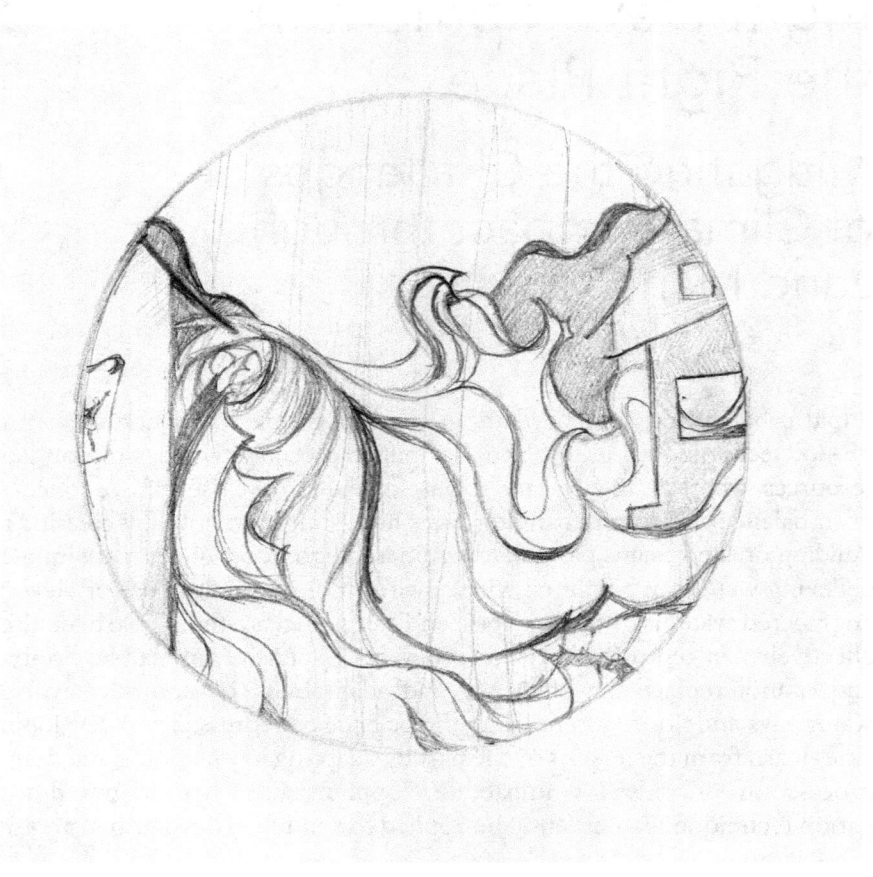

Drowning Earth

"Water, Water Everywhere ... nor any drop to drink."

Samuel Taylor Coleridge,
The Rime of the Ancient Mariner, 1832

The Rush for Land

Flooded streets have become an all too familiar way of life for much of the world's urban population, where more than half of such residents live on flood plains (Michaels et al., 2016). This is particularly acute in the densely populated low-lying coastal zones in Asia, including major cities such as Guangzhou, Ho Chi Minh City, Bangkok, Manila, Jakarta, Dhaka, and Kolkata. Recent years have witnessed increasingly severe and frequent flooding, which is only going to intensify with ongoing climate change (Abraham, 2018), yet rapid urbanisation is massively exacerbating the climate emergency, with continuing population growth projected to add 2.5 billion people to the world's urban population by 2050 and with nearly 90% of that increase concentrated in Asia and Africa (UN Department of Economic and Social Affairs Population Division, 2014). By 2050, Asia's urbanised population will have risen to about 64% and in China alone, there are already now at least 100 cities of more than one million residents. In India, 55% of the population is expected to be urban by 2050 and finding new land for these expanding city populations is beyond problematic.

So flooding is no longer just a problem for farmers living on flood-prone plains; water has become the nemesis of urbanites, where rapidly created new city development has spread uncontrollably at the expense of agriculture, woodlands, streams, and ponds. The huge city of Wuhan on the Yangtse River floodplain and one of the most populous of China's cities is now globally famous for the outbreak of the COVID-19 pandemic. However, in 2016 it experienced turmoil from a superstorm that resulted in multiple fatalities and the relocation of 1.4 million residents (Brant, 2016). Recently rated close to the foot of the Sustainability Index of 100 World Cities (Arcadis, 2018), but traditionally known as "the city of a hundred lakes", the chaos was just a small part of the week-long flooding which killed more than 180 people nationally, affecting 32 million people across 26 provinces and leading to losses of 50 billion yuan (about $7 billion) (Brant, 2016). Subsequently, the summer of 2020 proved to be even worse with southern, central, and eastern China and the Yangtze River Basin flooded by rains. The Three Gorges Dam was said to be on an "emergency footing" as it neared its maximum intake capacity by August, and flooding affected 63.46 million people, about 12% higher than the recent norm, causing a direct economic loss of approximately 178 billion RMB ($18 billion), with 219 people dead or missing and 54,000 homes having collapsed (ECNS, 2020a, 2020b). Such situations are now to be expected as commonplace. How did we get to this situation?

In the rush to develop more roads, homes, factories, and shops in order to feed the urbanisation frenzy, governments have turned a blind eye to that most basic concept of "Right Development in the Right Place" and grabbed at the cheap, flat, agricultural flood land previously and deliberately left clear from development. This has been replaced by engineered, high-value, high-risk urban development. Not only is such development irresponsible, it has also taken away the very land best suited to feeding burgeoning urban populations. From 1992 to 2012, the US lost 11 million acres of agricultural land with the best soil and weather conditions for growing food (Nosowitz, 2018). On top of the opportunity costs of lost food production, the potential costs of disaster far outweigh any short-term benefits, since the loss of existing natural drainage capacity sees urbanisation increase water runoff volume and peak storm discharge, raising flood risk (Ali et al., 2011; Dewan & Yamaguchi, 2009; Miller et al., 2002; Sayal et al., 2014). Development has increasingly been located without respect to traditional land management, knowledge, or sufficient concern for the natural forces of nature. For thousands of years, populations have located next to rivers – they are the lifeblood, facilitating trade, enabling agriculture, and providing resources. However, past generations have always been smart enough to know not to build directly on the flood plain, generally selecting higher ground for development and retaining agriculture on vulnerable land. Yet modern cities, concrete-caked and bitumen-baked, have fallen foul of both the arrogance and ignorance of a society that has been led to believe that natural environmental balance is unimportant and can be overcome with new technology and engineered systems built to manage stormwater, including underground drainage pipes, storage tanks, and deep tunnel systems, many of which have not been designed to cope with the intensity of the climate emergency. Daunting sea-level threats allied with continually intensified and more frequent torrential downpours are inevitable, yet many cities seem oblivious and ill-prepared for this. Climate Central suggests that 300 million people globally are currently threatened in living below what will be the average annual flood level in 2050, and three-quarters of those live in just six countries: China, Bangladesh, India, Vietnam, Indonesia, and Thailand (EU, Climate-ADAPT, 2020; Kulp & Strauss, 2019). Yet business-as-usual water management approaches remain prevalent in the concept of developing on low-lying flood and coastal plains and then attempting to rapidly remove ever-increasing floods of water through storm drain infrastructure, and in protecting land in the form of dams, levees, gates, and tunnels. The result is fatalities, flooded streets, and homes, submerged metro systems, huge economic loss, and an even more serious loss of natural systems and ecological diversity.

Wise Old Men

In the 1870s, the Back Bay Fens in Boston was a tidal salt marsh that had become foul-smelling and prone to flooding as the city developed around it. The challenge faced was one of sanitary engineering: to provide a storage basin for stormwater and to divert sewage flowing into the Fens so that the marsh could be restored to ecological health. The work of Frederick Law Olmsted reshaped the area to form a meandering stream bordered by wide reaches of low-lying marsh, creating a new landscape carefully designed to look natural (Berg, n.d.). Olmsted linked the Fens with the rest of an integrated park network along the Muddy River known as "The Emerald Necklace", which was envisioned as a common ground to which all people could come for healthful relief from the noise, pollution, and overcrowding of urban life. He designed paths and parkways to link the parks into the surrounding burgeoning neighbourhoods – a green-and-blue network at the heart of the city. It was around this time that the various planning professions originated and that of landscape architecture arose through the advocacy of its pioneering father, Olmsted. It continues to involve the systematic investigation and understanding of existing social and environmental systems in order to guide and adapt to future change. The scope of the profession involves site and development planning, stormwater management, environmental restoration, park and recreation planning, visual resource management, and green infrastructure planning, all at varying scales of strategy, design, and management; it certainly is not garden design. The decision-making approaches to development that have guided landscape architecture for 150 years have always had "sustainability" at their core. It was always considered "standard thinking". However, as the world leaps towards environmental crisis once again, "sustainability" is now a marketable commodity.

Let's skip to the world of post-war Europe, rapidly rebuilding with housing programmes and new towns. The new visionary is the Scottish landscape architect and city planner Ian McHarg, who during the 1950s and 1960s, from his position at the University of Pennsylvania and as a national celebrity with his own TV talk show, *The House We Live in*, pioneered the concept of "ecological planning". His 1969 book *Design with Nature* continues to be one of the most widely celebrated books on landscape architecture and land-use planning. He advocated an ecological sensibility that accepted the interconnected worlds of the human and the natural, and sought to more fully and intelligently design human environments in concert with the conditions of setting, climate, and environment – the true work of the landscape architect and in line with the rationale of Olmsted, who believed that the goal wasn't to make viewers see his work, but to make them unaware of it. McHarg served on several important panels and commissions, including the influential 1966 White House Commission on Conservation and Natural Beauty, in doing so befriending Ladybird Johnson and Laurence Rockefeller amongst other influential decision-makers. He set his thinking in radical opposition to what he argued was the arrogant and destructive heritage of urban-industrial modernity, a style he described as "Dominate and Destroy" (Massy & Niman, 2018). So what happened to the understood tenets of these luminaries. Why was their influential work and knowledge sidelined?

Seoul Understanding

As a means of learning from the past and in terms of the impacts of rapid urbanisation, there are few better references for rapidly urbanising cities to take as example than that of what happened to the Republic of Korea through its economic development plan initiated at the time of McHarg in the late 1960s, following the Korean War. The population of South Korean cities, and Seoul in particular, increased massively through industrialisation and unsurprisingly created many infrastructure, pollution, and environmental problems affecting the everyday lives of citizens. In the 1970s and 1980s, developers moved from the traditional built-up areas on higher ground to the undeveloped low-lying areas for site and land development (Banpo, Jamsil, Cheonho, Amsa, Siheung, Gimpo, Seongsan, Shillim, Janghanpyeong, Guro, Mokdong, etc.). Not only was this a high-risk policy, but the new areas were also developed without adequate consideration for stormwater facilities, resulting in repeated flooding. The loss of natural grounds, green belt, and farmland reduced the permeable green zones under which ground water could be recharged. The impervious surface expanded from 7.8% of the city of a population of 2.5 million in 1962 to that of 47.7% of a city of 10 million by 2010. Just 11% of surface water runoff from heavy rain ended up in low-lying areas in 1962, but this had increased to 52% by 2010 (Young, 2015). There are 40,000 basement housing units located in the flood-prone low-lying areas of Seoul. As well as the problem of surface runoff from the massive volume of stormwater flowing into these basements, the sewer pipes for basement housing are installed lower than the public sewage system; as a result, they back up and regurgitate horribly when it rains. After major flooding in 2010 and 2011, plans had to be established to invest heavily in order to change the city's flood control measures, which had previously been focused on utilising engineering facilities to control floods, into measures that accepted the natural environmental situations and adjusted back to those, whilst being more prepared and responsive by involving the population working at the micro-scale to minimise damage. Seoul adopted a water circulation system to restore natural water circulation and increase the amount of rainwater absorbed into the ground. The city removed highways and opened up underground rivers, such as Cheonggyecheon. It installed facilities that store and utilise rainwater, improved the permeability of roads and pavements, and empowered citizens to make use of rainwater. This type of new rainwater management is critical as it eases the burden on the existing sewage system and rainwater pumping stations, and helps the city to be more prepared for urban flooding. Seoul has had to transform its flood control policy to go beyond simple prevention to that of embracing the environmental, urban planning and transportation aspects, realising that the main elements that affect flood damage are a combination of rainfall, geography, land use, and the sewage system (Young, 2015).

Low-Impact Development

The realisation that water is a valuable resource must sink in fast. City rivers sent underground into concrete channels and storm drains can be "daylighted" again, as demonstrated in Seoul, injecting vigour into urban life while serving as flood absorbers. Meanwhile, cities are now starting to undertake disaster risk assessment, which is going to be an essential tool in shaping more enlightened thinking about where it makes sense to develop. Since it is unlikely to be immediately practical or possible to completely limit development on high-risk flood plains everywhere, the adoption of "Low-Impact Development" (LID) models in the short term that can minimise the deterioration of environmental quality must become the norm rather than the special. LID is not a new term; such models have been practised for millennia as being sensible and adaptive approaches to shaping the land with minimal impact when conventional approaches would be unacceptable. The ecologist Simon Fairlie, who coined the term, has described it as "development which, by virtue of its low or benign environmental impact, may be allowed in locations where conventional development is not permitted" (Fairlie & Land Is Ours, 2009). The US definition of LID is somewhat different and focuses more on the techniques of "sustainable urban drainage systems" (SuDS) or "water-sensitive urban design" (WSUD) as it is known in Australia, which generally follow a five-point approach to the efficient use of site stormwater: storing water runoff and releasing it slowly (attenuation); allowing water to soak into the ground (infiltration); slowly transporting water across the surface (conveyance); filtering out pollutants (filtration); and allowing sediments to settle out by controlling the flow of the water (sedimentation). Whilst the US and the UK definitions vary, both provide holistic and comprehensive approaches to land use planning that first aim to mitigate development impacts to the environment at a localised level through utilising 'right place' development principles and are common in addressing water impacts through internalising flow and management into a closed loop, whilst utilising harvesting techniques to provide sources of varied quality of water for reuse within the development scope, such as for irrigation, cleaning, or potentially even drinking water. Techniques generally include bioretention cells (rain gardens), cisterns and storage tanks, green roofs, permeable surfaces, and swales, all traditional land management techniques. High-tech or manufactured stormwater management devices are frequently integrated in the urban context that are able to capture or filter pollutants or aid infiltration. The spatial planning of LID is therefore critical, since surface and ground water systems need protection through buffers (Dietz, 2007), and implementation can be affected by a number of variables such as placement, selection of technique, design, construction, and upkeep that determine the volume of runoff (Muthukrishnan et al., 2004).

Cities as Sponges

Traditionally, Chinese cities have been extremely familiar with the need to configure their cities to water, especially those developed on the Yangtse and Yellow River flood plains which were constantly subject to flood. China formed some of the engineering marvels of the world, with parts of the Grand Canal dating back to the fifth century BCE and the 1,770 kilometres (1,100 miles) being constantly augmented and updated through dynasties over the next 2,000 years. Linking Beijing to Hangzhou and the Yellow River with the Yangtze, the canal has been the centre of trade and prosperity through centuries and includes dykes and lock gates, lakes and levees, with Marco Polo having recounted the Grand Canal's arched bridges, warehouses, and prosperous trade of its cities in the thirteenth century:

> And there are in it twelve thousand bridges of stone, for the most part so lofty that a great fleet could pass beneath them. And let no man marvel that there are so many bridges, for you see the whole city stands as it were in the water and surrounded by water, so that a great many bridges are required to give free passage about it ... At the opposite side the city is shut in by a channel, perhaps 40 miles in length, very wide, and full of water derived from the river aforesaid, which was made by the ancient kings of the country in order to relieve the river when flooding its banks. This serves also as a defence to the city, and the earth dug from it has been thrown inwards, forming a kind of mound enclosing the city.
>
> (Halsall, 1996)

Meanwhile, north of Hangzhou, prosperous trading canal-towns developed on the south Yangtze River surrounding Suzhou in sophisticated water networks, with waterfront houses amidst zigzag lanes, or as the Yuan Dynasty writer Ma Zhiyuan described in the classical verse 天净沙 • 秋思 "Tian Jing Sha, Qiu Si" ("Autumn Thoughts") "households amidst small bridges and murmuring brooks". These formed a unique architectural culture adapted to the landscape, breaking traditional rules of symmetry and regularity, and demonstrating the perfect combination of the traditional Chinese ideology of "Integration of Nature and Man" together with economics (Ruan, 2004). Land stewardship has developed over thousands of years based on learning through trial and error, and has enabled people to locate in safe places, keeping soil from eroding, and diverting water for irrigation. But in China's economic land grab during the last 30 years, such knowledge was jettisoned and the new development areas created on an unprecedented scale have been characterised on simplistic lines around grid road planning and inexperienced designers creating 'centres and axes' on pretty renderings that were able to convey simple story concepts to decision-makers not familiar with the multiple cultural, social, and environmental complexities of development. As a result, traditional landscape drainage has been swept away and replaced with insufficient, rapid dispersal systems and engineering control systems in the form of dams, levees, gates, and tunnels. The result is a massive and continuing threat of flood. But has China finally woken up to the Seoul factor or is it already too late?

In China, something called "sponge city" development has started to be all the rage and it is considered as being the solution to continuing water planning disasters. Finally, old knowledge has been given a new lease of life through a modern pitch. In 2014, China issued "Construction guideline for sponge cities in China: Low-impact development (LID) of storm-water systems" and this, as the name suggests, is closely based on SuDS/LID characteristics. By September 2015, the national government had rubber-stamped the development of 16 model "sponge cities" as an ecologically friendly alternative to the engineered urban solutions of modern China. This requires infrastructure retrofits of cites such as Xixian New Area in the north, with about 500,000 people right through to huge economic centre of Chongqing in the southwest with a population of 10 million. Each city received 400 million RMB ($63 million) a year for three years to implement projects. Sponge city construction evaluation has therefore become a significant issue for the Chinese government after such tremendous investment and as a result, the "SPC Construction Evaluation and Assessment Method" (EAM) to evaluate sponge city construction was also released in 2015. The EAM involves 6 first-level categories and 18 second-level categories, with 11 qualitative and 7 quantitative criteria. The 6 first-level categories are water ecology, water environment, water resources, water security, regulation and implementation, and construction completion rate (Li et al., 2019). By 2017, a further 14 cities had been added, including the major urban centres of Beijing, Tianjin, Dalian, Qingdao, Shanghai, and Shenzhen, resulting in 30 cities being selected as "pilots" for sponge city construction (Xia et al., 2017); however, the principles are being adopted and are spreading fast nationwide. Clearly a broad array of challenges are to be expected, from technical to physical, regulatory, institutional, community-based, and financial. An early study aimed at analysing both challenges and the opportunities indicated that the most dominant issues involve uncertainties and risks, and identified four factors as critical to success:

1. forming broad and diverse coalitions is essential in order to fully explore all possibilities, successfully pilot projects, and probe for system-wide changes to achieve beneficial outcomes;
2. further research efforts are necessary to examine the various techniques, performance levels, life/cost analysis, the range of multiple benefits, and other implementation factors;
3. enhanced communication and coordination are essential among agencies across all sectors, including stakeholders, government officials, staff, and practitioners; and
4. expectations should be tempered into understand that overnight success is difficult to achieve and that time will be required for education,

training, and experiential learning and that methods will need to be adjusted and honed in order to reduce risks

(Li et al., 2017).

It might be expected that the successful implementation of some sponge city concepts will not only bring about a necessarily more sustainable urbanisation process in China, but will also potentially contribute to wider related research and development through the vast amount of data and knowledge generation that will result. China's ability to conduct on-the-ground research through pilot projects at a significant scale potentially has benefits not just to the country itself, but also to other Asian countries undergoing massive urbanisation under significant threat from rising sea levels. The ability of China to rapidly mobilise and implement large-scale, fast-track policies has been clearly evident over the last decades. Unsurprisingly, results have been mixed, yet the country has typically adopted iterative techniques to undertake rapid change, learning continually on the job and improving upon previous mistakes step by step rather than adopting linear, deeply researched, and detailed proposals which take significantly more time to plan perfectly and are potentially never perfectly aligned to an ever-changing scenario. However, it would appear that for further improvements to develop through sponge city implementation, more site-specific regulatory frameworks need to be developed and relevant technical guidance needs to be included in project briefs. Whilst continual technical innovation can be expected, both product certification mechanisms and professional accreditation have typically been behind the curve. Moreover, there is a very poor base level of awareness and understanding of environmental issues within the population, including those in the educated classes, meaning that public outreach and education will be particularly difficult hurdles to jump. Yet the perceptions of climate risk that do exist suggest that improving basic education, climate literacy, and public understanding of the local implications of climate impacts are vital to public engagement and ongoing support for climate-related action. Unsurprisingly, because education, geographical location (urban/rural), and household income are the key predictors of climate change awareness, it means that those who are least aware are also generally those who are most at risk. Risk perceptions have been generally formed around dissatisfaction with local air quality and the role of local pollution appears to mistakenly shape the poor understanding of and lack of concern about climate change in general. In fact, China was identified as the nation with the least-concerned population about the risks from climate change of all 119 countries surveyed in the Gallup World Poll (Lee et al., 2015).

Is Anybody Listening?

At the Greater Bay Area Urban Design Conference 2020 in Hong Kong, themed on a "Critical Action Plan for the China GBA", keynote speaker Martha Schwartz, a renowned landscape architect and professor at Harvard Graduate School of Design, thrust sea-level rise to the top of the agenda with a wake-up call for leaders to take urgent action against the continued development of the Pearl River Delta flood plain and the ongoing land reclamation that continues unabated in the Bay Area (Schwartz, 2020). Nowhere needs to hear that call more than Hong Kong, where the sleepy government has yet to undertake a detailed flood risk assessment. Both the Climate Change Report (HKSAR. Environment Bureau, 2015) and the Climate Action Plan 2030+ (HKSAR. Environment Bureau, 2017) anticipate a potential rise in the annual mean sea level in the waters of the Pearl River Delta relative to the average between 1986 and 2005 of 32–53 cm by the midtwenty-first century (2046–2065) and by 63 cm–1.07 m by the late twenty-first century (2081–2100) respectively, and point out that a storm surge typical of a 1-in-50 year event today will become a 1-in5 year to 1-in-10 year event by 2021–2040. Such an event was Severe Typhoon Hato in 2017 and it was a painful lesson across the region, causing serious flooding, power outages, and contaminated drinking water sources. Even if not impacted directly, widespread and prolonged flooding of the Pearl River Delta region can cripple the ability of interconnected cities to function normally. Yet action isn't so quick to emerge; so far, only more studies have been commissioned to review anticipated climate change effects and reviewing current design standards in the Civil Engineering Department, whilst the can is "kicked down the road" once again with the statement that "there are longer-term considerations that will need to be discussed in the coming years." In the meantime, business as usual can be accelerated, with the government putting all its chips on red with a massive new-town development project themed "Lantau Tomorrow" and aimed at creating an island central business district (CBD) in rural Hong Kong waters. You couldn't make it up. Undaunted by the immense white elephant that was the building of the Hong Kong–Zhuhai–Macau Bridge and the dubious call to reclaim environmentally sensitive waters for an additional runway at the Hong Kong International Airport, "Lantau Tomorrow" promises the next jobs boost for the construction sector. It is shrouded behind supposedly meeting the needs for providing additional mass housing supply to the population and marketed as "smart" and "green" by the Civil Engineering and Development Department, the body tasked with delivering this Liveable City, but one only expert in building roads, bridges, and other grey infrastructure. It's a classic example of "the wrong development in the wrong place" and proof once more that governments are detached from dealing with the enormity of the problems they face.

Across the bay, on the east bank of the Pearl River estuary, further massive reclamation has been undertaken to build what will become the world's biggest exhibition centre at 500,000m^2 along with the 84.1 km^2 Binhai Bay New Area. The third runway at Shenzhen Airport is due to follow soon, all in extreme high flood-risk zones. The probability of extreme coastal flood disasters of high magnitude from rising sea levels increases significantly in the absence of proper protection and adaptation, and a region's flood vulnerability is in part related to its local level of socio-economic development. Reinsurance Company Swiss Re estimates that major flooding of the Pearl River Delta region would result in insurance pay-outs of US$35 billion and that the total economic cost would be "at least double, probably even more" according to its flood risk advisors (Moiseiwitsch, 2014). It is predicted that a sea-level rise of just 75 cm by the end of the century will result in more than 1.5 million people being displaced (Yu et al., 2018). Much of the southern part of the Pearl River Delta is just 30–40 cm above sea level, and with a population of 42 million and an economy half the size of that of Australia, according to Swiss Re, the region is the world's most-exposed flood zone.

It is critical for Hong Kong and the Pearl River Delta cities to urgently take flood risk more seriously and initiate more strategic and resilient development decisions, starting with naturalised landscape mitigation strategies led by environmental scientists and landscape architects, who have been advocating such measures for decades, but have typically been sidelined into undertaking cosmetic greening treatments to large-scale projects, which are primarily dominated by the more powerful engineering and architectural consultants, rather than engaging in holistic and scientific landscape applications at project inception, or "superficial embellishment", as the eminent landscape architect Hideo Sasaki once warned (Sasaki, 1950). This has been particularly true in China, where there is little formalised planning education and the profession remains somewhat unregulated and unaccredited. Thankfully, after Chinese President Xi Jinping suggested cities "should be like sponges", the term suddenly caught hold among architects, engineers, and urban planners. Yu Kongjian, the Dean of Peking University's College of Architecture and Landscape Architecture, and currently the pre-eminent figure in the landscape planning profession in China, has been successful in showcasing the "ecological approach" advocated by many landscape architects and has for some decades been a particularly conspicuous exponent of the socio-ecological planning approach of fellow Harvard Graduate School of Design alumnus McHarg (Yu et al., 2001). It may now be that Yu's lobbying and the mantra of McHarg is finally paying off and that government, developers, and planners in China are finally waking up to the massive urban problems generated by irrational and unbalanced development over the last two decades. With the scale of rapid development in the country continuing without respite, the impact of changes there can resonate globally and this makes China the urgent priority case for implementing better decision-making.

With the present climate emergency, torrential downpours will continue to intensify and become more frequent worldwide, bringing with them an increased threat of flooding and landslide. Whilst sea level rise will increase the storm surge risk to coastal towns and cities, low-lying areas and flood plains everywhere are at severe risk. It is surely common sense that new urban districts everywhere are located away from susceptible land areas and are allowed to develop in the right place – in places safe for both current and future generations, but without the destruction of valuable natural systems. These are not the cheapest places, the fastest places, or the easiest places to develop, but when "Putting Wellness First" these are the obvious places; places structurally well planned so as to ensure that the coming deluges can be slowed, stored, and water gradually released without causing flooding. Olmstead achieved these simple feats back in the nineteenth century; how can such a basic and traditional understanding have been so totally ignored by governments, planners, and engineers all the way into the twenty-first century?

References

Abraham, J. (2018, 8 February). Climate change is increasing flood risks in Europe. *The Guardian.* https://www.theguardian.com/environment/climate-consensus-97-per-cent/2018/feb/08/climate-change-is-increasing-flood-risks-in-europe.

Ali, M., Khan, S. J., Aslam, I., & Khan, Z. (2011). Simulation of the impacts of land-use change on surface runoff of Lai Nullah Basin in Islamabad, Pakistan. *Landscape and Urban Planning, 102*(4), 271–279.

Arcadis. (2018). *Citizen centric cities: The Sustainable Cities Index 2018.* https://www.arcadis.com/media/1/D/5/%7B1D5AE7E2-A348-4B6E-B1D7-6D94FA7D7567%7DSustainable_Cities_Index_2018_Arcadis.pdf.

Berg, S. P. (n.d). *Restoring Olmsted's vision: The art of urban landscape.* http://www.muddyrivermmoc.org/restoring-olmsteds-vision.

Brant, R. (2016). *China steps up flood rescue in Wuhan.* https://www.bbc.co.uk/news/world-asia-china-36732306.

Dewan, A. M., & Yamaguchi, Y. (2009). Land use and land cover change in Greater Dhaka, Bangladesh: Using remote sensing to promote sustainable urbanization. *Applied Geography, 29*(3), 390–401.

Dietz, M. E. (2007). Low impact development practices: A review of current research and recommendations for future directions. *Water, Air, and Soil Pollution, 186*(1), 351–363. https://doi.org/10.1007/s11270-007-9484-z.

ECNS. (2020a, 8 August). Three Gorges reservoir receives record water flow. *Chinanews.com.* http://www.ecns.cn/news/2020-08-20/detail-ifzzcmwe9699841.shtml.

ECNS. (2020b, 13 August). Floods will not threaten China's food security: authority. *Chinanews.com.* http://www.ecns.cn/news/2020-08-13/detail-ifzzcmwe9698272.shtml.

EU, Climate-ADAPT. (2020). *Flooded future: Global vulnerability to sea level rise worse than previously understood.* https://climate-adapt.eea.europa.eu/metadata/publications/flooded-future-global-vulnerability-to-sea-level-rise-worse-than-previously-understood.

Fairlie, S., & Land Is Ours. (2009). *Low impact development: Planning and people in a sustainable countryside: a report and guide prepared in association with The Land Is Ours* (2nd enlarged ed.). Jon Carpenter.

Halsall, P. (1996). Medieval sourcebook: Marco Polo – The glories of Kinsay [Hangchow] (c. 1300). In *The Book of Ser Marco Polo the Venetian concerning the Kingdoms and Marvels of the East,* trans. and ed. by Henry Yule, 3rd ed. revised by Henri Cordier (London: John Murray, 1903), Vol II., 185–193, 200–205, 215–216. https://sourcebooks.fordham.edu/source/polo-kinsay.asp.

HKSAR, Environment Bureau. (2015). *Climate change report.* Environment Bureau – Government of the Hong Kong Special Administrative Region. https://www.enb.gov.hk/sites/default/files/pdf/ClimateChangeEng.pdf.

HKSAR, Environment Bureau. (2017). *Climate Action Plan 2030+.* https://www.enb.gov.hk/sites/default/files/pdf/ClimateActionPlanEng.pdf.

Kulp, S. A., & Strauss, B. H. (2019). New elevation data triple estimates of global vulnerability to sea-level rise and coastal flooding. *Nature Communications, 10*(1), 1–12. https://doi.org/10.1038/s41467-019-12808-z.

Lee, T. M., Markowitz, E. M., Howe, P. D., Ko, C.-Y., & Leiserowitz, A. A. (2015). Predictors of public climate change awareness and risk perception around the world. *Nature Climate Change, 5*(11), 1014–1020.

Li, H., Ding, L., Ren, M., Li, C., & Wang, H. (2017). Sponge city construction in China: A survey of the challenges and opportunities. *Water, 9*(9), 594.

Li, N., Qin, C., & Du, P. (2019). Multicriteria decision analysis applied to Sponge City construction in China: A case study. *Integrated Environmental Assessment and Management, 15*(5), 703–713.

Massy, C., & Niman, N. H. (2018). *Call of the Reed Warbler: A new agriculture, a new earth.* Chelsea Green Publishing.

Michaels, G., Kocornik-Mina, A., McDermott, T. K. J., & Rauch, F. (2016, 12 December). Why are so many people still living in flood-prone cities? *The Conversation.* https://theconversation.com/why-are-so-many-people-still-living-in-flood-prone-cities-55281.

Miller, S. N., Kepner, W. G., Mehaffey, M. H., Hernandez, M., Miller, R. C., Goodrich, D. C., Kim Devonald, K., Heggem, D. T., & Miller, W. P. (2002). Integrating landscape assessment and hydrologic modeling for land cover change analysis. *JAWRA Journal of the American Water Resources Association, 38*(4), 915–929.

Moiseiwitsch, J. (2014, 7 July). Insurers consider likelihood of catastrophic storm in the Pearl River Delta. *South China Morning Post.* https://www.scmp.com/business/china-business/article/1548221/insurers-wary-flood-risks-china.

Muthukrishnan, S., Madge, B., Selvakumar, A., Field, R., & Sullivan, D. (2004). *The use of best management practices in urban watersheds.* United States Environmental Protection Agency.

Nosowitz, D. (2018, 22 May). 10 numbers that show how much farmland we're losing to development. *Modern Farmer.* https://modernfarmer.com/2018/05/10-numbers-that-show-how-much-farmland-were-losing-to-development.

Ruan, Y. (2004). *Water Towns South of the Yangtze River* [江南水乡古镇]. Zhejiang Photographic Press, Hangzhou, pp. 20–22, 60–62.

Sasaki, H. (1950). Thoughts on education in landscape architecture: Some comments on today's methodologies and purpose. *Landscape Architecture, 40*(4), 158–160.

Sayal, J., Densmore, A., & Carboneau, P. (2014). Analyzing the effect of land-use/cover changes at sub-catchment levels on downstream flood peaks: A semi-distributed modeling approach with sparse data. *Catena, 118,* 28–40.

Schwartz, M. (2020). Regenerating ecological services using the public realm landscape, *The Greater Bay Area Urban Design Conference 2020 – Wellbeing through Urban Design: A Critical Action Plan for Mega Region*, Hong Kong, 25 November. http://gbauda.com/conference-video/International.

UN Department of Economic and Social Affairs Population Division. (2014). *World Urbanization Prospects.* United Nations Department of Economic and Social Affairs Population Division.

Xia, J., Zhang, Y., Xiong, L., He, S., Wang, L., & Yu, Z. (2017). Opportunities and challenges of the Sponge City construction related to urban water issues in China. *Science China Earth Sciences, 60*(4), 652–658.

Young, R. K. (2015). Seoul's flood control policy. https://seoulsolution.kr/en/node/3525.

Yu, K., Li, D., & Ji, Q. (2001). Ecological design for landscape and city: Concepts and principles. *Journal of Chinese Landscape Architecture, 6,* 3–10.

Yu, Q., Lau, A. K. H., Tsang, K. T., & Fung, J. C. H. (2018). Human damage assessments of coastal flooding for Hong Kong and the Pearl River Delta due to climate change-related sea level rise in the twenty-first century. *Natural Hazards, 92*(2), 1011–1038.

Frames of Blue and Green 4

Adopting Green and Blue Infrastructure as the Fundamental Network to Plan Cities

Establishing connected human and ecological systems that promote resource conservation, health, and risk prevention should be the first priority of the urban planner and not the last. Reversing current practices, planning solutions must move rapidly away from development-led frameworks to that of first optimising natural system infrastructure and strengthening clear "go" and "no-go" areas for development infill in doing so. Understanding that Green Infrastructure works as the key component of urban design principles in shaping cities to be both highly functional and liveable, becomes essential to realising why is should be prioritised and funded upfront in order to reduce investor risk and improve return on investment. As well as demonstrating clear financial savings, there are further non-monetary benefits to Green Infrastructure in meeting environmental, social and corporate Governance (ESG) commitments, whilst for public realm-owned assets, how can the recurrent costs of management be factored in on top of the capital investment benefits?

DOI: 10.4324/9781003112488-5

Tree of Life

"To the eyes of the man of imagination, Nature is Imagination itself."

William Blake, *The Letters*, 1799

Missing Links

Networks and systems are connected; if they are not connected, they don't work. When cables are broken, electricity won't flow; when pipes are missing, systems leak; when roads don't meet, you can't drive on them. Hard, "grey infrastructure" networks dominate our cities and it's patently understood that such networks must be continually maintained, repaired, and upgraded. When different networks collide, they can cross over each other; one cable, pipe, or road can go over another, using tunnels or bridges, switches or bypasses to ensure their continuity of flow. But in the urban realm, two key infrastructure systems have been typically overlooked, which often don't flow, frequently don't connect, and usually don't cross. Not only are these systems not functioning properly, but traditionally they have not even been considered as being networks or worthy of planning in their own right.

The unheralded systems of urban infrastructure are those of "human landscape", made up of paths, tracks, alleyways, and informal desire lines, along with those of "ecological landscape", formed from rivers and streams, gardens, parks, slopes, and unutilised land. Both of these are subject to repeated system gaps, bottlenecks, blockages, barriers, and diversions that typically make them form patchworks rather than connected networks, and this seriously impacts their function. In the case of human systems, such blockages are manifest in health and safety impacts, whilst ecological systems are disrupted through environmental impacts. As such, these networks are not only important, but are also critical. Landscape systems need to be connected in the same way that highways, electricity grids, and telecommunications need to be networked. Unconnected green spaces are of limited value and there are essentially two main reasons for this. The first is environmental, where green space needs to support biodiverse habitats. Small remote areas can only maintain small remote "island" habitats where there is no ecological movement and the habitats cannot evolve. They lack resiliency and are highly vulnerable to change and its potential impacts. Second, in the same way that green space provides ecological movement, it is also able to provide valuable social movement in the form of recreational spaces. Interlinked areas create opportunities for more varied recreational opportunities, social contact, and movement. So, green space needs to provide a rich variety of habitat, diversity, and experience.

Planning for such systems, where both existing and proposed resources of multifunctional green and blue space are deliberately networked, whilst being commonplace in local government in North America, Europe and Australia, is much less so in the developing world, where urbanisation and population growth are at their most extreme and such planning is most needed. Labelled as "Green Infrastructure", the components can be cultural, ecological, developmental, agricultural, or recreational and include both managed and unmanaged green space (Foster et al., 2011; McMahon & Benedict, 2000). They consist of both public and private assets, can be with or without public access, and include urban, peri-urban, and rural locations. Together with "blue" landscape elements linked to pool and pond systems, artificial basins, or water courses, they form a "green-blue system" that can set clear parameters providing "go/no go" areas for growth and development. Using Green and Blue Infrastructure (GBI) to shape or direct where growth will go can protect essential ecological processes and systems, preserve working landscapes and resource-based industries as well as performing environmental services such as managing stormwater, recharging groundwater, reducing the urban heat island, and cleaning both air and water (McMahon & Benedict, 2000). Investing in GBI not only contributes to the environment but also creates direct and indirect positive regional effects (Vandermeulen et al., 2011).

Green Infrastructure systems, not road infrastructure, should therefore form the primary framework of both new and augmented planned areas as the best way to shape the pattern of development. Green space needs to be at the heart of city planning rather than an afterthought, and it all needs to be fully connected in order to allow flora and fauna to thrive and to allow people to move comfortably through it. Cities need green networks that are not severed by roads or buildings. Replanning to link existing green space and drainage ways with newly created environmental corridors (the bigger the better) should be a starting point in upgrading cities to meet the hardships caused by climate emergency. In identifying GBI resources, it is essential to recognise that linkage is key for connecting both natural areas and features, and for connecting people and programmes. Systems need to be designed that function at different scales, across political boundaries, and through diverse landscapes. Opportunities for linked inner-city green space should include agricultural allotments, temporary use of undeveloped sites or sites awaiting new development, private gardens, natural habitats (including wetland, natural grassland, and woodland), playing fields, cemeteries, country parks, and water bodies.

Most cities have not actively planned GBI networks as primary systems; however, their resources do often still manage to exist in part, having evolved piecemeal; fitting in around the surrounding grey infrastructure systems: the roads, the railways, the urban grid. They have often been formed as "SLOAP," an acronym for "Space Left Over After Planning": fragments of land remaining after the optimisation of all other networks and development needs, especially highways. Often these areas later become designated as "Open Space" or "Green Belt", and despite often being inaccessible, disconnected, sterile, poorly funded, unmaintained, and barely protected, are frequently allocated as designated green space provision for urban dwellers. They form awkward land patches where developers cannot develop and drivers cannot drive; they host drains, utilities, and level changes. Even specifically provisioned parks and rest areas are typically positioned because they are not needed by other functions rather than being positively introduced where they can best serve the community. Typically such facilities are ringed by multi-lane highways making access restricted, or are fenced off from adjacent areas and are laid out based on minimised maintenance commitments rather than maximised opportunities for amenity and urban enhancement.

The seeming unimportance given to GBI and its not having been systematically planned is threefold: stemming from the fact that the negative impacts are not immediately obvious; that such impacts have been difficult to attribute to particular deficiencies in Green Infrastructure; and that it has been almost impossible to quantify the impacts economically. This is no longer the case and considerable data now exists to illustrate the importance of primary planning for human and ecological systems, essentially "Putting Wellness First" and advocating a change in priority from simple, economics-based approaches to those addressing risk mitigation and of more sophisticated health and welfare-based solutions.

Man and Beast

So green space is able to provide valuable social access in the form of recreational spaces, activity nodes, meeting places, and safe walking connectors. Interlinked areas create wider opportunities for better-quality access and more varied recreational opportunities, social contact, and movement. There is increasing evidence that access to good-quality environments, particularly access to natural environments, is one of the easiest and most cost-effective ways of reducing social inequalities (Ward Thompson, 2013). The greatest economic benefits can be seen to those who are most disadvantaged. As advanced economies have become more aware of the prevalence of non-communicable diseases such as heart and lung disease, obesity, and diabetes, an urgency for more understanding has developed. Newly completed research in these areas suggests that access to urban woodlands can be particularly valuable, whilst breathing microbes from soil is good for mental health and can boost the immune system (Ward Thompson, 2018). Easily accessed green spaces supply opportunities for social interaction, walking, and talking, as well as the potential to undertake beneficial activities such as growing food. Contrast that with awareness of the health issues from walking alongside roads, where vehicle emissions should be of particular concern in the congested city street conditions found in dense city centres, not to mention the psychological stress caused by noise and safety issues relating to this environment.

As well as providing for human connection, green space needs to support diverse ecological interaction. If urban spaces are to have birds, butterflies, and insects, all acting as important pollinators, then suitable habitats are needed to support them. Small, remote areas can only maintain small, remote "island" habitats where there is no ecological movement and the habitat cannot evolve. These are highly vulnerable to change and particularly to the potential impacts of climate emergency. Green space therefore needs to provide a variety of habitats and diversity through as large an area as possible. Too much of the green space in cities is either "public park", which is highly maintained, poor in diversity, and sterile in type of use, or merely roadside tree planting, which has limited ecological and few recreational benefits. Better connecting isolated urban green space pockets and linking that to the natural environments of surrounding rural lands could have profound benefits for managing flood risk, enhancing the biodiversity of ecosystems as well as the accessibility of the population to adequate quality green space.

Creating GBI

Funding GBI upfront, as a primary public investment using a full range of available financing options, and grounding its programmes in sound, scientific land-use practice can, it seems, promote a sense of community (Bomans et al., 2010), help reduce crime, fear of crime, and anti-social behaviour (Kuo & Sullivan, 2001), as well as promote opportunities for community involvement and cultural diversity (Coley et al., 1997). It can further provide opportunities for exercise, sport, and active recreation, and can improve health as a result of increased physical activity, such as walking and cycling (Seymour et al., 2010). It also becomes an essential means to help protect, re-create, or rehabilitate landscapes, historic sites, or habitats lost or damaged by previous development. Subsequent improvements in environmental quality can facilitate better air and water quality, and can contribute to improved drainage and flood control.

The EU Green Infrastructure Strategy, adopted in 2013, highlights the actions necessary to be carried out under the European Commission, including integrating Green Infrastructure into key policy areas, improving the knowledge base, and encouraging innovation in relation to Green Infrastructure whilst assessing opportunities for developing a Trans-European Green Infrastructure Network (TEN-G). During the 2014–2020 programming period, it was estimated that Green Infrastructure would likely receive EU finance amounting to over €6 billion through public EU funds from various funding mechanisms, namely: LIFE+; the European Regional Development Fund (ERDF), the European Social Fund (ESF), and the Cohesion Fund; the European Agricultural Fund for Rural Development (EAFRD); and the European Fisheries Fund (EFF). Initial assessments of the exploratory work suggest that operating at an EU scale rather than at a Member State level significantly improves the benefit-cost ratio, contributes to social priorities in addition to environmental priorities, and importantly can also assist to attract private investment (EU Commission, 2012).

A large part of GBI potential exists in its capacity to manage urban stormwater drainage and the US Environmental Protection Agency has developed a "Green Infrastructure Modeling Toolkit" as a means to assist decision-makers in planning and implementing GBI as a stormwater and sewage management resource. The toolkit provides five modelling tools enabling communities, planners, and land managers to predict, quantify, and evaluate the performance and effectiveness of natural and engineered water infrastructure management practices at different levels of complexity. The model goes some way towards assisting in mainstreaming of GBI as a primary planning tool, allowing watershed scale modelling; however, GBI must consider the multi-use nature that provides for both social and ecological systems. Cities need regulatory procedures that are able to fully benefit from the cross-sector benefits of GBI, but integrating the various sectors of government is a common problem globally. An analysis of methods to mainstream GBI planning proposed that governments need to create new regulatory bodies that are able to reach over other branches in order to take bigger-picture views, identifying that close stakeholder engagement and urban forestry programmes can act as a means to help with the integration of systems when regulatory alignment is not in place, and that certification programmes developed by local government can certainly improve performance at different scales, as illustrated by the UK and India (Zuniga-Teran et al., 2020). The "Building with Nature Standards" used in the UK as a third-party certification method have been co-developed with both public and private stakeholders to provide evidence-based knowhow and guidance on delivering high-quality Green Infrastructure, whilst the Delhi-based Centre for Science and the Environment published *Green Infrastructure: A Practitioner's Guide*, supported by the Ministry of Housing and Urban Affairs, which outlines methods and strategies for water-sensitive urban design and planning, and is focused across multiple scales from city lots to regions (Rohilla et al., 2017). At the very least, planning space restricted from development is the minimal form of Green Infrastructure that allows spontaneous social and ecological processes to emerge.

The UK Landscape Institute has positively promoted Green Infrastructure as an integrated means for development since releasing a position statement in 2009, and it now forms the cornerstone of policy, influencing the UK government's National Planning Policy Framework and Natural Environment White Paper, the second National Planning Framework in Scotland, and Planning Policy Wales (Copas & Phillips, 2013, p. 1). The Institute provides significant guidance on how to deliver Green Infrastructure along with the following key recommendations for the various stakeholder parties:

- Local government should build GBI into the planning process as a primary requirement, particularly where it can fulfil the role of grey infrastructure in water and waste management in a resilient and cost-effective way.
- GBI often crosses administrative and operational boundaries, requiring multi-authority discussion and cooperation, but is even more cost-effective at larger scales.
- New development should seek to conform to and enhance an area's strategic GBI goals by liaising with communities and government, where even small interventions can contribute to the overall success of GBI.
- The effective planning, delivery, and management of GBI requires a shared vision where strategies, responsibilities, and actions need to be clearly established amongst diverse parties, inducing landowners, users, and managers.
- Long-term funding for management and maintenance is critical to the delivery of long-term benefits. Creative resourcing of such funding can increase multi-stakeholder buy-in and the costs need to be balanced against the savings from reduced flood risk, urban cooling, and health and wellness benefits.
- The multiple benefits of GBI are proven to operate on both the financial and ESG bottom lines, and go beyond that of just the project proponent to wide stakeholder opportunities. Decision-makers need to be able to focus the specific range of benefits that particularly resonate with their own objectives (Copas & Phillips, 2013, p. 17).

By embracing performance measurement to continue to evaluate built projects, the quality of designed and planned landscape systems can be elevated. Increased data is rapidly becoming available as research and recording methods improve, and this will be aided further with big data sharing platforms becoming mainstreamed. The Green Infrastructure Resource Library (GIRL) has been established by Dr Ingo Schüder of Brillianto for the Green Infrastructure Partnership as an ongoing database of documents, case studies, videos, tools, and other information about Green Infrastructure and its benefits (Green Infrastructure Partnership, 2020). As such continued study extends, the traditional understanding of the innate connections between landscape provision and the health of ecosystems, people, and economies can be highlighted and the benefits reinforced with scientific data.

As the specific body of knowledge related to GBI performance in particular grows, it can be expected to better inform public policy, reduce investor risk, and improve return on investment.

Applying GBI as a Key Component of the Futureproof City

Beyond its exceptional value for money and wide-ranging capacity, GBI is a key component of urban design principles in shaping cities to be both functional and highly liveable, including "Putting Wellness First" principles. Comprehending its versatility is essential in understanding why it should be prioritised and when it comes to "Reconsidering, Rethinking and Redirecting", GBI should be at the forefront regarding the replacement of grey infrastructure solutions with Green Infrastructure and redirected resource allocation. The following ten factors are proposed to summarise how to utilise GBI in order to enhance urban places and create adaptable, vibrant, and resilient futureproof cities within "Frames of Blue and Green":

Character: "Local Spaces Not Standard Places"

> *Use Green Infrastructure to promote character in terms of cityscape and localised street environment by responding to and reinforcing distinctive patterns of development and culture*

Enhance the quality characteristics of local environments through the use of GBI as a design feature, combined with other place-making strategies to catalyse economic development with desirable community amenities and improved aesthetics. Formulate design principles that respond to landscape character, vernacular, and sense of place, identifying opportunities for community stakeholder involvement through design and implementation in order to foster ownership and involvement, working to create a common vision for places that makes the best use of the land. Green Infrastructure can provide for multi-functionality as well as recognising the character and distinctiveness of different locations, and ensuring that policies and programmes respond accordingly. A holistic understanding of the social and environmental setting and sensitivities as they relate to Green Infrastructure is critical to understanding character and place.

Green Infrastructure investments are especially valuable in being a visible display of positive, localised investment in communities, whereas typical "grey infrastructure" is often hidden from plain sight as underground utilities, or exemplifies standardisation and modularisation rather than responding specifically and deliberately to the local environment. GBI facilities, by contrast, are bespoke, can increase property values, and can spur economic revitalisation by providing community amenities such as parks and water features. Increased greenery and tree canopy are proven to increase property values and the desirability of neighbourhoods, whilst the quality and management of green space is directly related to civic pride, community values, and local identity.

Continuity: "An Endless, Unbreakable Bond"

> *Use Green Infrastructure to promote the continuity of street frontages and blur the definition of street space, which provides a robust interface and interaction between the private and public realms*

Fully connect GBI in order to allow flora and fauna to thrive, and to best facilitate people to move safely and comfortably through it. The basic tenets of island biogeographic theory hold that bigger areas are more diverse and resilient, and by connecting areas and providing better linkages, ecosystems can broaden and flourish more easily. If you have a park that is surrounded by roads and urban development, it becomes an island; flora and fauna all find it difficult to both access and spread, and biodiversity opportunities are restricted. In identifying potential GBI resources, it is essential to recognise that the quality of the linkage between them is key. Disconnected "green space" isn't quality "Green Infrastructure".

Systems need to be designed that function at different scales, and across political and ownership boundaries through diverse landscapes. In creating any network, collaboration between diverse stakeholder groups is essential.

Quality: "You Get More Than You Pay for"

> *Use Green Infrastructure to promote public spaces and routes that are attractive, safe, and robust in terms of use, facilitate high levels of activity, and work effectively for all*

Measure the quality of GBI interventions to quantify water, energy, air quality, carbon sequestration, tree planting, bioretention, infiltration, permeable pavement, and water harvesting to create robust assessments of the value of this land application against other uses. Whilst it is often understood that access to green space in the city creates reduces stress levels, decreases negative mood, reduces feelings of depression, and provides other benefits to health and well-being, these remain hard to quantify. Furthermore, a number of recent studies appear to suggest that there may be a less direct correlation and that it may be inaccurate to conclude that an increase in green space provision alone will lead to a direct increase in well-being. Without clear qualitative attributes, the data suggests that poor green space can sometimes even have negative connotations. Smaller, well-conceived, designed, protected, and maintained spaces can be much more valuable as public assets than large, monotonous, and poorly designed or maintained areas.

Funding landscape is extremely cost-effective; however, obtaining data to demonstrate the health and wellness benefits, and thereby emphasise the need for funding has been difficult in the past. More recently, software models like InVEST are becoming available to map and value the goods and services from nature that sustain and fulfil human life. The term "Quality-Adjusted Life Year" (QALY) is used in economic evaluation to assess the value for money of medical interventions. QALYs can be used to evaluate programmes and to set priorities for future programmes. Public space results in a significant improvement to QALYs at low cost, since as an intervention, it can be applied to a very wide group rather than being person-specific. As an upstream intervention to public health, green space can have huge benefits (Ward Thompson, 2018).

Movement: "Plan First and Foremost"

Use Green Infrastructure to promote accessibility and local permeability by making places that connect with each other and are easy to move through both horizontally and vertically, putting people before traffic

Prioritise the creation of human scale movement networks that can utilise GBI resources and integrate them into a wider system. Natural areas, important spaces, cultural features, people, and activity programmes are best connected by Green Infrastructure rather than road infrastructure, and networks that connect more or less directly between high-usage places, entrances, and transport nodes are the most valuable. Pedestrian networks are typically appended to roadways and frequently do not correspond to the surrounding human desire lines, causing increased journey time on foot, reducing walking incentives, and directly impacting pedestrians with harmful micro-pollutants from exhausts, brakes, and tyres. Well-planned GBI pathways can reduce severance by roads, reduce barriers to ease of access, enhance flow volumes, and reduce safety risks.

GBI links need to be placed first and foremost in the shaping of urban plans before the needs of vehicles and other development choices, and not as an afterthought. A well-considered movement framework can harness GBI systems to provide wider choices for how people will make journeys and can include a more varied account of the different kinds of interrelated movement activity that urban development can generate, making quality connections to existing and potential facilities.

Legibility: "Focus on the Needs of All"

Use Green Infrastructure to promote legibility through forms of design and layout that provide recognisable routes, intersections, and landmarks to stimulate an understanding of opportunities and help people find their way around

Utilise landscape to introduce hierarchies, identifiable features and visual references that create unmistakeable clarity in orientation and barrier-free accessibility. Cues are necessary as the primary source of information in wayfinding. Varied edge conditions, foliage, and ground textures as well as contrasting colour can be used as the key elements that define particular circulation routes. Spatial organisation and components, such as sensory information and signage systems, including audible signals such as water, music, and birdsong, are critical elements of the built environment, and landscape spaces can provide natural applications beyond the scope of regulated street environments. Prominent landmarks and distinct settings within a given context help form a mental image of space, particularly enabling people with visual and hearing impairments to gauge where they are in relation to their immediate surroundings.

The compact urban form of cities means that the "sidewalks" are primarily related to traffic routes rather than human routes; they are festooned with highway architecture, barriers, and obstacles such as safety railings, road signs, traffic controls, and street lights. Pavements are typically too narrow for passing pedestrians and are further restricted by street trading, litter bins, delivery carts, bicycles, and excavation work, not to mention the challenges of steps and ramps that are particularly challenging for an ageing population and those with disabilities. A lack of universal design consistency, layout, and regular maintenance present some of the biggest challenges, yet such barriers can be eliminated through careful and thoughtful planning of Green Infrastructure interventions that demonstrate sensitivity towards the needs of all.

Adaptability: "It's Supposed to Change"

> Use Green Infrastructure to promote adaptability through forms of development that can respond to changing social, technological, and economic conditions

Proactively integrate GBI opportunities to respond to the ever-changing urban baseline conditions. GBI is more flexible and less costly than grey infrastructure and can meet the needs of both the unexpected of tomorrow and the unknown of the future. Development forecasting has assumed business-as-usual or traditional usage patterns, without anticipating shifts to be as fast or disruptive as they continue to be today, where the acceleration of change is increasing exponentially. This implies that the planning of cities, something usually carried out over several years and based on accumulated data and scientific study, is hugely out of sync with the current and future aspirations of society. The environment is constantly changing, and understanding flexibility and adaptability is a key proponent of quality urban design. GBI can be adapted to meet the wide variety of changing needs efficiently.

The 2020 COVID-19 pandemic illustrated catastrophic urban disruption for which governments were ill-prepared, requiring reaction, adaption, and regulation at an unprecedented speed in order to accommodate change. The resulting intense use of urban Green Infrastructure resources for human activity resulted from their adaptability and put pressure on existing grey infrastructure to be adapted to new uses, with streets and car parks reclaimed. In the face of adaptation to the climate emergency, Green Infrastructure development has become a key tool in strengthening resilience to the anticipated impacts of heightened intensity and regularity of severe climate events, including floods, droughts, and heatwaves, and acting as an insurance technique against such disasters. Prioritising the integration of GBI into key policy areas and funding streams as well as improving the knowledge base and encouraging innovation has become a cornerstone of the EU Strategy on Adaptation to Climate Change.

Diversity: "Health in Variety"

> *Use Green Infrastructure to promote diversity and choice through a mix of compatible developments and uses that work together to create viable and interesting places that offer a range of experiences responsive to local needs*

Diversify GBI systems by connecting a wide variety of contributing resources, both natural and manmade. Diversity helps to promote resilient systems, where a variety of differing responses to environmental change can strongly influence resiliency factors. Not all people and ecologies respond in the same way to challenges, opportunities, and risks. The range and prevalence as well as the spatial and temporal distributions of different environments can be crucial to the resilience or adaptive transformation of a social-ecological system, and thus have a significant bearing on human vulnerability and well-being in the face of environmental, socio-economic, and political change.

The continual expansion of towns, cities, and the hinterland that supports them has eroded both natural, native habitats and cultivated, ecological habitats, eventually leading to biodiversity loss and a reduction in systems that can react to adversity and change. The green environment thus becomes important in being able to support urban wildlife and human interactions that can adapt in the face of disruption. GBI planning typically incorporates tiered use intensity in order to create as great a buffer width as possible to more sensitive or protected resources such as water margins and conservation areas. In urban areas, "green" zonings for instance, can become an essential tool in the wider shrouding of Country Parks, Conservation Areas, or Sites of Special Scientific Interest, where only low-intensity access or use can be facilitated. Meanwhile higher-intensity uses can be proactively encouraged where these are most removed from the vulnerable systems.

Richness: "Unprogrammed and Multifunctional"

Use Green Infrastructure to promote informal urban interventions such as street markets that embody a sense of personalisation and detail, that can heighten community perceptions, and that allow people to use given places for different purposes

Reduce prescriptiveness on the use of Green Infrastructure spaces. Good design facilitates different users to adopt usage programmes that allow for multiple uses across different periods of the day and in different seasons. Free and open access to common space for non-prescriptive public use is compelling and critical for all parties, including developers and public bodies. GBI is not just a contractual obligation or a planning requirement; it is itself a catalyst for economic growth and fiscal gain. A thriving economy, along with healthy, inclusive, and engaged communities, enhances the desirability of an area, driving real estate values and civic pride.

"Keep off the Grass" is one of the top selling signs on Amazon today. It is indicative of an approach to green space that can be found the world over, one that planners and policy-makers must work together to counter. In cities, the strict regulatory control over the design of public spaces and the ratios between types of space has often created physical barriers between public space. The use of public open space under municipal by-laws provides notorious guidelines and rules that can often be perceived as overly restrictive. As well as "keeping off the grass", "not flying a kite", "not playing an instrument", or even "singing", in many urban parks you should also expect not to be able to play ball games, access water, ride a bike, hang your clothes, walk a dog, or light a candle. Management offices have further restricted movement and activities within public parks and green spaces in order to promote easy facility maintenance and public safety. Furthermore, through programming exactly what a public space should be used for, space becomes naturally restrictive to the point that anything else done in those spaces becomes forbidden.

Identity: "A Coat of Many Colours"

Use Green Infrastructure to promote urban "quarters" that exhibit a distinctive sense of place and that reinforce a sense of belonging

Enable GBI to respond to its local functionary needs, whether these are naturalised, contrived, protected, or commonplace, and contrast this with the systematic monotony of standardised grey infrastructure systems. Consider the opportunities resulting from the collage of characteristics reflecting the locality of a place and its needs, and provide definition and a sense of place at both nodes and along corridors. Places that develop true to their locality are likely to be sustainable and enjoyable, and to attract users and investment. Local ecologies should form an important part of character identity where localised factors along differing strands of a Green Infrastructure network include microclimate, urban form, culture, topography, building types, and materials; these will naturally nurture local distinctiveness.

Implementation policies need to avoid creating or imitating works of other styles; rather, they should develop an understanding of expressing the layers of location history and compliment this with the needs of the future. In a globalised world, international styles abound and as places begin to look increasingly generic, effective urban design policies and strategies have the clear potential to reinforce local character and create places with a real sense of identity. Green Infrastructure should highlight such character resources worth protecting and build this into planning policy.

Durability: "A Life Investment"

Use Green Infrastructure to promote the creation of lasting structures and the rehabilitation of older buildings with new uses to extend their lifespan

Understand that the profile of a landscape is not static; changes occur in its richness, evenness, and diversity, whether measured over minutes or millennia. Landscape change is fundamental to GBI, where it can be perceived as a sequence of ever-changing snapshots in an endless flow of moments. Landscape planning does not consider the implementation of any one specific moment of completeness; rather, the essence is to meet the varied needs of any particular perception at both a specific moment as well as a series of unknown future moments. Continuous evolution occurs to adapt to physical changes through the succession of plants, afforestation, soil deposition, agricultural practices, technology, and fashion, which see expressions of time over a number of years or decades. A tree planted today must try to serve the needs of generations for hundreds of years to come through adaption, durability, and care. As such, investing in GBI upfront might be considered extremely cost-effective in capital investment terms, but the recurrent costs must be well considered and built in, ensuring continuous and increasing long-term funding for maintenance, improvements, adaptions, and protections, as would be expected for any valuable asset.

Financing mechanisms need to be tailored towards the types of property ownership and potential benefits. Unlike traditional, public benefit infrastructure on publicly owned land, GBI can involve assets on property under differing ownership. It's especially important to highlight the non-monetary benefits of GBI to non-governmental property owners or agencies, as well as the clear financial savings. In economic terms, benefits are typically "public goods" rather than "private goods". For public realm-owned assets, an integrated finance strategy can include the linking of GBI investments with those of traditional grey infrastructure services. For example, budgets related to land development, street construction and maintenance, transportation, open space, wildlife conservation, stormwater management, and flood control or disaster relief are all potential contributors to GBI financing.

References

Bomans, K., Steenberghen, T., Dewaelheyns, V., Leinfelder, H., & Gulinck, H. (2010). Underrated transformations in the open space: The case of an urbanized and multifunctional area. *Landscape and Urban Planning, 94*(3–4), 196–205.

Coley, R. L., Sullivan, W. C., & Kuo, F. E. (1997). Where does community grow? The social context created by nature in urban public housing. *Environment and Behavior, 29*(4), 468–494.

Copas, R., & Phillips, I. (2013). *Green Infrastructure: An integrated approach to land use; Landscape Institute position statements.* Landscape Institute.

EU Commission. (2012). *The multifunctionality of Green Infrastructure*. Directorate-General Environment. https://ec.europa.eu/environment/nature/ecosystems/docs/Green_Infrastructure.pdf.

Foster, J., Lowe, A., & Winkelman, S. (2011). The value of Green Infrastructure for urban climate adaptation. *Center for Clean Air Policy, 750*(1), 1–52.

Green Infrastructure Partnership. (2020). *The Green Infrastructure Resource Library (GIRL)*. https://www.brillianto.co.uk/green-infrastructure/?q=GIRL-view.

Kuo, F. E., & Sullivan, W. C. (2001). Environment and crime in the inner city: Does vegetation reduce crime? *Environment and Behavior, 33*(3), 343–367.

McMahon, E. T., & Benedict, M. (2000). Green infrastructure. *Planning Commissioners Journal, 37*(4), 4–7.

Rohilla, S. K., Jainer, S., & Matto, M. (2017). *Green Infrastructure: A practitioner's guide*. Centre for Science and Environment. http://cdn.cseindia.org/attachments/0.91656700_1505301183_Green-Infrastructure-guide.pdf.

Seymour, M., Wolch, J., Reynolds, K. D., & Bradbury, H. (2010). Resident perceptions of urban alleys and alley greening. *Applied Geography, 30*(3), 380–393.

Vandermeulen, V., Verspecht, A., Vermeire, B., Van Huylenbroeck, G., & Gellynck, X. (2011). The use of economic valuation to create public support for Green Infrastructure investments in urban areas. *Landscape and Urban Planning, 103*(2), 198–206.

Ward Thompson, C. (2013). Activity, exercise and the planning and design of outdoor spaces. *Journal of Environmental Psychology, 34*, 79–96. https://doi.org/https://doi.org/10.1016/j.jenvp.2013.01.003.

Ward Thompson, C. (2018, 22 May). *An ecology of urban spaces* [Interview]. http://www.initiatives.com.hk/180926-an-ecology-of-urban-spaces.html.

Zuniga-Teran, A. A., Staddon, C., de Vito, L., Gerlak, A. K., Ward, S., Schoeman, Y., Hart, A., & Booth, G. (2020). Challenges of mainstreaming Green Infrastructure in built environment professions. *Journal of Environmental Planning and Management, 63*(4), 710–732.

Placing for Age

Adapting Urban Development for Diversity and Inclusivity

5

When considering the ageing population demographic across the developed world and the trends towards "ageing-in-place" and primary care in the community, it becomes apparent that our cities are barely age-cognisant and not remotely age-friendly. In fact, ageing carries negative connotations that need to be reappraised in terms of better understanding the variety of age conditions and the possibilities from utilising the benefits of ageing in society through continued learning, knowledge sharing, and wisdom acquisition. Shared research identifies what is valued by the citizens of ageing societies and the importance of introducing a far wider range of development models that are able to incorporate housing and care provision, along with augmenting civic infrastructure that can better meet the needs and expectations of more inclusive urban populations. Meanwhile, new smart technologies are expected to be increasingly important in providing remote knowledge and support to health-focused communities but ultimately cannot replace social support systems, requiring the development of new processes whereby they can work hand-in-hand.

84 Placing for Age

Immortals

*"In narrow circles thinking also narrows,
The more one expands, the greater the purpose."*

Friedrich Schiller, *Wallenstein*, 1911

Smart Ageing

The UN has pointed out that the world is experiencing a seismic demographic shift, one in which no country will be immune to the consequences (UN, Department of Economic and Social Affairs, 2015). While increasing life expectancy and declining birth rates are considered major achievements in modern science and healthcare, they are already having a significant impact on future generations. By 2050, the estimated 10 billion people on Earth, compared to 7.7 billion today, will be living longer and the balance of those aged 65 and over compared to the working-age population will have nearly tripled from 20% in 1980 to 58% in 2060 (OECD, 2021a). Japan, Finland, and Italy are the countries with the oldest populations, whilst South Korea, China, Greece, Poland, Slovakia, Portugal, and Spain have the fastest-ageing populations. Japan, currently the world's oldest major economy, has been aware of its standout problem with an ageing demographic for a long time. Although its birth rate is not as low as that of many other rich countries, about 28% of Japan's population is currently above 65 years of age and this will increase to 40% by 2060 (Statistics Bureau of Japan, 2019; Japan, IPSS, 2021). However, South Korea is on track to surpass Japan's problems, with 44% of its population reaching that threshold by 2060 (Ahn, 2020) and the country is expected to become the world's oldest society as early as 2045 (Shin, 2019). According to the World Health Organization (WHO), when an ageing rate exceeds 7%, it becomes an "ageing society", when it exceeds 14%, it becomes an "aged society", and when it exceeds 21%, it becomes a "super-aged society"; the "ageing rate" is defined as the proportion of a society's population aged 65 or older. It took just 17 years for South Korea to become an "ageing society", whilst Japan took 24 years for the same transition, and by 2017, South Korea had officially become an "aged society" (Kim & Jang, 2017). As of end of 2019, the ageing rate had climbed to 15.5%, exceeding earlier estimates, and is expected to become a "super-aged" society as early as 2026 (Ahn, 2020; Choi, 2018; Shin, 2019). The average life expectancy of Koreans rose from 65 years in 1980 to 82.4 years in 2016, yet the suicide rate for Korea's older people has remained highest among all Organisation for Economic Co-operation and Development (OECD) members and is coupled with the highest poverty rate for this group (OECD, 2014). In terms of an index formulated by HelpAge International, a London-based rights group for older people, to evaluate conditions for seniors, Korea ranked 60th out of 96 nations in 2015. Whilst Switzerland topped the list, it came after Japan, Vietnam and China, which were placed eighth, 41st, and 52nd respectively, and lower than Tajikistan and Guatemala (HelpAge International, 2015).

Extraordinary efforts will need to be exerted to make the super-aged society both more vibrant and supportive by potentially overhauling healthcare, insurance, pensions, housing, and transportation systems and revising legal codes to adapt to demographic changes which will all be part of the necessity of "Putting Wellness First". The shift caused by ageing populations in developed economies has in fact been exacerbated by the global trend towards urbanisation. The challenge of providing adequate urban care for older people has become pressing, yet the focus up to now has primarily been on providing adequate facilities for them, whereas the frequently presented preference for ageing-in-place, coupled with a clear necessity for increased "care in the community" that addresses the shortfall in public healthcare support, has in fact positioned the wider urban public realm as the critical battleground for support of the aged. Action set up by other advanced nations that have preceded South Korea in becoming aged societies can be taken into account, and Japan has more to teach than most. The WHO Global Network for Age-Friendly Cities and Communities has been established to foster the exchange of experience and mutual learning between cities and communities worldwide, and promote healthy and active ageing, and a good quality of life for their older residents (WHO, 2020b). But what does "age-friendly" mean?

It's important to understand that "age-friendly" can be interpreted as relating either to being friendly to "all ages", what might be termed "inclusive", or to a more narrow view in terms of meaning "senior-friendly" or "elder-friendly", which tends to focus on communities targeted solely at older people. The WHO suggests that "an age-friendly world enables people of all ages to actively participate in community activities and treats everyone with respect, regardless of their age". Furthermore "in an age-friendly community, policies, services and structures related to the physical and social environment are designed to support and enable older people to 'age actively' – that is, to live in security, enjoy good health and continue to participate fully in society" (WHO, 2020a). This contrasts somewhat with traditional models of age-friendliness that have focused on a narrow interpretation, such as that of the US model of "elderly communities" including the likes of "The Villages", Florida's largest retirement community, and "Sun City" in Arizona, the first concept originating back in the 1960s. These communities have limited demographics with most residents typically being over 75 years old. "An age-friendly city emphasises enablement rather than disablement; it is friendly for all ages and not just "elder-friendly" (WHO, 2007).

Age-friendly communities that developed in Japan over the same period interpreted things somewhat differently, as can be expected, despite the same aim to provide age-specific facilities. Tama New Town, located on hilly land in Tokyo's western suburb, is the largest new town ever developed in Japan and was formed during the period of rapid economic growth in the 1970s as a dense, suburban development to counter urban sprawl. Its design adopted modernist, mass-housing planning with age-specific concepts and starter homes aimed at young buyers, with five-storey walk-up buildings, small apartments, and facilities focused at the baby boomer generation. However, the new towns never quite fulfilled their planning intent and the upward mobility of the generation never matured, meaning that the community "aged in place", and this has become somewhat problematic in today's situation with the provision of facilities now unsuited to the demographic. Tama New Town faces acute challenges of continuity and transformation, so in the same way that the term "age-friendly" may be ambiguous in terms of its age intent, it's also important to recognise a distinction that facilities need to be not only "age-friendly", but also need to be "ageing-friendly" and incorporate flexible and "time-adaptive" design principles to accommodate successful "ageing-in-place" or "ageing-in-community" (Murata, 2018).

Japan reacted to the ageing problem with a multi-pronged approach, first introducing comprehensive Long-Term Care Insurance in 2000 geared towards the financing of government-approved care plans offering different care models, such as "living in assisted-care" and "home care and assistance with grocery shopping". Plans have continued to be improved by introducing wider care models that integrate healthcare, preventive care, and long-term care. Meanwhile, the government aims to pivot economics towards the sector with the creation of the MedTech and aged-care industries by tapping into Japan's historical advantage in industrial manufacturing, design, and customer service (Pang & Arivalagan, 2020). In this regard, the concept of "smart ageing" has been developed by Professor Hiroyuki Murata of the Smart Ageing International Research Centre. According to Murata, there are four conditions to smart ageing – cognitive stimulation, physical exercise, balanced nutrition, and socialisation – which all need to be the focus of the next generation of "ageing-friendly" cities and communities (Murata, 2018). Smart Ageing aims to promote continued learning, knowledge sharing, and wisdom acquisition, according to Murata, in order to reappraise the traditional negative associations of ageing in terms of deterioration of skills, reduction in mobility, and loss of potential, and instead bring to the fore anti-"anti-ageing" concepts on the ideas of gain, development, and growth, in the belief that "all individuals and societies are maturing intellectually whilst effectively dealing with the changes associated with ageing".

The China Crisis

Care provision for older people is a problem the world over, but in China the problems are somewhat different. In 1996, China officially required children to care for aged parents; however, due to the demographic imbalance resulting from the one-child policy of the 1970s, a massive burden has now developed on the young working population. With the move towards urbanisation coupled with an ageing population shift, the challenge in providing adequate care to older people is very real. With siblings being uncommon, one child must typically care for both parents and four grandparents (the 1-2-4 ratio). This requirement on the young working generation has put pressure on Confucian traditions which dictated that children were responsible for taking care of their elders. Typically, the close-knit Chinese family would together support new children, with the older generation minding youngsters whilst the parents worked. With the working generation now moving far off to the cities for jobs, they often have to leave both their own children together with their parents in their rural villages and thereby become absent parents. Even if grandparents move to cities to join their families, they are necessarily left alone during the day, yet because of the Chinese "hukou" restrictions not categorising them as city residents, they have not had access to government social services provision or medical support. The problem has been exacerbated by the significant impact on rural villages, which have become depopulated by all but a few older people. Recent trends have shown that urban workers would prefer to bring their families to the cities so that they can also take care of them whilst they bring up their children; however, the availability of affordable space, lack of services support, and the associated higher costs have become significant issues restricting this from happening more often.

Under such pressures, the new generations are having to cast off many of the traditional responsibilities that they carried, and their outlook growing up in a "new China" will by necessity be different from those of past generations. However, one thing is apparent – the key to population growth and the care of older people will remain closely intertwined. The current Y generation entering the employment market have big decisions to make; the obvious financial burden of maintaining up to six older family members themselves clearly acts to dissuade young people from having children themselves. For those who choose to do so, few will apply to have a second child under the more relaxed policy scenario, citing lack of time and space as key concerns in addition to of the obvious cost. The usual 1–2-4 scenario of a couple supporting one child and four parents may develop into a 0–2-4–8 where parents and grandparents replace the single child, which could have significant implications for housing and facility provision. Even the well-educated young urban population is finding it increasingly impossible to afford home ownership. This situation now prohibits them from even getting married, since men are under cultural pressure to be able to provide a house in advance and any such accommodation may need to be big enough to accommodate multiple generations, even before there are any children to consider.

China's thirteenth five-year plan hinted at the scale of the problem, stating that: "As an integral part of elderly care, families and communities are asked to take their share of responsibilities. Community elderly care centres will receive more government funding" (China, State Council, 2017). In 2008, the government of Beijing Municipality outlined the "9064" framework for the care model to be implemented by 2020, whereby 90% of older people are expected to spend their last stages of life at home and be cared for by their family (home-based), 6% are expected to enjoy their last stage of life at home with community support (community-based), and just 4% are expected to be supported by long-term care institutions (institution-based) (Wang & Long (2018); Yu & Rosenberg (2017)).

The vast majority of older people will need to live with their families through several stages of care under the same roof or in close proximity. Those older people who are active need highly varied offerings and to be well connected to regular mass transport and a local community, whilst this will need to be integrated with those who are also needing critical care in the same family. The concept of the "out-of-town retirement village" will have a limited market here. Many more older people are going to need to be supported in the cities, potentially independently, and yet still be closely tied to their families in developments which provide diverse and flexible, multi-demographic opportunities to age-in-place. Residential development will have to become increasingly focused on promoting "elder" attributes as the main sales focus, with expanded health and wellness issues coming to the fore. The inclusion or proximity to senior activities, learning, nursing, and critical care will prove more compelling than that of schools and kindergartens, yet the two may become drawn closely together. Real estate developers are going to have to provide increasingly dynamic and varied products to meet the demand (Wilson, 2018a).

The 2006 White Paper *The Development of China's Undertakings for the Aged* affirmed the government's "active" role in promoting the construction of homes for seniors (China, State Council, 2006). The China Guangzhou government, for instance, announced in 2014 that it had made available 53 areas designated with 51,000 bed spaces for the fast-track building of new care homes, where the number of older people in the city was anticipated to reach 1.75 million by 2020 (almost 20% of the population). Land for care facilities is allocated directly or through public auction, and developers, corporations, organisations, and individuals can work either with the government or independently to build the homes (*New Express*, 2014). However, the facilities are considered not-for-profit and, as such, concerns exist about how the financial models will work in tempting management operators into development. Of the 53 areas, just seven are designated for public care homes; currently 71% of care homes in Guangzhou are privately owned. Senior housing is still a relatively new concept in China and there needs to be significant regulation in the sector, which has yet to show any obvious trends, but is expected to follow those of the US, Europe, and Japan, where the sector has a broad spectrum, providing communities for the "active elderly" who do not need care and also to the very old and frail who need nursing support. Tailored products and facilities might include variations on active-adult communities, senior apartments, independent living, assisted living, memory care, nursing homes, skilled-nursing communities, and continuing care retirement communities (CCRCs). The US leads the way in this field and may offer examples of how the elder care sector might develop in China. Currently trends there show an increasing sophistication of the market and a response to the expectations of the post-war, baby boomer generation. The large, gated, age-restricted active senior housing communities like Sun City, that limited children's visits, are becoming a thing of the past. Communities are now expected to become intergenerational and encourage connectivity between residents and the community at large, where Green Infrastructure interventions can be particularly important and valuable. Active residents look to be able to enjoy the benefits of what the wider area has to offer, particularly within transit-oriented districts and walkable environments, where shops, restaurants, libraries, and theatres form a key component of their lifestyle choices. Within the development provision is the expectation of sports courts, pools, spas, activity spaces, and outdoor fitness and meditation areas. More attention is being paid to health and wellness values. Multiple dining venues are seen as a must, including a variety of price-point options suitable for diverse communities (Nyren, 2014).

What we can be sure of is that the China model (or models that develop) will be distinct from those of the rest of the world and whilst undoubtedly elder care development will incorporate many facets of overseas facilities and management procedure, it will need to find and develop its own path. But it may be a rocky road for many would-be care facility developers. Providing such attractive developments to the new wealthy urbanised populace in China is one thing, but questions arise as to how adequate facilities will be able to be provided in rural areas, or for the infirm or those on low incomes. Ageing-in-place at home is repeatedly cited as the most desirable solution; however, a multitude of problems appear to exist, not least as to whether there will be enough trained people available to provide suitable in-home care to support absent families. The whole subject is a very sensitive one in a culture in which respect and responsibility for older people is hardwired and people instantly panic over the very thought of not being able to take care of their parents adequately.

Are Urban Streets Fit for Ageing Populations?

The question of whether its city was fit for hosting an increasingly aged population became the focus of a two-year study by the Hong Kong Institute of Urban Design following the published results of the 2016 by-census (Wilson, 2019a). The proportion of the population aged 65 or older had increased from 12% in 2006 to a new high of 16% just ten years later, causing some alarm; in 1986 the figure was just 8%. Meanwhile, the median age of the population had been found to have increased from 39.6 years to 43.4 years from over the same decade, which means that by 2036, a massive 31.1% of Hong Kong's population is projected to be 65 years or older (HKSAR, Census & Statistics Department, 2017).

Already concerned about the poor urban environment in terms of universal access and environmental health within the city, the Institute decided to focus its attention on the evaluation of the urban realm in the eyes of its existing ageing population in an effort to prioritise both thinking and funding towards what would be needed in order to start to better future-proof both public and private capital works projects. A three-pronged approach was conceived in which research would first be undertaken that would be available as a focus for discussion at the 2018 HKIUD Conference "Actions for Active Ageing – Urban Design for All". The third and final post-conference stage would be to reach clear actions and objectives in terms of kickstarting a pilot project addressing the key urban design factors that would enable an ageing population to remain active, healthy, and engaged, thereby continuing to contribute to society and the community, and to reduce burdens of care.

The research aimed to explore both the physical and social issues of how the city can be more inclusive and why better urban design is essential in reinforcing the cultural ties in communities with an ageing population, including ideas of walkability, an active living environment, appropriate transport modes, intergenerational participation, healthcare, and mixed-use development. Objectives were generated in order to: outline the key aspects of the different "software" and "hardware" sides, leading to excellent and inclusive urban design – e.g. from policy, walkability, and housing perspectives; explore how best-practice case studies from innovative projects all over the world can be applied to the city; identify what will be needed, in specific policy and urban design terms, to effectively serve the ageing population; influence how the government plans for the city to adapt to the rapid ageing population growth; and to highlight the opportunities and challenges that professionals in the industry will face going forward.

To kick off the research study, a fact-finding exercise was initiated through an "Experiential Workshop" that included senior government policy-makers from a wide array of urban realm departments. Participants were able to "gear up" with an "elderly simulation suit", a patented invention of the Cycling & Health Technology Industry R&D Center (CHC) in Taiwan, developed by professionals including doctors, nurses, physiologists, and social workers. The simulation suit consists of several specially designed impediments such as weights, braces, elastic restraints, and a pair of visually impaired eyeglasses, which allow participants to feel how older people bend their bodies and to gain an insight into their physical experiences. Different adjustments are able to be made in order to simulate varying impediments and age simulations. With the assistance of volunteers, participants were engaged in a number of typical, outdoor, daily life activities in the centre of the city, including visiting a community centre, trying out the community facilities and fitness equipment targeted at older people in a park, and eventually experiencing different real-life hardships faced by older people, such as crossing streets, walking up steps and hills, using transport systems, and wayfinding.

A key part of undertaking the research was to build up a dataset that could highlight priorities in terms of identifying the key barriers and affordances to older people's urban activity. An online survey was developed that was undertaken by the workshop participants both "before" wearing the elderly simulation suit and "following" the exercise, the object being to gauge any change in perception between undertaking tasks in their current physical state compared with that of what they might expect in the future. Not only were participants able to understand how their physical condition will deteriorate as they age and recognise the difficulties associated with that, but they were also able to better empathise with seniors in the community. Nearly everyone has older family members or friends who need to be looked after, bringing a very personal relevance and perspective to the exercise.

A second "Experiential Workshop" was subsequently held using students from Chinese University Hong Kong, Tsinghua University, and Stanford University as participants, as a means to both educate tomorrow's urban designers and at the same time collect further data from a contrasting and youthful user group. The data generated for the study was based on the interactive surveys undertaken during the first and second "Experiential Workshops", as well as those from a third group generated from a continual Facebook survey, which acted as a control group representing the public perception of those who did not had the benefit of having experienced the simulation suit.

The study outlined a whole host of important issues needed for improvements in the urban environment, most of which would perhaps seem relatively obvious to most. For instance, all three groups strongly identified "Staying Active for Better Health, Freedom and Ability to Go Places" as the most important issue for older people to be "happy and well", reinforcing the needs of society in "Putting Wellness First". However, when asked the question "How well does our urban environment support active ageing?" a distinct differential was identified between the public's general perception and the documented considerations of those who had actively worn the simulation suit. Whilst the active participants of both of the first and second "Experiential Workshops" showed consistent results, with roughly two-thirds finding the environment "not really" suitable to active ageing, a much more positive perspective was provided by the general public, of whom almost half considered the environment to be perfectly acceptable. This was backed up by the results of the pre-survey undertaken by the senior government participants at the first workshop "before" they had undertaken their experiential workshop. The worrying realisation therefore exists that the problems of older people are not properly recognised either by the public at large or by those responsible for shaping the environment, including those who actually design and manage it in a compact, modern, and well-developed city like Hong Kong.

The third area of the study tried to identify what actually makes an age-friendly urban environment, where comfortable walking and convenient transport connections were seen as paramount to all survey groups. The importance of having barrier-free access and sufficient well located rest points was also consistently highlighted. The study identified the key elements that shape an age-friendly urban environment by dividing them into four subsets: safe infrastructure; supportive amenities; cognitive power; and well-being factors. When it comes to the provision of safe infrastructure, factors such as road crossing, narrow footpath widths, the presence of obstacles, and the steepness of gradients were found to be of far greater importance to the experiential groups than the public perception, whilst the presence of steps and uneven surfaces was considered the greatest urban safety hazard across all sectors. Solving such problems with ramps, lifts, wider pavements, and handrails is clearly substantiated, whilst supportive amenities highlight the strong need for the more frequent provision of toilets and seats as a means to reducing the barriers preventing senior citizens from walking long distances. When it comes to cognition and the ability of navigating the urban environment, expectation and actual experience again contrasted strongly. The study found that the difficulties in finding unknown places would constitute a strong deterrent to older people actively engaging with the unfamiliar, widening their activity base, or being required to attend at unknown locations (Wilson, 2019a). At the end of the day, maintaining connections with the community and having easily accessible places for a wide variety of activities in well-maintained and appropriate facilities is what makes older people most happy in the urban setting. However, these are not typically the driving criteria for the majority of decision-makers shaping the urban realm, who continue to primarily divert investment and attention to grey infrastructure, roads, and barriers.

Soup for All

There is a school of thought which holds that addressing demographic ageing issues could have been initiated earlier by Singapore, especially in the light of Japan's experience; however, the catalyst for such awareness seems to have been the realisation that one million of its citizens would be "elderly" by 2030, a figure that resonated with public and policy-makers alike. Yet, addressing the issue later has given Singapore certain advantages in terms of being better armed with an understanding of how to tackle the issues, as well as having more resources in terms of data and technology to address them (Tan, 2018). New types of communities are emerging, such as that recently completed at Kampung Admiralty, where high-density elderly housing units have been plugged into an existing community to provide integrated facilities of amenity, service, and medical support not just for the new development, but for the additional benefit of an existing wider catchment, whilst structuring a multi-age district-wide solution. Singapore continues to conduct research into how to widen the range of housing options to allow age mobility through downsizing to smaller units or providing multi-generational homes. A matrix of housing product supply and allocation should respond to an individual's needs, mobility, and functional capability rather than income groups alone (Tan, 2018). Communities need to allow for differing forms of ageing-in-place, both independently and with assisted living, community, or family support, as well as realising that understanding social needs is the key to providing a responsive physical environment where no "one size fits all". One interesting development is that of incentivising young couples to adopt housing within walking distance of their elders – what might be called the "soup model" of housing, whereby you can travel to your family within the time it takes to walk with a hot bowl of soup before it gets cold. By supplying financial subsidies to such couples, Singapore's government is financially recognising the significant benefits this can bring in terms of cross-generational support of both older people and the very young together (Wilson, 2019b).

Thus, it's becoming increasingly necessary to develop new and broad ranges of community-based assistance to meet ageing needs, including affordable and accessible housing, convenient transportation, work, education, and volunteer opportunities, access to health and support services, participation in civic and cultural activities, and intergenerational connections. Volunteers and non-governmental organisations (NGOs) are increasingly expected to fill the gaps left by insufficient public-sector funding, especially in developing countries, and might be expected to play an increasingly important role in supporting elderly residents. In the Philippines, HelpAge International is already on the ground with its local partner, the Coalition of Services of the Elderly (COSE), to encourage and assist the elderly in addressing important issues within the community. As well as health and nutritional support programmes for older residents, COSE also coordinates with the government to offer home care and psychological support, and to train volunteers for "active ageing" initiatives (COSE, n.d.).

Age segregation is particularly problematic in that it creates divides in society that contribute to ageism and deprive everyone of opportunities for intergenerational learning (Blumenthal & Lape, 2014). This tends to be less of a problem in Asian societies than it is in Western societies; however, by ensuring that communities are well planned for inclusivity and diversity, intergenerational interactions can be better encouraged to everyone's benefit. Children in particular can sustain the ability of older people to age-in-place, while conversely older adults can enrich the lives of the young and share their knowledge and skills (Nyren, 2014).

Governments, both local and national, must work out how to further urban regeneration without displacing communities, whilst financers, real estate companies, and designers must urgently start to meet the requirements of ageing demographics and their desire to stay within their communities and close to their families and caregivers. Housing development must become more diverse and innovative in the product mix that is put onto the market as well as being designed in ways that can increase the flexibility and easy adaptability of the accommodation to allow for future change. The traditional approach of specifically targeting distinctive demographic groups with real estate products suited to those markets brings with it the problem that in doing so, it's difficult to create interesting, diverse, and functional communities, whilst ageing-in-place becomes particularly problematic, since residents will need to move away to meet their changing life needs over time (Wilson, 2018a).

Looking to the future, there would appear to be significant assistance that technology can bring in terms of providing informed design, and Japan has focused on this. In terms of facilitating older person support, it might be possible to expect "smart" benefits through more remote supervision, initially through online appointments and consultation, assisted by digital testing and monitoring. Singapore has already made efforts towards creating dementia-friendly communities, whereby educating community members such as shopkeepers can make a difference, but there do appear to be many and particular opportunities arising through the development of smart systems and technological support. As a note of caution, the more technology and hard science is employed, the greater the need for more social science knowledge to balance it out. History shows that the one cannot go without the other, and our knowledge of the social impacts of technological change has always been impaired by time delay. Can this possibly change through the adoption of AI predictive modelling? The increased provision of common shared Big Data is going to continually make urban managers better informed and allow more targeted functional responses in urban development, whereas perhaps in the past, these have been more aspirational on the part of planners and city shapers due to the lack of hard information. The Singapore model follows a "mantra" that the provision of services should be based on three constructs: "Proximity"; 'Accessibility'; and "Convenience". Continued data-based research on social systems and the behaviour of older people in particular is able to help to provide solutions of the "Right Size and Right Site" for development programming (Wilson, 2019b).

As many developed countries increasingly face the problems of ageing populations, making our cities more age-enabled to all sectors of society become essential. Being active throughout ageing is important, and safe and easy accessibility to quality landscape areas that are part of the fundamental Green Infrastructure provision in particular makes it easy and enjoyable to get out on foot and allow for smart ageing to develop. Uneven paving, steps, a lack of rest opportunities, or insufficient toilet provision can all act as barriers to some people wanting to take a walk, whereas access to daylight, the natural environment, and sociable places act as incentives. It's the challenge of the journey from the home to the destination that has a key impact on decision-making. Catharine Ward Thompson highlights that "it only needs one little thing in the environment to be wrong or difficult to deal with to stop older people getting out and about, so the design of the physical environment is critically important … details such as having arms on seats to help get up or down and choosing materials that don't get too hot or cold can make a huge difference" (Ward Thompson, 2018).

In order to better understand the issues of keeping active, it is noteworthy that people are simply more likely to walk and exercise if they are outside rather than being indoors. Getting outside can also help to avoid social isolation and the resultant problems of loneliness and the impact on mental health (Thompson Coon et al., 2011). Ward Thompson also points out that the body needs Vitamin D from sunlight, whilst daylight can affect our circadian rhythms and have an impact on our sleep quality, and that developing technology that provides a "virtual or artificial landscape" can never replace the real thing. Better pedestrian environments, which are pleasant, shaded, and can activate the senses through hearing birdsong, smelling flowers, and enjoying the change of weather and season are important, and better Green Infrastructure provision can provide this. Interestingly, people appear to have differing attitudes to the type of landscape they encounter, based significantly on their childhood experiences; those who were used to "natural" woodlands and landscapes in their youth still seek them out when they are older, whereas enclosed, vegetated spaces can be threatening to those who were less accustomed to them in their youth. Some may find they "don't feel safe" or are "uncomfortable" with isolation, so cities need a variety of landscape types, suitable to different users – an "ecology of urban spaces", where they could also act to greatly enhance overall biodiversity (Wilson, 2018).

Ageing-in-place is going to require a difficult shift in the way in which societies think about the role of communities and the way in which services are delivered to individuals. Ageing can make it increasingly hard to perform certain tasks; there is a multi-layered complexity of needs that is initially fairly straightforward, but becomes increasingly challenging as a result of ageing, illness, or disability. Strong family and local support can allow individuals to remain within their homes and communities; however, it is the unchartered potential of the technology sector to be able to deliver remote monitoring and doctoring that may offer a radical change in support systems.

Public health is something that needs to work across all sectors and all environments, and investment in the urban realm as a public health tool is extremely low in cost and high in benefit compared to intensive corrective public medical costs. However, as with Green Infrastructure, it takes a long time to fully measure and witness the return on investment to society at large of quality urban place-making and of its recurrent maintenance cost – perhaps even decades. Urgently undertaking more studies to convince policy-makers and funding bodies of the real and valuable benefits that can be accrued from well-considered and universally inclusive urban environments might be seen as the key to maintaining ageing-friendly cities and undertaking "Placing for Age". However, it needs to go further, by identifying the importance not just of providing a variety of diverse facilities within neighbourhoods, but also ensuring that facilities are in the right places and with ease of access guaranteed to those who need them most. Yet some forward-thinking cities – those that are already understanding the needs for an urgent and radical change in mindset – are tearing up and reconsidering their existing urban plans and development processes with a view to re-envisioning and collaborating in order to plan more-resilient, age-appropriate living places, rethinking land uses to mitigate the challenges of climate impact, population shift, and technological change, and redirecting funding towards more cost-effective, integrated, and inclusive urban infrastructure. These are the futureproof cities that will lead the global race of the coming Digital Decade.

References

Ahn, J.-h. (2020, 29 September). Over 40% of Korea's population to be elderly in 2060. *Chosun Daily.* http://english.chosun.com/site/data/html_dir/2020/09/29/2020092901184.html.

Blumenthal, S., & Lape, E. (2014, 14 June). Aging in place: An intergenerational priority. *Huffington Post.* https://www.huffpost.com/entry/post_8756_b_6315082.

China, State Council. (2006). *The development of China's undertakings for the aged.* Information Office of the State Council of the People's Republic of China.

China, State Council. (2017, 6 March). *China issues five-year plan on elderly care.* http://english.www.gov.cn/policies/latest_releases/2017/03/06/content_281475586946296.htm.

Choi, J.-s. (2018, May 24). Childbirths fall to fresh record low. *Chosun Daily.* http://english.chosun.com/site/data/html_dir/2020/09/29/2020092901184.html.

COSE. (n.d.). *Health and active aging.* https://cose.org.ph/health-active-aging.

HelpAge International. (2015). *Global Agewatch Index 2015*. https://www.helpage.org/global-agewatch/population-ageing-data/global-rankings-table.
HKSAR, Census & Statistics Department. (2017). *Hong Kong population projections for 2017–2066*. Census & Statistics Department, Government of the Hong Kong Special Administrative Region (updated 14 May 2019). https://www.censtatd.gov.hk/press_release/pressReleaseDetail.jsp?charsetID=1&pressRID=4200.
Japan, IPSS. (2021). *Population projections for Japan (2016–2065): Summary*. http://www.ipss.go.jp/pp-zenkoku/e/zenkoku_e2017/pp_zenkoku2017e_gaiyou.html#e_zenkoku_II_A-2.
Kim, S.-m., & Jang, H.-t. (2017, 4 August). Korea officially becomes aged society. *Chosun Daily*. http://english.chosun.com/site/data/html_dir/2017/09/04/2017090401307.html.
Murata, H. (2018, 22 June). *Smart aging: Concept and implementation – Pitfall of age-friendly design based on Japanese Experience*. HKIUD Conference 2018: Actions for Active Ageing – Urban Design for All, Hong Kong.
New Express. (2014, 22 August). Guangzhou plans to build more nursing homes. https://www.xkb.com.cn/article_344818.
Nyren, R. (2014, 18/05/2018). Senior's housing outlook. *Urban Land Magazine*. https://urbanland.uli.org/news/seniors-housing-outlook.
OECD. (2014). *The suicide rate of the elderly in Korea is the highest in the OECD area*. https://doi.org/doi:https://doi.org/10.1787/eco_surveys-kor-2014-graph21-en.
OECD. (2021a). *Elderly population (indicator)*. https://doi.org/10.1787/8d805ea1-en.
OECD. (2021b). *Housing prices (indicator)*. https://doi.org/10.1787/63008438-en.
Pang, S. Y., & Arivalagan, Y. (2020, 18 February). These countries are most ready to deal with ageing populations. *World Economic Forum*. https://www.weforum.org/agenda/2020/02/what-are-japan-and-singapore-doing-about-ageing-population.
Shin, S.-j. (2019, 3 September). Korea to become world's oldest society in 2045. *Chosun Daily*. http://english.chosun.com/site/data/html_dir/2019/09/03/2019090301279.html.
Statistics Bureau of Japan. (2019). *Current population estimates as of October 1, 2019*. http://www.stat.go.jp/english/data/jinsui/2019np/index.html.
Tan, S. H. E. (2018, 22 June). *Designing for an age-enabled and inclusive community*. HKIUD Conference 2018 – Actions for Active Ageing – Urban Design for All, Hong Kong. https://www.hkiud.org/actions/aa/aa_180622.php.
Thompson Coon, J., Boddy, K., Stein, K., Whear, R., Barton, J., & Depledge, M. H. (2011). Does participating in physical activity in outdoor natural environments have a greater effect on physical and mental wellbeing than physical activity indoors? A systematic review. *Environmental Science & Technology*, 45(5), 1761–1772. https://doi.org/10.1021/es102947t .

UN, Department of Economic and Social Affairs. (2015). *World population ageing 2015 – Highlights*. https://www.un.org/en/development/desa/population/publications/pdf/ageing/WPA2015_Highlights.pdf.

Wang, Y., & Long, Y. (2018). Population aging and the construction of the modern pension security system. In *The development of security and whole care system for the aged in China* (pp. 1–24). Springer.

Ward Thompson, C. (2018, 22 May). *An Ecology of Urban Spaces* [Interview]. Guangzhou. http://www.initiatives.com.hk/180926-an-ecology-of-urban-spaces.html.

WHO. (2007). *Global age-friendly cities: A guide*. World Health Organization.

WHO. (2020a). *Global age-friendly cities project*. https://www.who.int/ageing/projects/age_friendly_cities/en.

WHO. (2020b). *WHO global network for age-friendly cities and communities*. https://www.who.int/ageing/projects/age_friendly_cities_network/en.

Wilson, B. D. (2018a). An outline to futureproofing cities with ten immediate steps. *Proceedings of the Institution of Civil Engineers – Urban Design and Planning, 171*(5), 202–216.

Wilson, B. D. (2018b). An ecology of urban space: Barry Wilson interviews Catharine Ward Thompson. *The Magazine of Urbanisation, 110*, 83–87.

Wilson, B. D. (2019a). Cities not fit for ageing populations. *Urban Design, 3*, 20–29.

Wilson, B. D. (2019b). The X Factor: Singapore's drive to urban excellence: Barry Wilson interviews Elaine Tan. *The Magazine of Urbanisation, 116*, 73–79.

Yu, J., & Rosenberg, M. (2017). "No place like home": Aging in post-reform Beijing, *Health & Place, 46*, 192–200.

Think Fast, Think Smart

Incorporating Opportunities in the Digital Revolution

6

The digital platforms fronting Big Data are facilitating an urban management revolution whereby buildings, spaces, vehicles, machines, and control systems can interact effectively and efficiently to micro-adapt to changes in environmental and human behaviour. As traditional projection models become obsolete, since the complexity of these interacting systems cannot be human-managed, an increasing incorporation of sophisticated artificial intelligence (AI) predictive solutions is taking hold. Whilst governments are now understanding the value of Big Data, they are not yet fully conversant as to its means of collection, processing, output, and storage; simultaneously, the concept of opening up and sharing information in the public domain is challenging. The coming "Digital Decade" will see spaces created where substantially more data and data sources can be made available for use in society, but who will be in control of these? The potential for cities to become learning machines is very real and they may become the test bed for rapid evaluation of myriad solutions to diverse eventualities, where comprehensive planning becomes a thing of the past, and continual, fast response, iterative citizen-based management becomes the new norm.

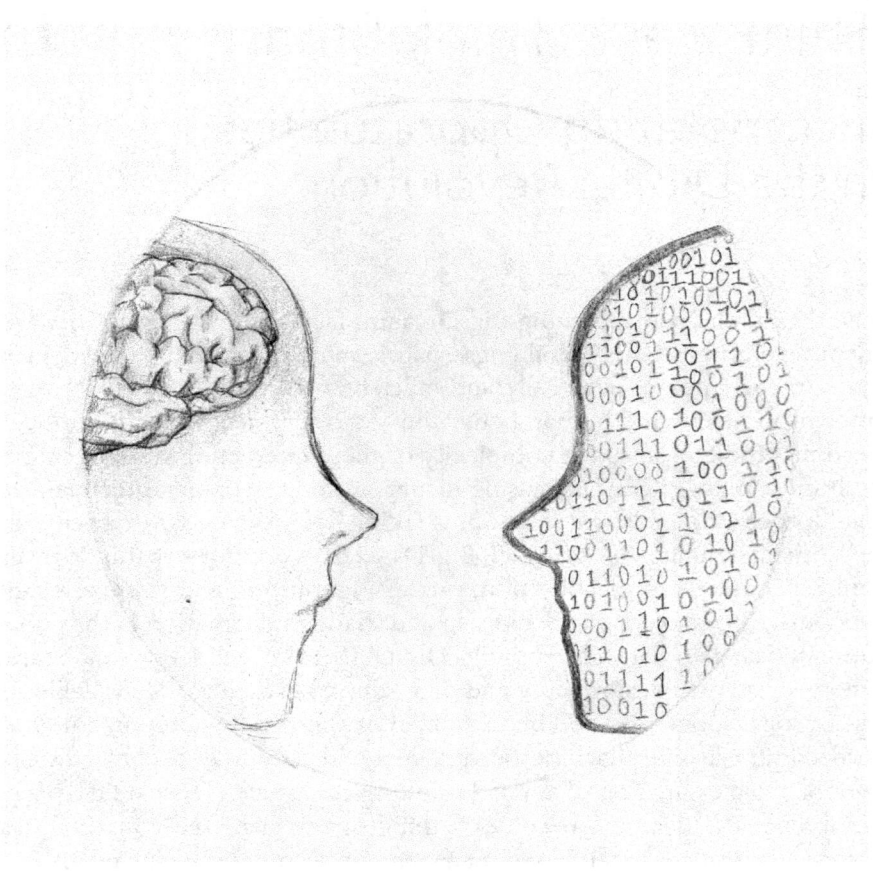

Thinking A Head

"The machine does not isolate man from the great problems of nature but plunges him more deeply into them."

Antoine de Saint-Exupéry,
Wind, sand, and stars, 1939

The Science of Complexity

A new generation of technologies is being increasingly developed and deployed into global urban management tools as part of what might be called "smart city" transformation, whereby buildings, spaces, vehicles, machines, and control systems can interact effectively and efficiently through micro-adaption to changes in climate and human behaviour. In theory, those cities that transition fastest and most thoroughly will not only become the most resilient, but will also be able to provide globally desirable living opportunities that attract the best minds and the highest-quality labour supply. The definition of a "smart city" is subject to wide interpretation, from almost anything and everything associated with "sustainable" management principles to more confined approaches focusing directly on connected information technology communication (ITC). Most mainstream approaches associate smart city concepts as predominantly technological interventions of some sort and it is evident that cities themselves are increasingly focusing on harnessing this growing power of technology, not only in adding capability in directly managing complex urban systems such as transport, buildings, and water systems, but also in being able to react to and predict continual fluctuations resulting from the myriad of natural system interdependencies in the chaotic urban realm, where every action has multiple reactions. For instance, whilst managing a metro system is a complex challenge in itself, understanding the multiple implications of change on other interrelated systems has been beyond the power of the human brain alone. A train arrival will kick off a chain of interrelated impacts: people flow both in and out of a station, their connections to other transport modes, waiting space, purchasing interactions, energy, air, noise, and temperature fluctuations, and telecommunications exchanges. The knock-on effects of any changes to the arrival of that train go beyond the rail network itself and outward into city-wide systems, the impacts becoming increasingly complex as our populations and cities continue to develop. Trying to anticipate the effects on urban behaviour through the fallout of the 2020 COVID-19 crisis highlighted the totality of social, environmental, and economic interdependencies. So, whilst systems are complex and interrelated, they have generally only been able to be considered in isolation. Transport planners prioritise traffic flows through optimised street capacity, junction interventions. and information access; however, they have not been in the business of being able to consider or accurately predict the social impacts resulting from barrier effects, or the health impacts through roadside air and noise pollution, or the opportunity cost of overlooking alternative public realm solutions. Other interfaces, such as bicycles and pedestrians, are incorporated, but have barely been considered, let alone prioritised.

Technology is now increasingly focused on trying to solve or at least optimise these "wicked problems", approaching the complex system riddles using AI or perhaps even augmented reality (AR). The means to achieve this are effectively the same as they have always been: collect information, organise it, analyse it, share it, and file it. Today's data essentially follows the same six stages: collect, prepare, input, process, output, and store. We have seen huge leaps forward in terms of processing, output, and storage in the past few decades in terms of speed and quantity, yet the key to further development for cities is the quantity of data that can be collected, how quickly it can be collected, and how it is prepared. The old adage of "put rubbish in, get rubbish out" (RIRO) is as true as it's ever been in relation to taking full advantage of AI and capabilities, so having good data is especially important for AI subsets like machine learning and deep learning, which gain greater capabilities over time by analysing large sets of data, learning from them, and ultimately making adjustments that make the applications more intelligent. So cities need *more* information about their environment and their people, they need information *faster*, and they need to *prepare* it effectively. Data whose size exceeds the capacities of standard contemporary data management tools is considered "Big Data" (Batty, 2013). The era of "Big Data" has arrived and is transforming our understanding of this world.

To this end, cities have for some time been working towards building up capacity for utilising spatial datasets and establishing spatial data infrastructure (SDI) platforms to manage big datasets, since everything (living, moving, or static) has some kind of spatial component and 80% of Big Data is associated with spatial information. Big Spatial Data (BSD) is therefore necessary in areas such as satellite imagery, the Internet of Things (IoT), Location-Based Services (LBS), and climate simulations (Huang & Wang, 2020). The US moved to establish its National Spatial Data Infrastructure (NSDI) in 1994 when President Bill Clinton signed Executive Order 12906 "to support public and private sector applications of geospatial data in such areas as transportation, community development, agriculture, emergency response, environmental management and information technology" (The White House, 1994). The NSDI was seen as part of the evolving National Information Infrastructure that would provide citizens with access to essential government information and thus strengthen the democratic process (US, FGDC, 1997). Over the years, as the NSDI evolved and was updated, it became a model for other nations and organisations around the world. The INSPIRE Directive, implemented in various stages, aims to create a spatial data infrastructure in the EU for the purposes of EU environmental policies or activities which may have an impact on the environment, coming into force in 2007 and implemented in stages, with full implementation required by the end of 2021 (European Commission, 2007a). Singapore's NSDI was set up in 2008 (previously it had been known as the Singapore Geospatial Collaborative Environment or SG-SPACE) and provides a mechanism to make authoritative geospatial data available for decision-making, public security, and cost-effective business (GeospatialSG, 2018). In 2011, the United Nations created the Committee of Experts on Global Geospatial Information Management (UN-GGIM) programme to "address global challenges regarding the use of geospatial information ... and to serve as a body for global policymaking in the field of geospatial information management" (UN-GGIM, 2011). New platforms are being created continually; by 2020, more than 100 nations had spatial data infrastructures, embracing open international standards for geospatial data and technologies to enable greater levels of data-sharing on topics that extend across administrative boundaries (US, FGDC, 2020). Analysing this spatial data makes it possible to learn how variables interact and why certain spatial relationships exist. It is becoming increasingly important for all urban management systems and no doubt smart city iterations will increasingly lean upon this BSD information, with future technological upgrades in terms of harnessing it more efficiently, effectively, and facilitating faster and theoretically more convenient urban living. However, there is growing discussion around the challenges that BSD brings as well as the opportunities, particularly in environmental sustainability regarding the huge data volumes produced, the different sources, structures, formats, scales, and resolutions generated, and the heterogeneity of data over space and time. In general, these challenges are less about the hardware and more about how to manage the huge volume of information and transform it into value (Sivarajah et al., 2017).

In terms of acquiring the amount of data needed to power meaningful outcomes, multiple data sources are rapidly emerging, such as cellular signalling, social media, smart cards, review forums, smart equipment, taxi services, and video cameras, meaning that governments, which previously generated and retained the majority of spatial data, are now having to engage with the private sector as key stakeholders. The concept of opening up and sharing information in the public domain, government to business (G2B), has been challenging in itself for many governments, where datasets are not in themselves standardised across departments and legal privacy issues exist in relation to sharing acquired information; however, receiving and integrating third-party information, business to government (B2G), becomes even more challenging. A recent study into the current state of SDI openness across Canada, the Netherlands, Australia, and Brazil, which were selected as being best practice, open-data countries, concluded that establishing a legislative framework is crucial in ensuring that a user-centred approach and open data availability are achieved, where the rules can be followed by all parties (including all layers of government, companies, industry, the academic community, and the public at large), and that compliance checking is embedded into the framework. The COVID-19 pandemic in particular has demonstrated to many governments the importance of spatial datasets being well organised and easily accessible across boundaries to improve decision-making (Mulder et al., 2020).

Importantly, in 2020, the EU issued *A European Strategy for Data* (European Commission, 2020a), a document outlining policy measures and investments intended to shape the data economy over the next five years, along with a communication on *Shaping Europe's Digital Future* (European Commission, 2020b), and also a *White Paper on Artificial Intelligence* (European Commission, 2020c) that indicates how the Commission will support and promote the development and uptake of AI across the EU. These documents are important as indicators of the way in which technology and data-sharing will be able to advance over what is termed Europe's "Digital Decade" (European Commission, 2020d). The strategy aims at creating spaces where substantially more data and data sources can be made available for use in society and the economy, whilst enabling those parties who generate the data to remain in control of it. It further intends to "create incentives for companies to share data, carrying out studies on the benefits of B2G data-sharing, and provide support to develop the technical infrastructure" (European Commission, 2020e). The plans focus on utilising legislation on data governance, access, and reuse as the framework to open up high-value, publicly held datasets and allow their free reuse, whilst the EU heightens investment in data processing infrastructure, sharing tools, architecture, and governance mechanisms in order to federate energy-efficient and trustworthy cloud infrastructure services along with a procurement marketplace for data processing services (European Commission, 2020a). This "Three Sustainability Pillars" approach adopts the social goals of expanding both the quantity and quality of digital access, skills, and innovation, along with protection against cyber threats, disinformation, and rights abuses through AI. Business can expect a rule-based environment with equity, protection, and support, whilst the climate-neutral goal for 2050 drives the environmental agenda for the digital sector. In the light of the fallout from the COVID-19 pandemic, the creation of a "European health data space" to foster targeted research, diagnosis, and treatment along with the expansion of super-computing capacity to develop innovative solutions for medicine, transport, and the environment seems apt. In summary, Europe appears to see itself as being somewhat behind the curve, perhaps in relation to the US and China, and intends to focus on "strengthening its digital sovereignty and setting standards, rather than following those of others". In doing so, it sets out its stall to support developing economies, digitalise establish standards, and promote them internationally to become a global role model for the digital economy (European Commission, 2020b).

Before the Digital Decade

On visiting the metro system in Shanghai, unsuspecting visitors may be both startled and bemused by the voice-interactive ticket machines at major stations across the city. This activation technology, developed by tech giant Alibaba, allows passengers to tell a ticket machine their specific destination and the machine will plan the best route for them and advise on the destination station. Payment is made by phone app and is particularly useful for unfamiliar travellers and tourists. Moreover, "it enables accurate communication with a smart device from a distance of up to five metres despite the extremely loud environment of the station, whilst people don't even need to use any specific word to active the machine", according to Yan Zhijie, the director of intelligent speech recognition at Alibaba's Institute of Data and Science Technology (Perez, 2017).

Guangdong residents use digital ID cards generated by the Wechat mini app named "Yueshengshi" to check in at hotels across the city. The card can be easily issued once the programme matches an applicant's face with the ID photo through Tencent's facial recognition technology. As a part of the efforts to build a "digital government", Guangdong province launched the "Yueshengshi" mini app in 2018 to enable local residents to process all livelihood services on their phones (Zhang, 2018).

The Shenzhen government housing lease platform is initiated in 2017, supported by integrating Tencent's technologies, including cloud computing, AI, Big Data, credit ranking, and digital payment (ECNS, 2017b) to provide a range of services, including undertaking rental transaction services, household registration, and subsidy applications, thereby shortcutting administration and information collection, and adding convenience in terms of making new leasing contracts (SZ. Gov, 2017).

The first intelligently themed public park opens in late 2018 in Beijing's Haidian district, empowered by search engine giant Baidu and equipped with a multitude of tech facility interfaces using face recognition, autonomous transport, and voice-interactive consoles. Face recognition cameras along the jogging track automatically record people's motion data and registered users do not need to wear hardware devices to see their performance details, which are recorded on interactive screens. Augmented reality Tai Chi lessons, autonomous buses, face recognition lockers, and smart voice pavilions allowing citizens to chat and check information on the smart screens have been introduced. The opening of the park is coupled with Baidu's ambitious plan named ACE, to promote solutions for "Autonomous driving", "Connected road", and "Efficient city" in building autonomous transport networks (Xinhua, 2018).

Brain surgery is conducted on a patient suffering from Parkinson's disease in 2019 through high-resolution live-streaming enabled by a 5G network, where the doctors in the operation room of PLAGH's Hainan Hospital, Sanya were able to undertake surgery through the real-time instruction of experts 3,000 kilometres away in Beijing (ECNS, 2019a).

More than 500,000 doctors register with Shenzhen's new 91160-Yunshan Medical Online Hospital in 2017 to provide patients with medical services such as online registration, doctor consultation, and electronic prescriptions through app and Web-based platforms. Yunshan Medical worked together with digital platform 91160.com to obtain China's first business licence aimed to help reduce visits for hospitalgoers; allowing people to manage their problems at home. National statistics show that out of China's more than 7 billion annual outpatient visits, nearly 60% are return visits and at least two-thirds of these could be carried out online (*China Daily*, 2017a).

Remote firefighting system guidelines are rolled out across China, connecting directly with buildings and providing improved functions, including automated alarm, inspection, and supervision provision, enabling fire and smoke recognition, monitoring of fire conditions, electricity leakage, and cable temperatures. Information resources, including live images of fire sites, the locations of firefighting teams, and major sources of danger near fire sites, are collected and maintained on a command platform held with public security departments. By the end of 2018, all high-rise buildings under construction are installed with the new surveillance systems and old buildings retrofitted with separate fire alarm and firefighting facilities (ECNS, 2017a).

Shared practice is observed in public security management in Shenzhen, where the country's first 5G-equipped police station adopts all key 5G applications, including AR glasses, patrol drones, and patrol robots, enabling remote and 24-hour police patrols (ECNS, 2019b).

The world's first rail-less train is tested in the city of Zhuzhou, in central China's Hunan province, moving at a speed of 70 km/h and carrying up to 500 passengers, the 30-metre, electrically powered train can travel 25 kilometres with a 10-minute charge. With sensors equipped onboard, it is able to plan its own routes and operate without a driver (*China Daily*, 2017b).

Equipped with the new technological applications in AI, Big Data, and the IoT, Shenzhen's first smart road opens after one year of construction. The 6.8 km Qiaoxiang Road provides a range of smart services through underground sensing and multi-functional lamp posts fitted with LCD screens, sensors, cameras, data networks, and other digital facilities, and is interfaced for future 5G micro-stations. The LCD screens are able to display bus information, traffic flows, community maps, transport facilities, and emergency notices. Sensors and CCTV cameras monitor air quality, road structure, and movements, with real-time feedback automatically adjusting waiting times for light control systems. The use of multi-functional posts is also able to reduce the number of traffic signs and camera poles on the road by 32% (Taicenn, 2019).

2020 and China's policy roadmap – the 14th Five-Year Plan – is developed with a dedicated section for technology development with the clear objective of becoming self-reliant in tech development, creation, innovation, and talent building, as well as establishing mass interdisciplinary and cross-regional innovation centres. Further investment in R&D shows seven frontier fields highlighted for further exploration: AI, quantum information, integrated circuits, life and health science, neural science, biological breeding, and aerospace technology (Wong, 2020).

A New Infrastructure

So tech infrastructure development is set to be one of the major factors contributing to economic development in China with so-called "New Infrastructure" such as 5G, forming a major policy direction. The 5G network is the latest important development of mobile wireless technology and provides faster data connections, opening the way to new industrial applications, and is essential in helping to build "smart cities" with widespread connectivity and a faster, more agile, and richer communications network than 4G. Essential in the goal of making unmanned driving a reality, 5G connectivity is also expected to bring unprecedented changes and new experiences in the fields of consumption and industry, education, and healthcare. By the end of 2020, China already had an estimated 690,000 5G base stations transmitting to consumers across the country compared with 50,000 in the US (Strumpf, 2020). China is considered one of the pioneers in 5G development and the issue has been high on the national agenda for several years. Things have moved fast. Early in 2013, the IMT-2020 (5G) promotion group, a platform for 5G research and international exchange and cooperation, was initially formed under the joint efforts of three government bodies: the Ministry of Industry and Information Technology (MIIT), the National Development and Reform Commission (NDRC), and the Ministry of Science and Technology (MOST). By 2015, the "Made in China 2025" initiative and the 13th Five-Year Plan both included 5G as an important development goal, and kicked off the R&D works building pilot networks. The government issued the operating licences for 5G networks in 2019, starting the full commercial services of the next-generation network technology and empowering the use of next-generation mobile devices and other new applications such as the IoT, virtual reality (VR), and autonomous cars which rely on extremely fast collection, processing, and output through multitudes of instantaneous and ever-changing spatial data points. The key to this development is faster networks – hence the importance of the 5G rollout. With Germany giving its agreement to allow leading 5G vendor Huawei to build out part of its 5G network there, among the world's major economies, only the US, the UK, India, and Taiwan plan to block Huawei 5G equipment (Boston & Woo, 2020). Huawei expects to add the digitised medical history and real-time health monitoring of half a billion people outside China to its cloud-based AI systems during the 2020s. Moreover, China's dominance in 5G gives it a head start in developing next-phase 6G broadband (Goldman, 2020).

Whilst the major technology companies spare no effort in promoting 5G, hailing it as the new urban revolution and introducing the benefits that it may bring to new applications and to smart city, smart transportation, and smart agriculture concepts, there are also many uncertainties surrounding the technology, such as the high cost of deployment, the timespan required for large-scale application and coverage, and the possibility of radiation risks caused by the large-scale construction of base stations. The network utilises different bandwidth frequencies from 4G, which can carry far more capacity and deliver ultra-fast speeds. However, the downside is that the range is much more limited, meaning parallel infrastructure needs to be developed. It's a completely different system and one which needs many more stations to cope with the short distances. 5G antenna will need to be "everywhere" and even if base stations get smaller, they will need to be installed on streets, buildings, and homes to give blanket coverage, with repeaters needed to extended the range and maintain consistent speeds in dense populations. The number of IoT terminals connected by 5G per square kilometre is expected to reach one million – ten times the density of 4G. It's likely that carriers will continue to use lower-frequency bands to cover wider areas until the 5G network matures, where modems and Wi-Fi routers are replaced with 5G small cells or other hardware to bring 5G connections into homes and businesses, thus doing away with wired internet connections. Building all this is expensive and takes time. Global mobile operator 5G capital expenditure is forecast to grow rapidly from a low base in 2018 to reach nearly $88 billion worldwide by 2023, thereafter follow a strong upward trajectory once rollout is in full swing (Sherrington & Dicks, 2018). Even markets like China, where 5G has been installed early on, will be continually adding boosters to improve coverage and capacity for years to come.

In an appeal to the EU in September 2017, currently endorsed by more than 390 scientists and medical doctors, a moratorium on 5G deployment was requested until proper scientific evaluation of the potential negative consequences has been conducted (Hardell & Carlberg, 2020; Nyberg & Hardell, 2017). In a Senate hearing, US Senator Richard Blumenthal blasted both the Federal Communications Commission (FCC) and the Food and Drug Administration (FDA) for being responsible for the failure to conduct any research into the safety of 5G technology and instead engaging in bureaucratic finger-pointing and deferring to industry. Senator Patrick Colbeck and Dr Sharon Goldberg famously testified against the deployment of 5G because of the reported adverse effects on health from wireless technologies in a 2018 hearing (RF Safe, 2018). A Bill sponsored by Senator Anna Kaplan went before the New York State Senate Health Committee in late 2020, requiring a study to be conducted by the Department of Health, the Department of Environmental Conservation, and the Office of Information Technology Services to evaluate the health and environmental impacts of 5G and future-generation wireless systems technology and small cell distributed antenna systems in the state (Kaplan, 2020). The International Agency for Research on Cancer (IARC) at the WHO in May 2011 classified Radio Frequency (RF) radiation in the frequency range of 30 kHz to 300 GHz to be a "possible" human carcinogen (Group 2B) (Baan et al., 2011). There is a suggestion that since the IARC evaluation, the evidence on human cancer risks from RF radiation has been strengthened based on human cancer epidemiology reports, animal carcinogenicity studies, and experimental findings on oxidative mechanisms and genotoxicity, and that the IARC category should be upgraded from Group 2B to Group 1, a human carcinogen (Hardell & Carlberg, 2020). A major international review of the relevant radiation safety guidelines by the International Commission on Non-Ionizing Radiation Protection (ICNIRP) outlined that there is insufficient data for a meaningful health risk assessment. Whilst it noted concerns over links between long-term exposure and certain types of cancer, and some evidence from epidemiological and animal studies, these remain controversial and "restrictions have been set to ensure that the resultant peak spatial power will remain far lower than that required to adversely affect health. Accordingly, 5G exposures will not cause any harm providing that they adhere to the guidelines" (ICNIRP, 2020).

5G: Urban Revolution or Tech Hype?

So it appears that there is no stopping the 5G rollout, even if there are health and wellness concerns. The potentials in smart city processes will not be held back and the speed of implementation is a global political race between cities and nations. In order for Big Data analytics to collect, prepare, input, process, output, and store real-time information and solve the complex problems of interrelated urban systems, superfast highways are needed. One particular field receiving increasing attention is that of "complexity science", which has emerged in the last decade and is an approach to systems and problems that are dynamic, unpredictable, and multi-dimensional. Whilst this has primarily been developed in the healthcare sector, its appropriateness for considering the interconnected relationships and parts making up the city seems undeniable. Unlike traditional "cause and effect" or "linear thinking", complexity science is characterised by non-linearity appropriate for the complex world in which we live in the early twenty-first century. It uses new theories that allow us to look at age-old problems with a fresh perspective that leverages the use of powerful computation and the large datasets that are offering us new insights into the fundamental workings of our interconnected world of networks, globalisation, and sustainability. A "Futureproof City", then, is one that is going to have to rely significantly on solving wicked problems through data analytics and to develop long-term resilience in both physical and social terms to meet the necessities of climate and ecological emergencies, population growth, and ageing, as well as mass migration and urbanisation. A "Futureproof City" is going to need new approaches that include a rapid movement towards sustainable and optimised transport modes; transitions from individual ownership to shared economic models; and the adoption of previously untried housing models that address density issues. To do this, improved leveraging of data with better digitisation, utilisation, and analytics is essential in order to predict the wider problems that cover social and environmental equity, and beyond those simply of economics, which has traditionally been the case.

Possibly the Digital Decade is about to meet an urban revolution, whereby regular and real-time data will be able to facilitate significantly better planning and optimal use of facilities and resources. It will allow decision makers to "get under the skin and into the real issues" of providing appropriate urban fabric by measuring previously unmeasurable impacts and conflicts and thereby facilitating "Putting Wellness First" principles to guide and dominate the development agenda. Substantial, integrated, and robust information, previously in short supply, should be immediately available to make better-informed decisions regarding the multi-layered costs of continuation of investment in business-as-usual practices and the ever-increasing risks of development in the wrong place, as compared to the holistic returns that can be provided through Green Infrastructure investment and the creation of age-friendly urban communities with safe and dependable housing provision, and clean and car-free streets.

According to Guo Ping, Huawei's rotating chairman, during his address at the 2019 Shenzhen Smart City Forum with International Friendship Cities: "Every 'smart city' goes through four steps of transformation." He calls this the "Maslow Model" for smart city development, where the first step is creating a modern ICT infrastructure foundation for ubiquitous connectivity, and he considers that 5G and AI are today as significant as the discovery of electricity at the end of the nineteenth century. Building up both physical and digital security is a necessary second step, whilst the third step leverages public–private cooperation in the digitalisation process. The culmination is the urban "Digital Brain", a city-wide system that integrates data across all government agencies and businesses to create social value (Guo, 2019). Shenzhen aims to be the first city with a "Digital Brain" and is already implementing activity in the second and third tiers, whereas most "smart cities" around the world seem to be struggling with both the first-level platform and particularly the second-level security issues, and are yet to harness the potential benefits of public–private co-operation, yet it will surely come, even if not as fast as in Shenzhen.

Once fully "Thinking Fast, Thinking Smart", our cities will then perhaps prove to be the solutions to the future and not the problems. Our "Futureproof City" will not only optimise complex systems, but will also be able to expect the unexpected, be as prepared as possible for such eventualities, and, when they arise, have the necessary systems in place to deal calmly and immediately with the outcomes. In the summer of 2019, the Shenzhen Special Economic Zone Construction & Development Group Co. Ltd invited international scholars, professionals, and urban thinkers based locally and from relevant fields to gather together at the Smart City salon, "5G – Urban revolution or tech hype?", for a roundtable discussion on the various impacts of 5G on the speed and development of cities, and how they were witnessing those changes (bwpi, 2019). It then seems that Shenzhen is the appropriate place for any such conversation, clearly being the pilot of China's smart transformation, a home to the country's leading tech companies, and offering an example to the world for Chinese technological creativity. The views expressed at the roundtable outlined both the optimism and uncertainty of what might lie ahead:

> *The unknown, long distance outcomes led by 5G impacts to society are not an obstacle to understanding the principles which would determine this development. Firstly society will face a new layer of data capable processing. I could see that every individual's movement, interaction, needs, body condition, etc. will be integrated into our apps in real time, eventually becoming a strong parameter in people's choices and daily routine based on their personal lifestyle. Secondly it's not only about having more data but how it's going to be processed. We could witness how the internet opened a new door to many minor entrepreneurs, urban locations, marketing research, and others. Ideally, larger data processing will support the strengthening of the weak, aiming to converge the undeveloped area in providing basic living standards. Thirdly IT offers an opportunity to rethink our planning methods. When thinking of device personalisation, it doesn't mean running away from collective principles, rather an implementation of what Lao Tzu sees as the stage of reaching "great integrity", breaking things into pieces in order to arrange them in harmony. This is how I see the role of "networked personalisation", not to make chaos of individuals, but to allow them a greater contribution to city planning and setting new parameters.*
> (Jimi Lee Jaksa, Associate Architect at AECOM)

> *It is an interesting idea to imagine a city with all sorts of modern technologies. What makes up a "technology city" might include better ways to match resources (demand and supply), better sharing of resources and better learning. On the other hand, these changes should also lead to the opportunities for people to see more "experimental cities" and find new ways of urban development by means of pioneering and trying. Such changes are likely to be seen first in cities such as Shenzhen. I hope that such new technology applications can better promote "collective action" in urban communities.*
> (Alain Chiaradia, Associate Professor at the Faculty of Architecture, Department of Urban Planning and Design, University of Hong Kong)

> *The implementation of 5th generation telecommunication will probably be a natural evolution from the 4th generation rather than a disruptive change.*

Although it is more advanced, the implementation is limited to densely inhabited areas which could limit its impact at [a] global level. The impact on urban lifestyle instead will be obvious. It is hard to imagine what this new system will bring in the future – countless applications in communication, goods and people logistics, but we all see that the introduction of any new technology is often linked to an improvement of the speed. 5G will possibly allow us to quickly run many applications and exchange data on a large scale in real time. In other words it will allow us to perform tasks faster and speed up our lives. Can we still accept that? Will we reach our physiological limits? In the contemporary lifestyle where there is no clear boundary between working time and free time, this "speed-up" may create a scary scenario that affects our daily lives rather than just working performance. The 5G promo video we saw today shows that as well. Nowadays our lives are more closely connected with technology and networks than ever before. As designers and city planners we should always be aware of their impact on society and environment, so that we can respond properly and focus on the real targets: to improve work and living places; to boost the efficiency of work, rather than sacrificing the quality of life.

(Danilo Trevisan, founding Director, Aleatek Group)

5G technology can bring huge changes to the all industries besides "smart cities", such as changing the environment of factory production to a more controlled environment. In addition, 5G also intends to add more "connections" among countries, societies and groups, making people's lives more closely connected global society. Combined with AI and other technologies, it is highly likely to bring greater creativity and productivity to the society.

(Jelena Lucic, Managing Consultant (Asia), epi Consulting)

I believe that 5G technology could bring at least 2–3 step changes to us in the future, and people are constantly expecting such changes. For example, 5G may change some operational models, such as providing better data monitoring and improving decision-making efficiency in some areas. But the real changes that 5G will bring may be completely different from what people expected.

(Louie Sieh, Assistant Professor, Department of Architecture and Civil Engineering, City University of Hong Kong)

5G will bring "quantitative" changes in the short term, just as the exponential growth from 2G to 3G to 4G will lead to faster transmission speeds. On the other hand, the "quality" of data is another dimension that needs to be considered and will face challenges.

(Benjack Phillips, Executive Director at AECOM)

5G technology may inevitably change people's lives in cities, but the change might be insignificant compared to the impact on rural people. 5G, as a new form of infrastructure, could bring huge benefits to underdeveloped and developing countries such as India and Africa, which previously had insufficient infrastructure, making it much easier to do business and potentially empowering vulnerable populations and addressing poverty.

(Yang Zhenyuan, Lecturer at the School of Architecture and Urban Planning, Founder, Space Making Lab, Institute of Architectural Design and Research, Shenzhen University)

We all agree that 5G will significantly increase efficiency that will be beneficial to the lifestyle, our work, travel, and will also support smart city building. Design can take the advantages. However cities are different from one to another, they have unique characters and issues. There are also critical challenges we are all facing such as global warming, sea level rise, identity, habitat and place making that require designer to make prioritized responses. With the technologies, design needs strong principles as guidance to arrive right actions, that can really make our cities better and more resilient.

(Lou Zhihang, Associate, Urban Design, SOM, Hong Kong)

5G is strictly a new form of infrastructure. Perhaps its biggest impact will be in regards to the haves and have-nots. The Greater Bay Area is well positioned to give itself a massive competitive advantage not only in having a superior system but also in having access to large amounts of data points via the Chinese reality. More interesting is the spatial impacts this could have in people's daily lives. Although this will not happen instantaneously, the changes this can bring to having more adaptive and immediately responsive cities, codes, and ways of living. The potential for more dynamic uses of public space, more spaces given to people, less to cars, financial systems, immediate feedback loops can impact taxing models, and on the relationship with the natural environment; immediate feedback and consequences for harming or helping our planet are not yet clear, but 5G "paves the way" digitally for the real world spaces in our city to behave very differently.

(Jason Hilgefort, Founder, Land+Civilization Compositions/Institute for Autonomous Urbanism)

References

Baan, R., Grosse, Y., Lauby-Secretan, B., El Ghissassi, F., Bouvard, V., Benbrahim-Tallaa, L., Guha, N., Islami, F., Galichet, L., & Straif, K. (2011). Carcinogenicity of radiofrequency electromagnetic fields. *The Lancet Oncology, 12*(7), 624–626.

Batty, M. (2013). Big data, smart cities and city planning. *Dialogues in Human Geography, 3*(3), 274–279.

Boston, W., & Woo, S. (2020, 16 December). Huawei gets conditional green light in Germany as government approves Security Bill. *Wall Street Journal.* https://www.wsj.com/articles/huawei-gets-conditional-green-light-in-germany-as-government-approves-security-bill-11608117504.

bwpi. (2019, 26 June). 5G – Urban revolution or tech hype? 5G and the Smart City, Shenzhen.

China Daily. (2017a, 7 April). Shenzhen's first online hospital opens. *China Daily.* http://www.chinadaily.com.cn/business/tech/2017-04/07/content_28831212.htm.

China Daily. (2017b, 24 October). World's first railless train on test run. *China Daily.* http://www.chinadaily.com.cn/china/2017-10/24/content_33642711.htm.

ECNS. (2017a, 31 October). China to pursue smart firefighting. *Chinanews.com.* http://www.chinadaily.com.cn/business/tech/2017-04/07/content_28831212.htm.

China Daily. (2017b, 19 December). Tencent partners with Shenzhen for rental platform. *Chinanews.com.* http://www.ecns.cn/business/2017/12-19/285082.shtml.

China Daily. (2019a, 17 March). China performs first 5G-based remote surgery on human brain. *Chinanews.com.* http://www.ecns.cn/news/sci-tech/2019-03-17/detail-ifzfmzhu2192467.shtml.

China Daily. (2019b, 29 April). China's first 5G police station unveiled in Shenzhen. *Chinanews.com.* http://www.ecns.cn/news/society/2019-04-29/detail-ifzhtktn3339785.shtml.

European Commission. (2007a). *About INSPIRE.* https://inspire.ec.europa.eu/about-inspire/563.

European Commission. (2020a, 25 November). *A European strategy for data.* https://ec.europa.eu/digital-single-market/en/european-strategy-data.

European Commission. (2020b, 25 November). *Shaping Europe's digital future.* https://ec.europa.eu/info/strategy/priorities-2019-2024/europe-fit-digital-age/shaping-europe-digital-future_en.

European Commission. (2020c). *White Paper on artificial intelligence – A European approach to excellence and trust.* https://ec.europa.eu/info/sites/default/files/commission-white-paper-artificial-intelligence-feb2020_en.pdf.

European Commission. (2020d, 16 September). *President von der Leyen's State of the Union Address: Charting the course out of the coronavirus crisis and into the future.* https://ec.europa.eu/commission/presscorner/detail/en/ip_20_1657.

European Commission. (2020e, 19 February). *Experts say privately held data available in the European Union should be used better and more.* https://ec.europa.eu/digital-single-market/en/news/experts-say-privately-held-data-available-european-union-should-be-used-better-and-more.

GeospatialSG. (2018). *The GeospatialSG programme.* Singapore Land Authority. https://www.geospatial.sg/about.

Goldman, D. P. (2020, 30 November). Huawei hits 5G critical mass with Germany's approval. *Asia Times.* https://asiatimes.com/2020/11/huawei-hits-5g-critical-mass-with-germanys-approval.

Guo, P. (2019, 14 May). Shenzhen Smart City Forum with International Friendship Cities, Shenzhen.

Hardell, L., & Carlberg, M. (2020). Health risks from radiofrequency radiation, including 5G, should be assessed by experts with no conflicts of interest. *Oncology Letters, 20*(4), 1–15. https://doi.org/10.3892/ol.2020.11876 .

Huang, B., & Wang, J. (2020). Big spatial data for urban and environmental sustainability. *Geo-spatial Information Science, 23*(2), 125–140.

IARC. (2012, 12 June). *ARC: Diesel engine exhaust carcinogenic.* https://sabiasque.pt/images/stories/ambiente/pr213_E.pdf.

ICNIRP. (2020). Guidelines for limiting exposure to electromagnetic fields (100 kHz to 300 GHz). *Health Physics, 118*(5), 483–524.

Kaplan, A. (2020). *New York State Senate Bill S7922,* An act in relation to directing the study of the health and environmental impacts of the implementation of 5G and future generation wireless network system technology and small cell distributed antenna systems in the state. https://www.nysenate.gov/legislation/bills/2019/s7922.

Mulder, A., Wiersma, G., & van Loenen, B. (2020). Status of national open spatial data infrastructures: A comparison across continents. *International Journal of Spatial Data Infrastructures Research, 15*, 56–87.

Nyberg, R., & Hardell, L. (2017). *Scientists warn of potential serious health effects of 5G.* http://www.5gappeal.eu/the-5g-appeal.

Perez, B. (2017, 5 December). Shanghai subway to use Alibaba voice and facial recognition systems in AI push. *South China Morning Post.* https://www.scmp.com/tech/enterprises/article/2123014/shanghai-subway-use-alibaba-voice-and-facial-recognition-systems-ai.

RF Safe. (2018). *Senator Patrick Colbeck testifies: Health effects from wireless technologies and 5G.* https://www.rfsafe.com/senator-patrick-colbeck-testifies-health-effects-from-wireless-technologies-and-5g.

Sherrington, S., & Dicks, D. (2018). *Mobile operator 5G Capex forecasts: 2018–2023.* http://img.lightreading.com/heavyreading/hr20181221_esum.pdf.

Sivarajah, U., Kamal, M. M., Irani, Z., & Weerakkody, V. (2017). Critical analysis of Big Data challenges and analytical methods. *Journal of Business Research, 70,* 263–286.

Strumpf, D. (2020, 9 November). U.S. vs. China in 5G: The battle isn't even close. *Wall Street Journal.* https://www.wsj.com/articles/u-s-vs-china-in-5g-the-battle-isnt-even-close-11604959200.

Shenzhen Government Online. (2017). *Shenzhen housing rental supervision service platform.* http://www.sz.gov.cn/en_szgov/services/personal/accommodation/platform.

Taicenn, (2019). *The first smart road in Shenzhen City.* https://www.taicenn.com/news/the-first-smart-road-in-shenzhen-city-28602311.html.

UN-GGIM. (2011, 27 July). Committee of Experts on Global Geospatial Information Management, 47th plenary meeting.

US, FGDC. (1997). *A Strategy for the NSDI.* https://www.fgdc.gov/policyandplanning/A%20Strategy%20for%20the%20NSDI%201997.pdf.

US, FGDC. (2020). *National Spatial Infrastructure – Strategic Plan 2021–2024.* https://www.fgdc.gov/nsdi-plan/nsdi-strategic-plan-2021-2024.pdf.

The White House. (1994). Executive Order 12906: Coordinating Geographic Data Access, Office of the Press Secretary, Washington D.C. https://govinfo.library.unt.edu/npr/library/direct/orders/20fa.html

Wong, D. (2020). What to expect in China's 14th Five Year Plan? Decoding the Fifth Plenum Communique. *China Briefing.* https://www.china-briefing.com/news/what-to-expect-in-chinas-14th-five-year-plan-decoding-the-fifth-plenum-communique.

Xinhua. (2018, 2 November). Baidu empowers Beijing park with AI technologies. *China Daily.* http://www.chinadaily.com.cn/a/201811/02/WS5bdbf693a310eff3032863dd.html.

Zhang, Q. (2018, 6 November). Digital IDs accepted at hotels in Guangdong. *Shenzhen Daily.* http://szdaily.sznews.com/MB/content/201811/06/content_499109.html.

Empowering the Future   7

Transitioning to the Stored Energy Economy

With battery development a key component towards efficient renewable energy utilisation and with it the move away from fossil fuels, advancements will see a variety of diversified products being rapidly developed to meet the wide and contrasting range of commercial applications requiring varied performance and with tumbling price points. The age of electric storage will in particular offer inexpensive, decentralised, and rapid energy supply to urbanising populations in developing countries, and with that the opportunity to create new services and parallel income streams. Meanwhile, new electric mobility modes, including micro-vehicles, civic and fleet vehicles, transporters, and even aerial vehicles, emerging in the shared economy of developed cities will transform how people get around. From horse carriage to railway carriage to motor carriage, mobility revolutions have taken place unexpectedly rapidly in the past. Sharing economies and automation can accelerate the drive to car-free city centres and green, clean-air districts.

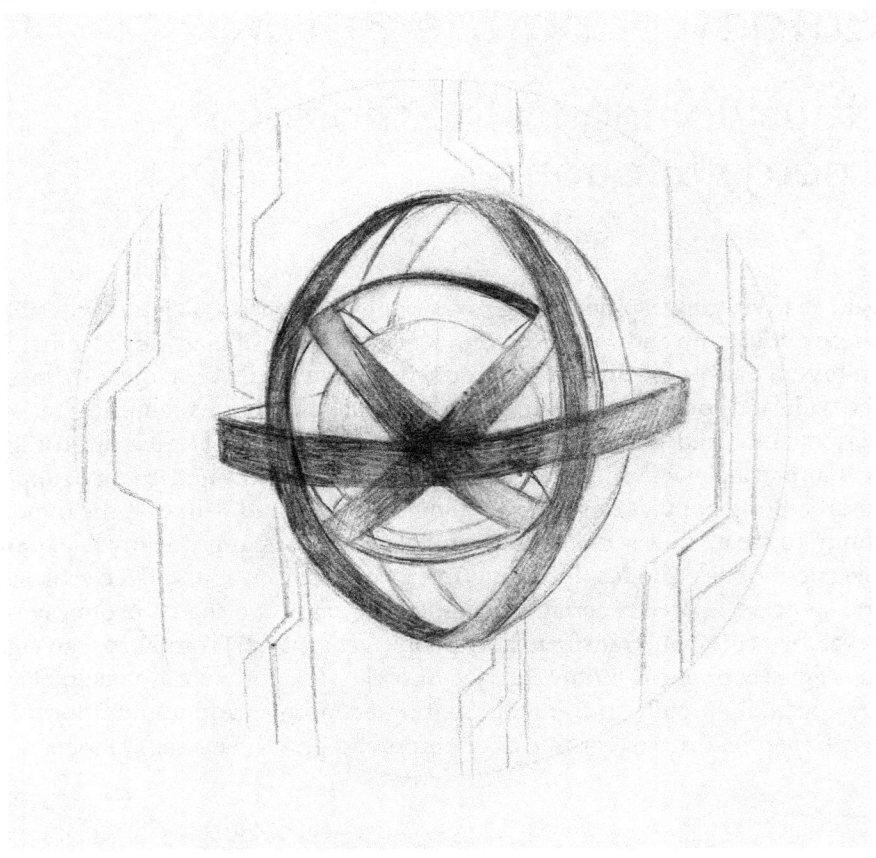

Dyson Sphere

"We will make electricity so cheap that only the rich will burn candles."

Thomas Edison, *Statement to a reporter*, 1879

Decentralising Supply

Another beautiful morning in Africa and residents of a remote South African community emerge excitedly from their dwellings, gathering around a truck loaded with solar panels. Rapid technological development has brought green, cost-effective, alternative electricity options to numerous African towns and villages that are away from existing power grids. Until recently, the only option to get power to their communities was waiting for governments, municipalities, or utility companies to find it politically expedient, financially possible, or even profitable to bring electric grid power to them; in developing countries, this can be a never-ending wait as the costs of establishing grid infrastructure are often prohibitive. Yet communities now have new electricity options available to them through solar systems, as efficiency continues to rise, storage capacity improves, and costs tumble. With funding of just US$1.5 million, 30,000 units can be supplied over a three-year period to 600 off-grid villages, supplying 20 W solar supply systems with generators to 20,000 homes in the most rural areas, and 10,000 units of higher-capacity 100 W / 250 W to homes and families with an ability to establish economic bases (bwpi, 2017). More than 75 public tenders for mini-grid projects were published in Africa during 2018 and 2019, with new regulations framing the development released, national targets for rural electrification defined, and international funding to promote the development of off-grid solutions increased (Infinergia, 2020).

For those living in the developed world who are worried about the details of everyday life such as getting a job, meeting work deadlines, paying the rent, or even choosing where to go on holiday, it's hard to contemplate some of the more basic constraints of life. Yet an estimated 1.2 billion people, roughly 16% of the global population, do not have access to electricity and many more suffer from supply that is irregular and of poor quality (International Energy Agency, 2016). Around four-fifths of these are predominantly in rural areas and whilst still far from complete, progress in providing electrification in urban areas has outpaced that in rural areas by a ratio of more than two to one since 2000. As recently as 1991, 10% (1 15 million people) of the Chinese population were without electricity. Since 2014, China has managed to link all its population, both urban and rural, to an electric supply, mostly though massive increases in the reach of a supply grid fed by polluting fossil fuels. For countries without the same huge economic growth potential as China, meeting such a basic need remains a distant aim.

Off-grid systems can be used in many different ways, but are particularly useful for direct water pumping to divert water easily and cost-effectively, either for drinking or irrigation purposes. There exists great potential for cooperative ownership which can be a lever for small agricultural societies without a supply of mains electricity or where economic reasons make the choice obvious. The United Nations Development Programme (UNDP) established a partnership with Chinese high-tech energy company Zhenfa New Energy that focused on the manufacture, distribution, and export of solar, wind, and biomass power by jointly undertaking new energy and environment projects. Zhenfa recently rolled out a solar-powered aquaculture project in the arid Shaanxi province, supported by the local government, whereby a whole village is able to self-supply electricity whilst generating profits from both fish farming and the sale of excess electricity to the grid. Solar integrated agriculture became the new buzz phrase when China's National Energy Administration included it in its regulatory language in 2015, highlighting clear incentives for those who combined solar power generation with agricultural applications (Godfrey, 2015). Currently the market is in its infancy, lacking standardisation, regulation, and management knowledge, and coherent policies will be essential in these areas in terms of facilitating the market to develop. However, the growth of this sector seems undeniable when coupled with the potential to reinvigorate rural economies, tackle food supply problems, and at the same time meet energy needs and environmental emissions targets.

With mass labour migration to the cities, which is a global issue, and rural economies increasingly devastated by climate impacts through flood, drought, and environment change, finding new livelihood opportunities and economies of scale that provide a counterbalance to depopulation through unprecedented financial attractions to youthful, rural, working populations has become essential. Not only do rural incomes currently lag significantly behind those in urban areas, but there is also a huge disparity between the two in terms of education, healthcare, and lifestyle opportunities. A new generation of agricultural workers must be able to develop stable and well-remunerated incomes in order to be able to contribute to solving the food supply and security issues caused by burgeoning population growth. Earning incomes through electricity generation could fulfil this aim. Of course, this is not a new concept and production models adopted by countries such as Denmark, through the use of individual and community co-operative energy generation, offer good examples of how to invigorate developing rural communities being left behind in the race to urbanisation. Wind power has gained a very high level of social acceptance in Denmark, with the development of community wind farms playing a major role in this process. Families have been offered tax exemptions for generating electricity within their own or an adjoining community, and as far back as 2001, wind turbine cooperatives had already installed 86% of all the current wind turbines in the country. While this could involve purchasing a turbine outright, it was more often the case that families purchased shares in wind turbine cooperatives, which in turn invested in community wind turbines (Gipe, 1996). Initial subsidies providing 30% of the capital cost in the early years were gradually reduced to zero. Surplus produced energy can be connected to the national grid at market charge rates, although there is a feed-in charge. Wind power generation has increased significantly year on year and accounts for an increasingly large share of Denmark's electricity consumption, growing from 39% in 2014 to 47% in 2019, spurred by the passing of a new climate law which requires the share of electricity sourced from combined renewable power to reach 100% by 2030 (Gronholt-Pedersen, 2020). Although many countries tried to subsidise green technology in the latter half of the previous century, most failed to make a viable industry.

Compared with the financial and logistical challenges of power grid expansion, decentralised power supply is considered to be cheaper, faster, and easier to get started, and becomes a viable solution for individuals, communities, private-sector initiatives, and governments. They are able to launch incentives for decentralised system installation without necessarily worrying about how long it will take to recover the initial investment (Oswald et al., 2015), since in many cases the options remain a stark choice between provision or non-provision. New ways of financing renewable energy projects in rural areas are emerging, and the quality and reliability of solar panels and small wind turbines has risen significantly, whilst increases in output have seen costs fall dramatically, making them a serious alternative to supplement or replace existing technologies like diesel generators. The price for electricity in many places in the world is now at a level where the payback time for self-supply is less than five years.

Whilst the opportunities to manifestly change rural lives are compelling, power supply is also undergoing a revolution in well-developed and urbanised regions, and self-supply is on the rise, with populations facing more choices than ever, which is forcing power companies to change their business models in order to create new income streams. Importantly, with the development in the storage sector, it will also soon be possible to store electricity much more cheaply than it is today. In the US, working through the "Green Power

Partnership" of the Environmental Protection Agency (EPA), self-supply arrangements vary, with some sources being directly connected to consumers, whilst others have renewable sources remotely located, and power then being grid supplied. Consumers retain ownership of Renewable Energy Certificates (RECs) associated with their electricity generator in order for it to be considered green power self-supply. Upfront capital investment can be offset through tax breaks and incentives at the local, state, and federal levels in order to help reduce purchasing costs; however, ongoing maintenance and operation costs along with the duties of owning a renewable electricity system still need to be considered. Organisations as diverse as the University of Missouri, H-E-B Grocery Company, IKEA, and the City of San Diego are using this procurement option to supply their green power from a variety of sources, including on-site owned solar arrays, wastewater methane plants, landfill gas facilities, and wind turbines (EPA, 2020). Apple's 175-acre "spaceship" Campus 2 at Cupertino, California sits amid 805,000 square feet of solar arrays. The 17 megawatts (MW) of solar panels on the roof of the "spaceship" and 4 MW of fuel cell storage provide 75% of the building's daytime electricity, with the rest coming from a nearby 130 MW solar farm. IKEA's total ownership and commitments now include 920,000 solar modules on its sites and 547 wind turbines in 14 countries, two solar farms with 1.5 million solar panels, and more than 920,000 solar panels on the roofs of IKEA stores and warehouses. IKEA is transitioning to become climate positive by 2030 (IKEA, 2020; Ingka Group, 2020).

With the change in government in the US in 2021, the country is expected to return to the fore of technology development in the field in order to meet anticipated new climate initiatives. Already on the floor of the Senate are various green bills and the American Energy Innovation Act passed into law at the end of 2020 (T&D World, 2020). This Act supports innovation for broad swaths of the energy sector, including nuclear, energy storage, geothermal, and solar; yet, although clean energy proponents support these provisions, they will not go far enough to meet the rigorous targets of the 2030 climate goals after the US rejoined the Paris Agreement, with expectations of many more comprehensive clean energy bills passing through Congress in the near future (Morehouse, 2020).

Bottlenecks Ahead

In typical solar-based, utility-scale, battery storage systems (mini-grids), the battery is the biggest issue in both capital and operational expenditure terms. In remote locations where there is no or limited technical support available, reliability becomes the key factor and so for these usually small to medium-scale systems, typically of less than 1 MW, lead-acid batteries are still the most commonly used technology. They offer a lower cost per nominal kWh, are mainstream, and are relatively easy to maintain. However, their high sensitivity to temperature and low depth of discharge along with their short lifetime are problematic, and the harshness of many off-grid environments means that many mini-grid solutions often have a significant failure rate. Less than 35% of the mini-grids installed in Senegal between 1996 and 2011 are still functional today (Posséme, 2020; US AID, 2019). Nevertheless, new solutions have emerged in recent years to tackle this issue, such as containerised and standardised systems in which every component is pre-assembled at the manufacturing stage and even the solar panels are bundled, coming with easy set-up folding systems, meaning that the container only needs to be transported to the relevant site and directly unfolded. This approach manages to address most of the difficulties that often appear in custom-made projects, such as missing pieces, theft, the vagaries of component supply, and the poor quality of installation. In a mini-grid battery project in Martinique, the output of a solar photovoltaic (PV) farm was supported using a 2 MWh energy storage unit, which was able to ensure that electricity could be fed to the grid at a constant rate, which avoided the need for back-up generation, and almost 130 MWh of battery storage systems have been implemented in Hawaii to provide similar smoothening services for both solar PV and wind power. However, mini-grids are being predominantly deployed in developed countries, including Australia, Germany, Japan, the UK, the US and other European countries. The Hornsdale Wind Farm in Australia is one of the largest systems in terms of capacity utilising 100 MW / 129 MWh, Lithium-ion (Li-ion) battery storage from Tesla. Meanwhile in New York State, a high-level demonstration project using a 4 MW / 40 MWh battery storage system demonstrated that the operator could reduce almost 400 hours of congestion in the power grid and save up to US$2.03 million in fuel costs (IRENA, 2020). As a result, lithium batteries are becoming increasingly utilised for mini-grids; however, despite supplying 99% of new storage capacity today, they are not ideal and get very expensive if their use is scaled up for continual supply over many hours. Similar to the wind and solar cost reductions, storage costs have seen a sharp decrease, in particular for lithium, whilst non-lithium technologies are also rapidly beginning to move down the cost curve and reveal areas where lithium is not an ideal fit for the application. Such new storage technologies as zinc-air, sodium-nickel, and sodium-ion have been trialled in recent years with varying rates of success. There remains a need for more reliable technologies that will improve performance and lower system ownership cost (Possémé, 2020).

So research continues into developing alternative products that focus on providing differing storage characteristics, drawing power from just about every source imaginable, with researchers at Imperial College London, for example, looking into bromine-based batteries, flow batteries, and fuel cells (Reed, 2020; Silverman, 2020). Currently there are two main challenges to energy storage technology. First, there is the need to develop diverse battery platforms beyond those currently available that are able to meet the varied cost and performance metrics for multiple different applications. A single battery technology is simply not viable; the energy storage requirements for electric vehicles, for instance, are distinctly different from those for stationary energy storage and, instead, a diverse set of appropriate battery platforms, each specifically designed for a class of applications, needs to be developed. Second, existing technologies are still not yet well enough developed to meet all of the required performance metrics for any given application, which are often themselves in conflict, such as frequent use cycles and long life, high energy density and low cost, and fast-charging and no safety risk (Trahey et al., 2020).

Whilst the proliferation of wind and solar resources is creating its own push to develop cheaper, long-duration storage, many organisations, utility companies, states, and nations are now upping their targets for clean energy to meet their 2030 carbon targets, and as the price of energy storage continues to fall, increasing deployment in new areas can be expected to become even more attractive. Commercial Li-ion battery pack prices, which were above $1,100/kWh in 2010, fell 89% in real terms to $137/kWh in 2020. By 2023, average prices will be close to $100/kWh and are expected to fall to $58/kWh by 2030 (Henze, 2020). The industry is becoming increasingly resilient to changing raw material prices, with leading battery manufacturers moving up the value chain and investing in cathode production or even mines, and enjoying gross margins of up to 20% with their plants operating at utilisation rates over 85%. Daixin Li, a senior energy storage associate at Bloomberg New Energy Finance (BNEF) suggests that increasingly diversified chemistries currently being developed in the market result in a wide range of prices and that battery manufacturers are racing to mass-produce diversified high energy-density batteries using new chemistries that will potentially come to market as early as 2021. Lithium iron phosphate or Li-ion (LFP) is currently the most cost-competitive alternative, contributing to the lowest reported cell prices of $80/kWh, and is currently utilised by the majority of Chinese electric vehicle power sources. So the road to achieving $100/kWh by 2023 looks clear despite the likelihood of bumps along the way, including the potential for commodity price increases regardless of recent smoothing in the market, yet beyond that date there remains a good deal of uncertainty about the speed of transition in battery development, and particularly towards the all-important 2030 targets. The progress of continued technology research into batteries perhaps goes hand in hand with "self-supply" and "electric vehicle" take-up, and there is much less certainty regarding how the industry will reduce prices even further from $100/kWh down to the BNEF expectations of $58/kWh by the end of the decade. This is not because it is unlikely, but rather that the various paths and options that might occur before 2025 are divergent. One possible path is the possibility of progress with the development of solid-state batteries which could be manufactured at 40% of the cost of current Li-ion batteries when produced at scale and would completely disrupt the market. To do this, reductions would need to come from materials, manu-facture, new technology, and the creation of new supply chains, none of which happens overnight (Henze, 2020).

Personal Charge

The advancements that are being made in battery technology are most likely going to reshape the rural landscape in the coming years and will be the key to the success of renewable supply. However, battery storage can also be expected to have profound implications on urban domestic power utilisation. In-home batteries have in fact become increasingly popular in recent years. The US Energy Storage Association reported a 10% increase in residential storage deployments from the final quarter of 2019 to the first quarter of 2020. The earliest adopters were largely interested in back-up power, but there is growing interest in the potential of home batteries as a tool to manage solar panels, electric vehicle charging, and demand response (US Energy Storage Association, 2020). Tesla has brought standardisation to the high-end domestic market with its "Powerwall", a large-scale, heavy-duty power bank offering 7kW of power and standing more than 1 metre tall (45"). Paired with rooftop solar supply, it is designed to "store energy, detect outages and automatically become an energy source if the grid goes down" and offers a ten-year warranty (Tesla, n.d.). Similar luxury market products are offered by competitors Sonnen, LG Chem, and Enphase, tapping into the emerging grid services opportunities. These home storage products are primarily developed for utilising self-supplied "green" power, storing it and using it to cut electricity bills rather than sending it back to the grid, an upmarket version of the solar kits currently being rolled out across Africa. Stored electricity can power an electric vehicle, can serve daily power needs such as lights, components, and refrigerators, and can reduce family energy consumption towards net zero, whilst helping to form more resilience in the face of electric grid outages in the event of natural or human-made disasters that are becoming more frequent. Connecting self-supply directly to a fixed grid means energy is generated during the day and thus sold at low peak tariffs, but still needs to be purchased for night or peak use. Utilising energy storage enables self-supply to be utilised at peak hours, which is when in fact it is most needed. The problem with lithium batteries is that they only hold enough energy to power an average American home for a couple of hours rather than days, so scaling the size to fit exact needs becomes important. The potential and excitement then comes with the continuing advances in technology already discussed, along with the cost reductions that come with these, meaning that when a self-supply battery is now connected back to the grid, this allows owners to utilise opportunities to generate and store free energy that can be sold to utilities during peak demand times. That could lower the need for increased sources of peak power demand such as expensive "peaker plants" or a costly upgrade in transmission and distribution lines, especially if utilities also invest in complementary large-scale projects. Two energy companies in Australia have utilised Tesla's bigger solution generally reserved for commercial and utility applications, the 105kW (420kWh) "Powerpack" and inverter system, in order to create a new shared "PowerBank" as a community alternative to individual Powerwalls in the city of Mandurah. The project is led by the government-owned Western Power and the energy company Synergy. The energy capacity is available to 52 families with solar installations in Meadow Springs. The Energy Minister Ben Wyatt commented at the project launch that: "At a cost of $1 per day, each customer participating in the 24-month trial will be able to 'virtually' store up to 8 kWh of excess power generated during the day from their solar PV systems in the battery. They will then be able to draw electricity back from the PowerBank during peak time without having to outlay upfront costs for a behind the meter battery storage system" (Lambert, 2018).

Perhaps even more interesting is the heightened opportunity for every single urban dweller, building, or institution, even those without access to any energy generating source at all, to still be able to own a large-scale, domestic powerbank, which is charged from the grid overnight at a low peak cost and then used during high demand peaks or resold back to the energy grid as a revenue stream. The product is then no longer "high end", but becomes a mass-market application, and in this way the whole population can become "peak demand smoothers" rather than "peak demand users", and smart applications can allow power utilities to optimise the power supply needs, putting power storage capacity into the "commons" and leaving individual citizens as micro-power suppliers, thus avoiding the need for municipal-scale capital investment in battery storage. Moreover, there are also opportunities to resolve issues relating to the large-scale investments expected for electric vehicle charging infrastructure, whereby decentralised home storers would be able to flexibly address the widespread supply requirements. A pilot programme is underway in New Hampshire by an Ontario-based company, Liberty Utilities, that should be able to lead the way and help outline initial costs and benefits of how individual residential energy storage might be spread across the state. The utility has supplied batteries for the homes of 100 customers and over the next two years will analyse the value offered both to customers and to the grid. Participating customers pay US$50 a month for ten years or about US$5,000 upfront for the installation of two Tesla Powerwall batteries, each of which retails for around US$6,500 excluding hardware and installation. They will also be enrolled for new time-of-use rates, which vary based on the time of day. However, the utility will own the batteries and will be able to draw from them to help meet demand during peak hours (Thill, 2020). The project is planned to be rolled out by adding 150 new households as well as introducing a "Bring-Your-Own-Device" programme with the option of purchasing a home storage battery from another provider. In this way battery aggregators can bid to provide an additional 2.5 MW of capacity, which is equivalent to about 500 batteries (Liberty Utilities, 2019). The results of Liberty's test run could help determine how residential batteries are deployed across the state and will no doubt influence other electric utilities. A bill recently introduced into the New Hampshire state legislature would forbid utilities from owning "behind-the-meter" batteries unless the New Hampshire Public Utilities Commission determines, based on this pilot, that utility ownership is in the public interest. If utilities own the batteries, some advocates say it could prevent competition and customers could end up paying more than they should. As more domestic storage options are unveiled over the next few years, a variety of options are likely to emerge, depending on location and market.

A Battery for Life

The future of energy storage and batteries appears further heavily tied to the transformation of the vehicle sector from petrol to electric. In fact, the future direction of both urban and rural environments is significantly linked to the progress of battery development. So much of humanity's surroundings are visually impacted by the presence of power towers, filling stations, or overhead cables, yet in the future, these surroundings may feature energy banks, charging points, or power boards. Bob Lutz, former vice chairman and head of product development at General Motors, has for some time been predicting huge stranded assets in traditional motor vehicles by 2025, as manufacturers retool their production in a switch to electric vehicles (EVs) and municipalities automate public transport systems (Lutz, 2017). The global EV market demand was estimated at over 2.3 million units in 2019, boosting the existing stock to 7.2 million vehicles, equal to about 2.6% of global car sales. This is a tiny part of a huge global vehicle market, but one that is about to explode under a set of new market drivers. As technological progress in the electrification of two and three-wheelers, buses, and trucks advances and as the market for them grows, the range of EVs is expanding significantly (International Energy Agency, 2020). Incentives are continually being offered through government initiatives to promote the manufacture and sale of EVs, and this is about to accelerate under the increased pressures of meeting new emissions regulations relating to the 2030 climate goals in both Europe and China which were announced in 2020 and 2021. At the same time, the Indian government announced its plans to spend US$1.4 billion to subsidise sales of hybrid and electric vehicles until 2022. These regulations pose major challenges for the automotive industry, since manufacturers will face potential penalties amounting to several billion dollars unless they increase their EV penetration rates significantly. The year 2019 saw the German government and car manufacturers agree to raise cash incentives by 2025 under the "Environment Bonus" plan for battery-powered cars, which will reach US$6,680 per vehicle, and the car industry will cover half the cost. Germany plans to ban the sale of all new internal combustion engines by 2030. Norway aims to have 100% of its cars either an electric or plug-in hybrid unit by 2025, and the Netherlands plans to ban all petrol and diesel car sales by the same year, whilst France aims to end its petrol and diesel car sales more sluggishly by 2040 (Nicholas & Lutsey, 2020). The UK brought its previous targets forward by ten years in 2020 in order to phase-out the sale of new petrol and diesel cars and vans by 2030 as a means to achieve its stated climate, air quality, and energy security ambitions, and adopted a 100% zero-emission new car sales goal for 2035 (HM Government, 2020). Meanwhile, China, which already has almost half the global EV stock and where 1.1 million electric vehicles were sold in 2018, has signalled a shift in policy away from subsidies while implementing quotas. In its 15-year EV draft plan, Beijing set a target for EVs to account for 25% of annual new light-vehicle sales and 20% of new car sales by 2025 (Berman, 2020).

If Lutz is correct, then the majority of these government targets look overly cautious and completely out of touch with the bigger changes in the market. Manufacturers are already retooling and repositioning to gain market share in the new order, which is certain to hit a rapid tipping point once EVs are close to price parity with conventional vehicles. With the discussed predictions of average battery pack prices at US$101/kWh by 2023, it is at around this price point that automakers in some markets should be able to produce and sell mass-market EVs at the same price and with the same margin as comparable internal combustion vehicles. Furthermore, with the writing clearly having been on the wall for some time and with the climate environment clearly signalling the end for the internal combustion engine, one wonders both how many manufacturers will continue to be bullish in developing new models of traditional vehicles and, perhaps more tellingly, how many potential vehicle purchasers would remain determined to stick to obsolete technology that will rapidly have no resale value. The purchasing of a traditional power vehicle becomes an increasingly risky business week by week and the market teeters on the brink of a rapid conversion which will undoubtedly see the masses of stranded assets Lutz anticipates, and one where EV's simply become identified as "vehicles" once again, whilst conventionally-powered vehicles become distinctive as "fuel vehicles" (FVs).

The transitions in both the automotive industry away from FVs and the energy supply industry away from fossil fuels are well under way and gathering extreme momentum. The speed of both shifts relies heavily on energy storage and in particular in the short term on the capacity for Li-ion batteries in making further progress in terms of costs, energy density, and cycle life. BYD, the world's largest maker of rechargeable batteries based in Shenzhen, has developed its "blade battery", a type of LFP which is said to be safer and cheaper than many EV batteries as it doesn't include the costly element cobalt. LFP technology is not new, but the battery architecture has improved its energy density, which makes it more acceptable for wider use. This battery type is ideal for forklifts, bicycles, and electric cars, and is also gaining popularity as a home storage option. Even Tesla is using LFP batteries from Chinese maker Contemporary Amperex Technology (CATL) for its Shanghai-made Model 3. Whilst the industry outside of China has been continually pushing for longer-range performance from EVs and moving to more expensive nickel-rich chemistries in order to achieve that aim, China has not seen the same imperative and has focused on technologies more suited to urban travel modes with shorter operational distances and more repeated performance characteristics, including bus and taxi fleets, and municipal service vehicles. These don't need to travel ultra-long distances on one charge, but do need low price points to make them accessible to markets, and their pack prices at US$80/kWh are far more competitive than those technologies that use more expensive elements.

A lack of charging facilities also doesn't seem to have hindered the rollout of EVs in China, with private owners charging at home and finding range and duration perfectly adequate for the vast majority of trips. A lack of charging infrastructure is often stated as a hindrance to EV market growth, along with variations in charging load and lack of standardisation. China's success in putting five million EVs on the road in the last decade has been built on a clearly articulated vision, consistent planning, coordinated action, city-level innovation and leadership, policy implementation, and the continued adaptation of policy tools to meet the changing market (He & Jin, 2021). Different countries have their own standards, such as CCS (Europe, the US, and Korea), CHAdeMO (Japan), and GB/T (China). Some electric manufacturers such as Tesla have focused on overcoming this obstacle by having their own charging network. The UK is one of the few governments that actually has a comprehensive strategy for electrification, with both an official Office for Low Emission Vehicles (OLEV) and an electrification strategy called the Road to Zero strategy. This anticipates that the vast majority of drivers will choose to charge at home; however, the strategy aims to provide charging options to the third of households that don't have off-street parking through adding street charging pillars and integrated lighting poles. This will have not only significant implications for the visual quality of the urban fabric and street environment, but would also seem to continue to promote the use of private vehicles in urban locations, which seems to go against current policy and tends to negate rapid transitions to more sustainable transport modes, including public transport, walking, and biking. Therefore, this could also be hugely expensive and wasted infrastructure deployment. The US is adopting a different approach, placing emphasis on charging facilities being made available at stations, workplaces, and public destinations, and letting utility providers and the market provide suitable locations for other service provision. These have developed along interstate highways and public parking lots across the country (US National Renewable Energy Laboratory, 2020) and locations can be pinpointed by using the Alternative Fueling Station Locator app tool from the US Department of Energy's Alternative Fuels Data Center (Alternative Fuels Data Center, n.d.).

It seems clear that renewable energy resources will have a huge role to play over the next decade as supply prices plummet and fossil fuels are significantly replaced as both means of electricity supply and direct fuel sources in order to address pollution and climate emergency concerns. Harnessing the power of these renewables efficiently will be critical and battery storage will be at the rockface of change, carrying the ability to transform both rural and urban economics and societal behaviour. Independent generation through micro-wind turbines, solar panels, or other small-scale decentralised renewable systems can free rapidly urbanising areas in the developing world from dependency on the power grid, allowing new forms of development models to emerge, whilst the rapid and continued advancements in storage technology offer wide opportunities to expand economic options. Power storage is likely to bring somewhat unforeseen changes to the physical environment, which could be significant depending upon how they are integrated and regulated by national governments. Yet the role of energy storage should rapidly touch the lives of all and can empower developing urbanising economies in particular to move away from their anticipated fossil fuel reliance in the immediate future and generate new revenue streams for the masses by allowing storage and supply to be provided by everyone, unleashing urban potential and "Empowering the Future".

References

Alternative Fuels Data Center. (n.d.). *Alternative fueling station locator*. https://afdc.energy.gov/stations/#/find/nearest.

Berman, B. (2020, 1 April). China backslides on electric car quotas while extending subsidies. *Electrek*. https://electrek.co/2020/04/01/china-set-to-backslide-on-electric-car-quotas-while-extending-subsidies.

bwpi. (2017). *Simple solar tech generates new lives*. http://www.initiatives.com.hk/170407-simple-solar-tech.html.

EPA. (2020). *Self-supply*. https://www.epa.gov/greenpower/self-supply.

Gipe, P. (1996). *Community-owned wind development in Germany, Denmark, and the Netherlands*. http://www.wind-works.org/cms/index.php?id=61&tx_ttnews[tt_news]=506&cHash=fcb13537bd5b8ec990858ce72560f0e2.

Godfrey, M. (2015, 27 January). How farmers can help grow China's solar power. *South China Morning Post*. https://www.scmp.com/comment/insight-opinion/article/1693178/how-farmers-can-help-grow-chinas-solar-power.

Gronholt-Pedersen, J. (2020, 2 January). Denmark sources record 47% of power from wind in 2019. *Reuters*. https://www.reuters.com/article/us-climate-change-denmark-windpower/denmark-sources-record-47-of-power-from-wind-in-2019-idUSKBN1Z10KE.

He, H., & Jin, L. (2021). *How China put nearly 5 million new energy vehicles on the road in one decade.* https://theicct.org/blog/staff/china-new-energy-vehicles-jan2021.

Henze, V. (2020, 16 December). Battery pack prices cited below $100/kWh for the first time in 2020, while market average sits at $137/kWh. *BNEF.* https://about.bnef.com/blog/battery-pack-prices-cited-below-100-kwh-for-the-first-time-in-2020-while-market-average-sits-at-137-kwh.

HM Government. (2020, 18 November) *Government takes historic step towards net-zero with end of sale of new petrol and diesel cars by 2030.* https://www.gov.uk/government/news/government-takes-historic-step-towards-net-zero-with-end-of-sale-of-new-petrol-and-diesel-cars-by-2030.

IKEA. (2020). *Ingka Group increases its sustainability investments by 600M EUR over next 12 months* https://www.ikea.com/us/en/this-is-ikea/newsroom/ingka-group-increases-its-sustainability-investments-by-600m-eur-over-next-12-months-pubded3e0c9.

Infinergia. (2020). *Mini-grid for village electrification – 2020 edition.* https://www.infinergia.com/en/mini-grid-market-report.

Ingka Group. (2020). *IKEA Finland completes acquisition of three new wind farms, to support its renewable energy generation.* https://www.ingka.com/news/ikea-finland-completes-acquisition-of-three-new-wind-farms-to-support-its-renewable-energy-generation.

International Energy Agency. (2016). *World Energy Outlook 2016.* https://doi.org/doi:https://doi.org/10.1787/weo-2016-en.

———. (2020). *Global EV outlook 2020.* https://www.iea.org/reports/global-ev-outlook-2020.

IRENA. (2020). *Battery storage paves way for a renewable-powered future.* https://www.irena.org/newsroom/articles/2020/Mar/Battery-storage-paves-way-for-a-renewable-powered-future.

Lambert, F. (2018, 5 November). A new Tesla "shared Powerbank" launches as a community alternative to individual Powerwalls. *Electrek.* https://electrek.co/2018/11/05/tesla-shared-powerbank/#more-78368.

Liberty Utilities. (2019). *Liberty Utilities home battery storage pilot approved.* https://new-hampshire.libertyutilities.com/alstead/liberty-utilities-home-battery-storage-pilot-approved-.html.

Lutz, B. (2017). *Kiss the good times goodbye.* https://www.autonews.com/article/20171105/INDUSTRY_REDESIGNED/171109944/bob-lutz-kiss-the-good-times-goodbye.

Morehouse, C. (2020). *Senate works to pass comprehensive energy bill in 2020 as renewables sector vies for more aid.* https://www.utilitydive.com/news/senate-works-to-pass-comprehensive-energy-bill-in-2020-as-renewables-sector/591844.

Nicholas, M., & Lutsey, N. (2020). *Quantifying the electric vehicle charging infrastructure gap in the United Kingdom.* https://theicct.org/sites/default/files/publications/UK-charging-gap-082020.pdf.

Oswald, A. J., Proto, E., & Sgroi, D. (2015). Happiness and productivity. *Journal of Labor Economics, 33*(4), 789–822. https://doi.org/10.1086/681096.

Possémé, B. (2020, 12 November). The outlook for mini-grids. *Energy Storage News.* https://www.energy-storage.news/blogs/the-outlook-for-mini-grids.

Reed, G. (2020). *Imperial energy storage startup reaches final of New Energy Challenge 2020.* https://www.imperial.ac.uk/news/206653/imperial-energy-storage-startup-reaches-final.

Silverman, D. (2020). *Imperial pioneers innovation in clean energy sector.* https://www.imperial.ac.uk/news/195020/imperial-pioneers-innovation-clean-energy-sector.

T&D World. (2020). *U.S. Senate passes American Energy Innovation Act.* https://www.tdworld.com/utility-business/article/21151118/us-senate-passes-american-energy-innovation-act.

Tesla. *Powerwall.* https://www.tesla.com/powerwall?redirect=no.

Thill, D. (2020, 27 July). Small batteries but high stakes for New Hampshire home energy storage pilot. *Energy News Network.* https://energynews.us/2020/07/27/northeast/small-batteries-but-high-stakes-for-new-hampshire-home-energy-storage-pilot.

Trahey, L., Brushett, F. R., Balsara, N. P., Ceder, G., Cheng, L., Chiang, Y.-M., Hahn, N. T., Ingram, B. J., Minteer, S. D., Moore, J. S., Mueller, K. T., Nazar, L. F., Persson, K. A., Siegel, D. J., Xu, K., Zavadil, K. R., Srinivasan, V., & Crabtree, G. W. (2020). Energy storage emerging: A perspective from the Joint Center for Energy Storage Research. *Proceedings of the National Academy of Sciences, 117*(23), 12550–12557. https://doi.org/10.1073/pnas.1821672117.

UNDP China. (2013). *China Human Development Report. 2013: Sustainable and liveable cities: Toward ecological civilisation* (G. Luchsinger, Ed. Vol. D668 Archival Library of Chinese Publications CIP Data H.Z. (2013) No.122691). China Translation and Publishing Corporation.

US AID. (2019). *Off-grid solar market assessment – Senegal.* Power Africa Off-Grid Project. https://www.usaid.gov/sites/default/files/documents/1860/PAOP-Senegal-MarketAssessment-Final_508.pdf.

US Energy Storage Association. (2020). *U.S. Energy Storage Monitor Q4 – Executive Summary.* Wood Mackenzie Power & Renewables. https://energystorage.org/resources/industry-resources/us-energy-storage-monitor.

US National Renewable Energy Laboratory. (2020). *EV charging stations continued strong growth in early 2020, NREL report shows.* https://www.nrel.gov/news/program/2020/ev-charging-stations-continued-strong-growth-in-early-2020-nrel-report-shows.html.

Unleashing Urban Potential

Repurposing Streets to People's Needs

8

Significant areas of the public realm are dedicated to vehicle use at the expense of other, more productive investments. With the imminent death of the internal combustion engine due to health concerns and climate imperatives, combined with the increasingly limited access of private vehicles in cities, the land available to be released from standard roads and parking can be radically transformed for the better. How will this change land utilisation, how can parking be repurposed, and what should the immediate approaches be to urban parking in transition? Many cities are initiating remarkable and rapid transformations, adding cycle paths, wider pedestrian pavement, and safer, slower streets, yet advances in smart technologies and particularly automated safety and response systems that can accompany fully automated vehicle districts should allow much more significant repurposing of streets back to civic spaces for interaction, play, and pleasure.

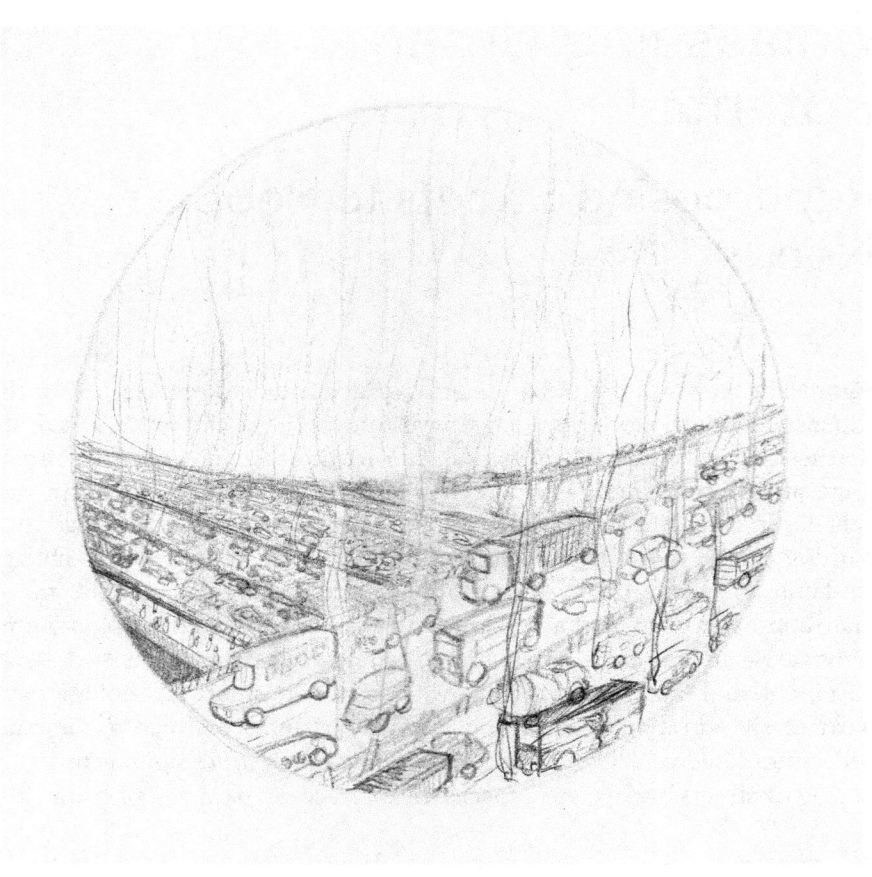

Tox-city

"God made the country, and man made the town."

William Cowper, *The task*, 1785

End of the Road

Road traffic injuries are the leading cause of death for young people aged between five and 29 years and claim 1.35 million lives every year according to the UN World Health Organization (WHO), while 50 million more are injured. More than 185,000 of these deaths are children (WHO, 2020) – over 500 children every day. Road deaths are higher than deaths from any illness – more than malaria, more than tuberculosis, more than HIV – and exceed the combined annual casualties of all of the world's armed conflicts. It's a figure that equates to the COVID-19 pandemic happening every single year. What it seemingly isn't is a figure that is newsworthy. The theme of the Fifth UN Global Road Safety Week was #SpeakUp, calling for strong leadership to push strategic, evidence-based action to save lives on the road. Moreover, 93% of these fatalities, which cost most countries 3% of their GDP through loss of effective labour supply and diverted household savings, occur in underdeveloped and developing countries, which only support around 60% of the world's vehicles. Half of the deaths are not vehicle users, but people who just happen to be in the vicinity, in "the wrong place at the wrong time", including pedestrians and cyclists, and rates of road traffic death are three times higher in developing countries than in developed countries (WHO, 2020). For developing countries in a phase of motorisation, as is the case in China today, roads are often built without due consideration for the changing times in which we live or for the communities they have to pass through. Vehicles are killers and with most of the future population explosion focused on developing nations in Africa and Asia, further vehicle growth and a business-as-usual approach to road-based urban development will kill millions more. Unfortunately, rates of road traffic deaths in Africa and Southeast Asia are already the world's highest at 26.6 and 20.7 deaths per 100,000 of the population respectively according to a UN report, whilst Africa has the highest proportion of pedestrian and cyclist mortalities (accounting for 44% of deaths) and in Southeast Asia, the majority of deaths are riders of motorised two- and three-wheelers, representing 43% and 36% of all deaths respectively (WHO, 2018). The cornerstones of the UN "Safe System" approach developed to cut road deaths in half by 2025 are "safe roads and roadsides", "safe speeds", "safe vehicles", and "safe road users", all of which must be addressed in order to reduce fatal crashes and serious injuries (WHO, 2020). In cities, all of these factors are also shaped by the design and regulation of the urban environment, which, to all intents and purposes, nowadays relates to roads, the planning for roads, and the design of roads.

Roughly 60,000 new cars are taking to China's streets each day, fuelled by the need to keep the economic boom at full tilt. According to the State Statistical Bureau, the country had only 0.5 million cars on the road in 1990 (China, National Bureau of Statistics, 1989), but this number had exploded to over 43 million privately owned cars by 2011 (China, National Bureau of Statistics, 2011) and a whopping 261.5 million by 2019 (China, National Bureau of Statistics, 2020), when almost 21.5 million new passenger cars joined the roads (The Global Economy, 2019), meeting the forecasts of reaching 22 million in 2020 (Wang et al., 2012). That accounts for half of all the cars sold globally (The Global Economy, 2019). Conversely, in the US, car sales have decreased year on year following their peak in 1986 at almost 11.5 million (Wards Auto, 2017) and 30 years later, annual sales were roughly only one-third of that number, with the downward trend being expected to continue (The Global Economy, 2019). Yet the number of "wrong time wrong place" road deaths while walking or riding a bike reached 7,140 in 2018; the highest since 1990 and an alarming 41% increase since 2008 (National Highway Traffic Safety Administration, 2019). Road deaths are not road deaths anymore, they are street deaths. At the city level, streets have also been rapidly absorbing new private vehicles, in densely compact Hong Kong, for example, at the alarming rate of over 4.6% per annum for the last decade (HKSAR, Transport Advisory Committee, 2014). In a similar fashion to the US, the trend of critical and fatal road traffic accidents has been decreasing over the same period and in 2014 Hong Kong had the lowest number of fatal accidents since 1955, despite the growth of vehicle numbers (Hong Kong Road Safety Council, 2018; HKSAR, Transport Department, 2020). In the UK, during 2013, 1,713 people were killed in road accidents reported to the police, the lowest number on record, and half the figure recorded in 2000, whilst 21,657 people were seriously injured, a 43% decline compared to 2000. Highways and transport departments will surely want to pat themselves on the back for this; however, it seems clear that it is the safety features built into the latest vehicle models that have powered the continued drop in fatalities. The number of deaths in the latest vehicle model released each year has fallen by nearly two-thirds in the past decade. In 2013, new cars had a lower fatality rate than cars fresh off the assembly line did just a few years earlier. The broad decreases in fatality rates stem from several factors. The increased use of child restraints and seatbelts has saved thousands of lives as compliance of mandatory seatbelt laws from the 1980s onwards started to kick in. Furthermore, laws that restricted driving privileges for young drivers have also reduced fatalities. But safety experts say that the critical factor in reducing the number of deaths has been the snowballing improvements to vehicle-safety technology. Safety improvements – in particular, electronic stability control systems that make vehicles less likely to flip over – are responsible for at least some of the drop in deaths. They also empower drivers to feel safer and drive faster. The twenty-first-century car is bigger, safer, and faster than ever. Sitting perched up high, with the music and AC on, it becomes easy to disassociate yourself with the speed, noise, and air rush outside at street level. So efficient are the engines and so reliable are the brakes that speed restrictions seem to go against the very purpose of the vehicles. The vast majority of drivers are not maniacs and do want to behave responsibly, but clearly the established use of speed limits on roads is not working, even in a developed society like Britain. The British Parliament estimates that "most drivers and pedestrians think speeds are generally too high but 95% of all drivers admit to exceeding speed limits" (Parliament, House of Commons, 2002).

Analysis of road accident data presented by both Dr C. B. Chow and Dr Joey Li of the University of Hong Kong appeared to indicate clear geographical disparities in Hong Kong traffic accidents (Chow, 2015; Li, 2015). Whilst severe injuries and deaths are in fact lowest in the dense urban areas, the outlying new towns and their surrounding rural areas exhibited the highest risks, especially to car drivers and passengers. However, pedestrians, the group at highest risk of traffic accidents, are found to be at greater risk in the dense urban areas where collisions are more likely. The "Grim Reaper's Road Map" substantiates these figures for the UK, showing the places where people are most likely to die in a car crash (Shaw et al., 2008). The lowest rates are found in urban areas, with London, Newcastle, Greater Manchester, and Cardiff having particularly low rates. In rural areas, where car use is more often necessary and where average speeds are higher, rates can be many times greater. The worst place for road deaths is the north of Scotland. By contrast and not surprisingly, the risk to pedestrians of being hit by vehicles is at its most severe in busy urban centres.

Urban Effects

So urban streets are the least safe place for cyclists and pedestrians, and for those in developing countries they are beyond hazardous. But it doesn't stop there. Awareness of the health issues from vehicle emissions are of particular concern in congested city street conditions, not to mention the psychological stress resulting from noise and safety issues. Emissions include particulates from diesel engines, nitrous oxide, volatile organic compounds, carbon monoxide, and benzene, whilst metals such as copper, iron, and manganese interact with acidic sulphate-rich particles already in the air to produce a toxic aerosol (Harrison et al., 2012). A WHO study found that diesel fumes directly cause an increase in lung cancer (IARC, 2012), whilst 4.3 million deaths a year are linked to exposure to outdoor air pollution (WHO, n.d.), and the global fraction of air pollution-related premature deaths by tailpipe emissions alone is just under 12% or about 500,000 (Anenberg et al., 2019). Among children, air pollutants are associated with increased acute respiratory illness, increased incidence of respiratory symptoms and infections, increased duration of respiratory episodes, and lowered lung function. A statistical study in California of children with cancer under six years old found that living near smog results in a 5–11% increase in cancer risk (Heck et al., 2013). Asthma, the most common chronic disorder of childhood, is on the rise in the US and in other industrialised nations. During the 1980s, the prevalence of childhood asthma increased by nearly 40% (Weitzman et al., 1992). Many different factors have been associated with asthma, but several studies have linked particulate air pollution with exacerbations of asthma in children afflicted with the disease, whilst research indicating that infants whose mothers were exposed to higher levels of ultra-fine particles (UFPs) during pregnancy are much more likely to develop asthma (Wright et al., 2021). Young children generally spend more time closer to the ground by virtue of both their shorter stature and the nature of their typical physical activity; therefore, they experience greater exposure to pollutants emitted close to the ground, such as automobile exhaust and high-density pollutants brought downwards by gravity. In addition, when the sources of air pollutants such as cars are close to playgrounds and other areas where children play, children and infants in strollers may be heavily exposed (International Programme on Chemical Safety et al., 1986).

It's not just exhaust fumes that are likely hurting us. There is an urgent need to start paying more immediate attention to air pollution caused by tyre, brake, and road wear because this won't be solved by a switch to electric vehicles (EVs) (Georgia Institute of Technology, 2017). Brake dust, tyre fragments, and even tiny bits of the road can get into the air and these make up a similar proportion of the airborne particulate matter (APM) resulting from vehicle use as exhaust emissions (Harrison et al., 2012). Whilst brake pad dust may be reduced through EV adoption because these mostly utilise regenerative braking which doesn't use brake pads most of the time, tyre and road dust will remain a serious problem. Several countries and regions have implemented or are in the process of implementing programmes to improve tyre efficiency and safety, such as the US, Japan, the

EU, and South Korea (Pike, 2011). Rating and labelling programmes along with drawing up compliance standards are important first steps in this process, enabling both consumers to select and ensuring manufacturers offer more efficient tyres. The installation of tyre pressure monitoring systems (TPMS) as a safety and efficiency measure should become an effective strategy in reducing wear, aided by the global spread of the technology.

We can ask the question "what are brakes for?" The answer has to be "to allow vehicles to go faster". Continued improvements in braking systems since the invention of the motor vehicle have allowed drivers to accelerate and decelerate rapidly to such a point that traffic management in the last few decades has been focused on limiting speeds and managing smooth flows. Both fuel consumption and exhaust emissions vary significantly with the variability of vehicle speed. A steady speed is the key to reducing the emission of harmful pollutants. Whilst lower speeds require less intense wear on brakes, driver behaviour in minimising unnecessary braking and avoiding excessively rapid acceleration are key environmental features. As such, traffic management features such as "stop lights and speed bumps" can adversely impact air quality, and the effective use of traffic signal systems to improve air quality requires visionary design and committed institutional coordination that appears to be beyond most governments at present.

The widespread availability and affordability of car travel has provided many freedoms to society. Cars offer the potential to travel to almost any destination, at whatever time, with passengers and luggage and a minimal need to plan ahead. They have made it easier to keep in touch with friends and family, and to reach a wider range of job opportunities, but these benefits have been obtained at a substantial price and one that generally falls most heavily on the poorest and most vulnerable in society – those who are generally unable to benefit from private vehicle use themselves suffer from the effects of other people's travel. The negative impacts include deaths, injuries, stress, air and noise pollution, and the loss of social cohesion (Douglas et al., 2011). In the UK, the cost of community severance and the loss of social cohesion, the so-called "barrier effect" due to transport infrastructure, is classified as an "impact that is currently not feasible to monetise"; however, research from the Institute of Transport Economics in Oslo suggests that it is even greater than the estimated cost of noise pollution and almost equal to the cost of air pollution (Kay, 2011). The UK Department for Transport estimated the costs to urban areas in 2009, based on excess delays, accidents, poor air quality, physical inactivity, greenhouse gas emissions, and noise pollution as being up to £56 billion, significantly more than the revenue generated by road taxes (HM Government, 2011).

Road planning and engineering efforts in most cities have changed little in the last 50 years in terms of road layout and speed control, in line with the lack of modernisation in the planning and construction industries as a whole. Highways and transport departments are preoccupied with absorbing the increased traffic volumes on the roads, repeatedly widening them and providing increased design volumes for traffic. Their understanding of the complex interrelated problems is not holistic and in order to keep pedestrians "safe" from these "improved" roads, they need to be marginalised behind endless concrete barriers, corralled by steel railings onto pavements that are often insufficient in width to allow adequate movement, and marshalled into threatening subways, inconvenient elevators, and onto endless footbridges. The impact to cities and on their citizens, particularly older people, has become increasingly damaging. With streets designed and shaped primarily for vehicles, pedestrian crossings are dictated by traffic rather than pedestrian needs, there is an inefficient use of space, they are cluttered with signs and obstructions, and they are standardised, monotonous and lack interest, character, and diversity. Things can get even worse if EV charging facilities are allowed onto streets as the UK is currently proposing. The essential challenge for newly industrialising governments is to shirk traditional, urban transport solutions that are primarily focused on providing benefits to the individual, and to protect all of their citizens with frameworks and policies which strike a balance for the interests of wider society, whilst being equitable for both this and future generations. Hopefully the knowledge that will be increasingly derived from the processing of big spatial data will better help to facilitate changes in this direction, which seem to be beyond human planning capabilities alone.

Street Cleansing

City governments are starting to wake up to the fact that their towns and cities will be increasingly locked into direct global competition for inward investment, tourism, economic activity, and employment, with ever more up-to-date information about each and every urban centre becoming available around the world. If a city is packed with noisy, polluting traffic, is subject to legal action for its failure to address toxic air pollution, and has continued high incidences of road traffic congestion and accidents, then it will increasingly be out of touch with coming societal changes and will struggle both in terms of investment and labour supply (Murray, 2011). Both health and safety concerns together with the sharing economy are also ringing the death knell for the private motor vehicle in cities, whilst it's also inevitable that a variety of automated modes will be the only vehicles in cities in the not too distant future as safety, efficiency, insurance costs, and congestion all influence the market. A recent study suggests that private car ownership across the US will decrease by a whopping 80% compared to its peak levels by 2030 (Garfield, 2017). With the move towards EVs, the car industry will have most likely already shifted significantly away from business as usual, meaning that finding fuel stations, repair shops, or spare parts for old-tech, combustion engines will be impossible in urban areas. At this current moment in time, to be building new roads and the supporting infrastructure for old technology in and around cities is just burning money, increasing health and safety impacts, and extending the inefficient use of valuable land. This is a particularly important lesson for developing economies. Stopping road "improvements", limiting access, adapting them to new uses, and starting to remove them completely will help create more liveable cities and will hasten a rethink of how cities should operate. It is time to "Reconsider, Rethink, Redirect".

Trends in developed nations are showing a movement away from city road building and upgrading projects to that of streets dedicated to wider public use solutions, such as dedicated bus and cycle lanes, shared streets, and pedestrianisation schemes. Not only are new roads rarely being built, but existing streets in urban areas are being torn up, narrowed, greened, and redefined. The last 20 years has seen the green shoots of change in traffic management in many of the world's towns and cities, with continued research producing innovative traffic design and management solutions aimed at providing improved road safety and traffic flows, whilst enhancing the quality of the public realm for residents through which vehicles have to pass. New concepts are constantly being trialled and most important in this has been the realisation that walking and cycling are the preferred means of transport in cities, whilst incorporating high-speed, standardised highway design threatens pedestrian and bicycle safety, as well as reducing the mobility of city dwellers and the quality of the environment in which they live.

The Dutch road traffic engineer and innovator Hans Monderman is not considered a household name, yet he silently influenced the lives of many thousands of European citizens and is recognised by his peers for first challenging assumptions during the 1980s about the use of standardised engineering approaches to street design. His approaches reject the usual means of direction, priority, and control whilst promoting the planning of public space around people and their contextual surroundings rather than the motor vehicle. Monderman found that the traffic efficiency and safety of streets improved when the urban realm was reconfigured to encourage each person to negotiate their movement directly with others. His most famous design approach is "Shared Space", which typically calls for removing regulatory traffic control features such as kerbs, lane markings, signs, and lights, and replacing intersections with roundabouts. His policies and new methods were first adopted for seven European pilot projects in Fryslân, Emmen, and Haren, (the Netherlands), Ejby (Denmark), Bohmte (Germany), Ipswich (the UK), and Ostend (Belgium). Findings showed pedestrian and economic activity greatly increased, whilst traffic speeds reduced significantly, and delays and congestion fell. Surveys of drivers, cyclists, and pedestrians indicated increased satisfaction and confidence with the new arrangements, although the concept has been challenged by some older citizens and particularly the blind and partially sighted. Subsequently, similar or modified urban street redesigns using these principles have become widespread in Europe and have even been adopted in the US. Exhibition Road in London was given a major makeover in 2012 that brought these principles to the fore.

In fact, London is now a different city from that of 20 years ago since the introduction of the Congestion Charge policy to its central area. Buses are flowing freely, public bikes are for hire on street corners, and cafes are sprawling over pavements previously occupied by vehicles. The Congestion Charge policy, introduced in 2003, remains one of the largest charge zones in the world and aims to reduce congestion whilst raising funds for London's public transport system. The scheme is on the point of being expanded extensively across the city as the mayor's vision for "Healthy Streets" takes hold. During the first ten years since the introduction of the scheme, gross revenue reached about £2.6 billion up to December 2013. From 2003 to 2013, about £1.2 billion (46%) of net revenue was invested in public transport, road and bridge improvement, and walking and cycling schemes. Of these, a total of £960 million was invested in improvements to the bus network. An overall reduction of 11% in vehicle kilometres travelled had been recorded in London between 2000 and 2012. By April 2019, the Ultra Low Emission Zone (ULEZ) was launched within the Congestion Charge zone with the aim of reducing toxic air pollution and protecting public health (Transport for London, 2020).

In 1998, the Transport Research Laboratory reported that "signposted" 20 mph (32 km/h) speed limits on individual roads only reduced traffic speeds by about 1 mph and delivered no discernible reduction in accident numbers, but that 20 mph "zones" achieved average speed reductions of 10 mph, along with child pedestrian accident reductions of 70% and child cyclist accident reductions of 48%. "20's Plenty for Us" is a voluntary organisation that campaigns for the introduction of a default 20 mph speed limit for residential streets and urban streets. By seeking to obtain implementation across a complete local authority or community, the organisation believes that worthwhile speed reductions can be achieved without the usual physical calming features. It terms this type of intervention "Total 20". No physical calming measures are required. A report subsequently published in 2008 estimated that following the introduction of 20mph zones in London, a reduction of casualties by 45% and those killed or seriously injured (KSI) by 57% occurred (Transport for London, 2003). In September 2020, the city announced plans for a 20 mph speed limit in central London across 8.9 km of roads, following a consultation showing public support for lower speeds. Europe and America have introduced a whole gamut of initiatives ranging from congestion charging to speed cameras, car-free zones, low-speed streets, removal of on-street parking, the Dutch system of "woonerf", Shared Space, and "home zones" or "living streets" as introduced in the UK. However, the biggest improvements can be made through removing roads altogether and adapting urban areas for comfortable, safe walking and biking. The pedestrianisation of city centres began to gain popularity in Europe about 50 years ago and is now a feature of most developed city-centre plans (Melia & Shergold, 2016). The sort of measures used include the shading of pathways, attractive paving materials, the use of materials to dissipate heat, integration with public transport stations, landscaping, and better pedestrian corridor links with major destinations. The provision of adequate pedestrian facilities improves air quality by keeping traffic away from sensitive, high-exposure locations and by encouraging walking as the preferred mode for short trips. A study of Nuremberg in Germany shows that significant improvements in air quality have been achieved since pedestrianisation was introduced in the city centre in the early 1970s (European Commission, 2004).

Visiting historic Oxford, 100 km northwest of London, requires leaving the car on the outskirts of the city in one of five large and well-appointed car parks and taking a shuttle bus a short distance into the city centre on dedicated bus lanes. Once inside the heart of the town, the central area is widely pedestrianised with high-quality surface finishes and crowded with activity and businesses free from excessive vehicle emissions. Oxford operated the first "Park and Ride" public transport scheme in the UK, initially with an experimental service operating part-time from a motel on the A34 trunk road in the 1960s and then on a full-time basis from 1973. Implementation of public transport Park and Ride bus services in the UK accelerated in the 1980s and 1990s, with schemes ranging in size from an allocated area with space for fewer than ten cars to multiple dedicated sites catering in total for nearly 5,000 cars. Schemes predominantly serve a single town or smaller city, with adoption most often found in historical centres where the irregular and narrow streets mean that the effects traffic congestion are heightened and streets cannot easily be widened. Introducing more expensive, rail-based Park and Ride modes can only be considered appropriate for larger metropolitan areas. Since its first introduction in Detroit in the 1930s (Bullard & Christiansen, 1983), Park and Ride has been recognised as an effective way to promote public transportation and reduce traffic in urban areas (Bolger et al., 1992; Duncan & Cook, 2014; Niblett & Palmer, 1993). Using strategically located Park and Ride facilities as part of an optimally integrated planning framework can improve net social benefit dramatically and encourage commuters to shift from car mode to transit and Park and Ride modes, reducing travel costs for all users across the system, and can easily be expanded to consider strategies such as congestion pricing to achieve an improved level of social welfare (Song et al., 2017) – a key lesson for urban centres in developing countries.

The last few decades have seen a complete re-evaluation of the benefits of the motor vehicle in developed cities and after years of implementing street-widening and traffic engineering schemes at vast cost to the taxpayer, it has finally been realised that building more roads encourages more traffic volume, which in turn of course causes further congestion whilst decreasing the value, character, and liveability of our cities. Strong movements now prevail in which streets are increasingly restricted to fast-moving traffic and priority is placed on returning to pedestrian and cycle use, both in the inner cities and within suburban residential areas.

The Unbearable Costs of Parking

Whilst roads facilitate car journeys, it is actually parking that generates them. The land area dedicated to vehicles in many American cities is over 50% and whilst European cities are typically closer to 25%, it's still a vast area of public realm provided at the expense of other, more productive investments (McCahill & Garrick, 2012). Traffic congestion rightly attracts tremendous attention, but parked cars shape daily urban life to an even greater extent. Off-street parking typically consists of dull, uniform, paved space or is hosted in banal parking structures, whilst on-street parking narrows streets, reduces safety, causes congestion through waiting and searching, creates a hostile street environment, and blights both the air quality and appearance of streets. Land use patterns have changed to reflect car use, with shops and services feeling compelled to provide vehicle parking areas. Society has become hardwired to accept increasing levels of car dependency. Where building density is low, parking is extremely land-intensive and where density is high, parking is capital-intensive, making its cost substantial in either case. Moreover, parking tacitly subsidises those most able to afford car ownership, since vehicles are parked most of the time and ownership is easier if a car can be cheaply and reliably stored when it is not being driven. In those countries where minimum parking requirements are established together with land development in order to ensure adequate parking supply, such as the US and China, the cost of parking is aggregated into the cost of development, thereby increasing the prices of all goods and services sold at sites offering parking. Transport planner Donald Shoup suggests that the external cost of parking in cities may be greater than all the other external costs combined, where, for example, minimum parking requirements increase the cost of constructing a shopping centre by up to 67% if the parking is in an above-ground structure and by up to a whopping 93% if the parking is underground (Shoup, 2014).

Focusing urban areas on mass-transport solutions together with the use of shared vehicles, including cars, bikes, taxis, scooters, and other micro-vehicles (MVs), would relax parking requirements significantly, as such vehicles can be employed 24/7, whereas private vehicles are parked for the majority of their lives – an incredibly inefficient use of space and resources. Removing on-street parking to free up urban space and removing minimum parking quotas would create the potential for more interesting spaces, more greenery, and more efficient land use. Just think what can be done without all that wasted space. First and foremost, authorities need to desist from setting minimum parking requirements in urban planning and replace this with maximum limits. Minimum requirements are intended to satisfy anticipated peak demands for parking for every form of land use, be it home, work, school, restaurants, shopping centres, and hundreds of other land uses. Because peak demands occur at different times of the day and may last for only a short time, several parking spaces must be available for every motor vehicle, resulting in tremendous inefficiencies. Whilst minimum parking requirements produce a very localised benefit – they ensure that every form of land use can accommodate all cars "drawn to the site" – this local benefit comes at an extremely high price to the whole city. Minimum parking requirements increase the density of both parking spaces and cars. More cars create more traffic congestion, which in turn provokes calls for more local remedies, such as street widening, intersection flaring, intelligent highways, and the subsequent need to provide further additional parking. More cars also produce more exhaust emissions. Transport engineers do not consider the price of parking as a variable in estimating parking generation rates; providing free or low-cost parking generates trips.

Urban planners allocate land use density so that new development will not generate more vehicle trips than nearby roads and highways can carry. Minimum parking requirements therefore distort transportation and land use. Restricting parking can limit trips, reduce road pressure, and free up development space.

Whilst some degree of parking provision may ultimately be required for large buildings and for servicing, emergencies, and other occasional necessities in urban areas, new development, both residential and commercial, should not be allowed to generate extra vehicle trips. London's iconic Swiss Re Tower, which is commonly referred to as the "Gherkin", has just five car parking spaces allocated, which are utilised solely by two-wheel transport anyway, whilst Western Europe's tallest building, the Shard in London at 310 m (1,016 ft), contains just 48 parking spaces taking up the room usually required for just eight cars. Served by a valet, a driver parks in a space and gets out of the car, which then disappears into the ground. It is then parked automatically into a store and can be called when needed. Such automated parking solutions have been common in Japan for decades to guard against on-street parking and efficiently park limited numbers of vehicles in high-cost locations.

Adaptable Streets

Urban places can be radically different in the future if that's what their citizens want. Vehicles, MVs, bicycles, and people can co-exist harmoniously, traffic can flow better with narrowed space, and they can be safer places, wonderful, engaging places in which to live. Urban places can be created with careful urban design, making unique streets structured around green infrastructure networks, but political will and determination will make the essential difference in terms of improving the fabric of cities. The advocation for change being realised by Paris, Milan, London, Madrid, Barcelona, and multiple US cities that have enacted street closures, bike lane implementation, free public transport, and other measures during the COVID-19 crisis has demonstrated just how easy it actually is to facilitate rapid urban change. Perth, Auckland, and Boston are among the cities that automated crossing signals so that pedestrians don't have to touch "beg buttons" that may be contaminated. Bogotá, Mexico City, and Berlin all expanded their cycling networks. These rapid actions were not years in the making and were not expensive; they were iterative, flexible, and adaptable, and the most successful of them were implemented in consultation with local residents and community groups in new ways of bottom-up planning and stakeholder buy-in.

These slow streets or shared space iterations raise the potential for a radically different vision for streets in towns and cities in the future. With sufficient professional support and political determination, this could hold the key to reversing the long-lamented decline in the quality of streets across the world, where cars and traffic are likely to remain an inevitable component of our social and economic structures, especially in developing countries. If the findings from the increasing number of Shared Space schemes continue to demonstrate the positive outcomes from treating drivers as intelligent citizens, governed by the same social protocols that underpin civility in other public places, there is hope that the segregated world of post-war urban planning will no longer need to blight the coherence and quality of the built environment. Of course, change is difficult to accept, so there is always going to be resistance. For instance, the city of Oakland in California, which rapidly implemented over 70 miles of street restrictions during the COVID-19 pandemic, was generally hailed for its swift and bold actions. Yet the local residents and interest groups that city officials anticipated would benefit from these "Slow Streets" pushed back, having not been consulted or involved in the decision-making process. A further period of much more detailed refinement was required, whereby officials stopped following their own planning ideas and adopted suggestions from local groups and residents, involving them so that they could take ownership of the process.

In Sweden, a series of national pilot schemes called "Future Streets" and "Street Moves" launched in September 2020 under the national innovation body Vinnova focused on the single-street level and allowed the community to pay direct attention to "the space outside your front door . . . and that of your neighbours adjacent and opposite" according to Dan Hill, Vinnova's director of strategic design. Through public workshops and consultations, residents were encouraged to control the use of their immediate street space, whether for parking or other public uses. This approach has already been rolled out experimentally at four sites in Stockholm, with three more cities about to sign up. By rethinking the public realm as a series of critical sections of community connecting space, the project seeks to break through assumptions of streets as primarily places to move and park cars (O'Sullivan, 2021). The basic tools being used by Street Moves are inspired by the American "parklet" model which arises from the urban activism of what are known as "park(ing) days", initiated in San Francisco in 2005 by experimental architects REBAR. They consist of modular street furniture kits designed to fit the dimensions of a standard parking space, and these can be used for the temporary (or even permanent) adaption of the space. Such units have been increasingly adopted across Europe, where modules can be easily and cost-effectively exchanged if they do not meet expectations or when circumstances change – to include sitting areas, planting, or bike parking, for example. The city of Oslo has used parklets as an important contribution to "Bilfritt Byliv", Oslo's car-free city life project, in which cars were phased out of the city centre by 2020. The City Council undertook a five-year plan to transform an area of 1.3 square kilometres into a better urban environment, believing that a more varied and welcoming city space could be developed with input from city residents of all ages, businesses, and interest groups. In 2017, six designated pilot areas were the first to experiment with the initiative and 700 parking spots for private cars were removed by the summer of 2018. Understanding the difficulties brought by people's resistance to change, implementation was carried out gradually, with car restrictions being introduced temporarily and then evaluated before moving to a permanent change, allowing adjustments as necessary (World Cities Culture Forum, n.d.). Parklets played a leading role in providing temporary installations, the hope being that this modular approach will generate new services and solutions linked to planning, green areas, e-commerce, and mobility. Future iterations should demonstrate modules that continually adapt and upgrade to meet changing times and needs, yet the key issue in innovation is experimentation. The pilot projects in both Stockholm and Oslo focus on developing healthy and vibrant street environments through directly involving residents in the displacement of their surroundings, and developing and testing different solutions in real-life conditions (Hill, 2020).

Mobility through Technology

By having more people using one vehicle, carpooling has historically been seen to reduce each person's travel costs such as fuel, tolls, and the stress of driving, and has been seen as a more environmentally friendly and sustainable way to travel, since sharing journeys reduces carbon emissions, traffic congestion on the roads, and the need for parking spaces. The advent of the shared-vehicle age takes this to a whole new level, with fewer vehicles doing the same number of trips, being readily available for use, and rarely needing to park. This means removing private parking from the urban public realm is not only possible but inevitable and will radically change our cities once fully regulated and integrated into policy. Technology advances are only going to make app-based mobility services more accessible, safer, and absolutely essential in providing third-party transportation spatial data to urban managers, leading to private vehicles in cities becoming too costly for both individuals and society as a whole. Users of the modern city need to disassociate themselves from the conception of car ownership being associated with personal growth and achievement, which is being used to sell cars to the urban masses in developing countries. This is a brilliant piece of marketing hogwash continually fostered by car manufacturers to sell vehicles; it's not at all necessary and probably not even beneficial to use a car in the city, and most of those who do, often only do so at weekends, preferring public transport for weekday commuting. However, it is desirable to be able to use a private vehicle from time to time and, in fact, to be able to use lots of different kinds of vehicle at different times: a safe one for the family; a soft-top for the summer; a red one to show off to friends; an executive model for clients; and a van for moving all those boxes. Vehicle-sharing residential communities or associations can provide all this, along with cheaper insurance, regular maintenance, and efficient, dedicated parking. Going one better, the app-taxi model offers chauffeured driving and dedicated pick-up options. Large city dwellers need to adapt to the concept that owning a car is not acceptable to the common good, cannot benefit from the common space, and cannot abuse the common health. Those who wish to live in cities need to understand that they cannot own a car unless they can pay for the significant privilege of doing so and that storing their vehicle can only be done on their own facilities. The UK's decision to enable EV charging on residential streets is seriously misguided ill-considered, and is seriously at odds with other stated air pollution and climate goals aimed towards improved urban living quality for all (HM Government, 2018). Cities need to be considering how they are going to be removing private vehicles and transform streets into more healthy, safe and productive places than being used simply as car charging facilities.

So a city built on public transport is all very well in concept, but the private vehicle has been extremely successful in being able to deliver people door to door in all weathers. The problem of getting that final trip from the train or bus stop to your destination has always been problematic, especially when carrying goods, suffering from physical infirmities, or simply just avoiding the rain. The sharing economy is already addressing this "holy grail" of urban transport planning – the "last mile problem". Multiple-mode, transport-sharing options already exist in cities in the form of cars, vans, trikes, bikes, electric bikes, scooters, and other MV solutions to suit differing needs, and it can be expected that a multitude of new transport modes will emerge with advances in technology. Those cities geared to high-speed, wide bandwidth data services such as 5G are going to be the first that will be able to introduce autonomous vehicles (AVs) into their transport fleets and as a consequence will reap the significant opportunities provided towards reshaping their cities more flexibly and efficiently. AVs already function in ways that are completely different from existing motor vehicles, essentially freeing themselves from the traditional "rules of the road" and potentially liberating the planning and design of streets, since they can pass easily through data-managed ground or even airspace. Roads no longer have to be "roads"; they can be "places" affording AV access. So who needs their own car when shared vehicles not only have the ability to drop you "door to door" but automated aerial vehicles (AAVs), currently being rolled out in beta versions in China and Germany, can even take you "door to floor", utilising roof spaces, refuge floors in tall buildings, terraces, and large balconies (Zart, 2017)? Buildings and apartments can be adapted to even have their own skyports. How are planners building in the flexibility to take such changes into account? Whilst it will take time to regulate airspace and costs to fall so that the technology is available to the masses and not just the few, this is the undeniable future. The immediate and most obvious benefit from AAVs is their potential to carry out civic emergency response duties to fire, medical, and security needs (Burgués & Marco, 2020; Merino et al., 2005). Much of the way in which streets have been developed has been in order to service buildings, particularly in the event of fire, and China is already incorporating AAV response into its urban fire-fighting response. Providing automated aerial access for fire and maintenance services through high-level, externally accessed hatches, whether for fighting fires or cleaning windows, means that vehicle access requirements on the street and around buildings can change. Building codes on emergency vehicle access (EVA) can be relaxed and building arrangements can become more varied and flexible.

Activating Places and Transitioning Modes

The car still has a place in the city of tomorrow, but it will be a much more limited one. Mass transit, supplemented with MVs and driverless service vehicles, will undoubtedly form the key part of urban public transport solutions in forward-looking cities where "Putting Wellness First" is the key driver of civic responsibility. Shared and fleet vehicle pools, benefiting from the coming data revolution, will necessarily replace the personally owned vehicle, with recurrent costs and space restrictions making them unsustainable. But transitioning to this model will take time and the start must be made during the coming decade, from ensuring new urban development in expanding cities has extremely limited car parking provision and at the same time removing existing car parking (the generator of journeys) from urban and community centres, and replacing the roads that serve them with streets that serve people. In so doing, urban spaces can become both safe to be in and positively activated for a variety of users, with the valuable and limited space used more equitably, efficiently, and effectively through the provision of green infrastructure and ageing-friendly interventions. The first steps in this process have already been taken and can continue by progressively eliminating on-street parking and placing well-regulated taxi-app services and other shared solutions for micro-mobility at the forefront of an urban transport planning revolution supported by free mass transit for all. The transition for "Unleashing Urban Potential" can start with these ten common-sense actions:

1. Reject existing road traffic projections and re-evaluate outdated city planning concepts in the context of today's rapid societal changes, technological advances, and unsustainable development.
2. Restrict the allowable parking space provision in new-build development to minimal numbers in order to discourage future car journeys.
3. Implement restricted access schemes to central urban areas to reduce non-essential car journeys and generate funding for alternative public transport uses.
4. Develop alternative street programmes with residents and community groups to create safe places and remove access to through-traffic.
5. Progressively remove on-street parking and develop automated parking lots where essential to achieve efficient space utilisation.
6. Develop pedestrian and bicycle/micro-only green infrastructure corridors and enforce their right of way over cars to achieve more equitable utilisation of public space.
7. Promote hierarchies of small-scale, automated people-mover and light transport solutions to address "last mile" travel connections from transport hubs.
8. Develop and implement rigorous urban road speed restriction, reconfiguring minor streets to 10km/h, 20km/h, and 30km/h design standards in dense urban areas for safer streets, and use technology to enforce compliance.
9. Promote well-regulated "app"-based taxi and car-sharing initiatives.
10. Embrace data-sharing innovation for improved real-time complex systems management.

References

Anenberg, S., Miller, J., Henze, D., & Minjares R. (2019). *A global snapshot of the air pollution-related health impacts of transportation sector emissions in 2010 and 2015*. International Council on Clean Transportation (ICCT), Climate and Clean Air Coalition (CCAC). UN Environment Programme.

Bolger, D., Colquhoun, D., & Morrall, J. (1992). Planning and design of park-and-ride facilities for the Calgary light rail transit system. *Transportation Research Record, 1361, Light Rail Transit: Planning, Design, and Operating Experience (Papers presented at the Sixth National Conference on Light Rail Transit, held in Calgary, Alberta, Canada, 24–27 May 1992)*, 141–148.

Bullard, D. L., & Christiansen, D. L. (1983). *Guidelines for planning, designing and operating park-and-ride lots in Texas*. Texas Transportation Institute (No. TTI-2-10-74-205-22F). https://static.tti.tamu.edu/tti.tamu.edu/documents/205-22F.pdf.

Burgués, J., & Marco, S. (2020). Environmental chemical sensing using small drones: A review. *Science of the Total Environment, 748*, 141172. https://doi.org/https://doi.org/10.1016/j.scitotenv.2020.141172.

China, National Bureau of Statistics. (1989). *China statistical abstract, 1989*. Praeger. https://catalog.hathitrust.org/Record/007107987.

China, National Bureau of Statistics. (2011, 10 October). *Communiqué on national expenditures on science and technology in 2010*. http://www.stats.gov.cn/english/NewsEvents/201110/t20111010_26508.html.

China, National Bureau of Statistics. (2020, 28 February). *Statistical communiqué of the People's Republic of China on the 2019 national economic and social development*. http://www.stats.gov.cn/english/PressRelease/202002/t20200228_1728917.html.

Chow, C. B. (2015). *Geo-spatial analysis on burden of childhood traffic injuries in Hong Kong 2001–2012*. Making Our Road Transport Safer for Children, Hong Kong.

Douglas, M. J., Watkins, S. J., Gorman, D. R., & Higgins, M. (2011). Are cars the new tobacco? *Journal of Public Health, 33*(2), 160–169.

Duncan, M., & Cook, D. (2014). Is the provision of Park-and-Ride facilities at light rail stations an effective approach to reducing vehicle kilometers traveled in a US context? *Transportation Research Part A: Policy and Practice, 66*, 65–74.

European Commission. (2004). *Reclaiming city streets for people: Chaos or quality of life?* Office for Official Publications of the European Communities. https://ec.europa.eu/environment/pubs/pdf/streets_people.pdf.

Garfield, L. (2017, 4 May). Only 20% of Americans will own a car in 15 years, new study finds. *Business Insider*. https://www.businessinsider.com/no-one-will-own-a-car-in-the-future-2017-5?r=US&IR=T.

Georgia Institute of Technology. (2017). Brake dust may cause more problems than blackened wheel covers. *ScienceDaily*. https://www.sciencedaily.com/releases/2017/03/170303091332.htm.

The Global Economy. (2019). *Passenger car sales: Country rankings*. https://www.theglobaleconomy.com/rankings/passenger_cars_sales.

Harrison, R. M., Jones, A. M., Gietl, J., Yin, J., & Green, D. C. (2012). Estimation of the contributions of brake dust, tire wear, and resuspension to nonexhaust traffic particles derived from atmospheric measurements. *Environmental Science & Technology, 46*(12), 6523–6529. https://doi.org/10.1021/es300894r.

Heck, J. E., Wu, J., Lombardi, C., Qiu, J., Meyers, T. J., Wilhelm, M., Cockburn, M., & Ritz, B. (2013). Childhood cancer and traffic-related air pollution exposure in pregnancy and early life. *Environmental Health Perspectives, 121*(11–12), 1385–1391.

Hill, D. (2020). *Mission-oriented innovation in practice*. Creative Bureaucracy Festival, Berlin, Germany. https://creativebureaucracy.org/program/festival-2020/mission-oriented-innovation-what-is-it-and-does-it-work.

Hong Kong Road Safety Council. (2018). *Road Safety Council Annual Report 2018*. https://www.roadsafety.gov.hk/doc/annual2018/index_en.html.

HKSAR, Transport Advisory Committee. (2014). *Report on study of road traffic congestion in Hong Kong*. Government of the Hong Kong Special Administrative Region.

HKSAR, Transport Department. (2020, 19 July). *Accident Trend since 1953*. Government of the Hong Kong Special Administrative Region. . https://www.td.gov.hk/en/road_safety/road_traffic_accident_statistics/accident_trend_since_1953/index.html.

HM Government. (2011). *Creating Growth, Cutting Carbon–Making Sustainable Local Transport Happen*. Department for Transport. https://www.gov.uk/government/publications/creating-growth-cutting-carbon-making-sustainable-local-transport-happen

HM Government. (2018). *The road to zero: Next steps towards cleaner road transport and delivering our industrial strategy*. Department for Transport. https://assets.publishing.service.gov.uk/government/uploads/system/uploads/attachment_data/file/739460/road-to-zero.pdf.

IARC. (2012, 12 June). *ARC: Diesel engine exhaust carcinogenic*. https://sabiasque.pt/images/stories/ambiente/pr213_E.pdf.

International Programme on Chemical Safety, Commission of the European Communities, United Nations Environment Programme, International Labour Organization, & World Health Organization. (1986). *Principles for evaluating health risks from chemicals during infancy and early childhood: the need for a special approach (9241542594)*. https://apps.who.int/iris/handle/10665/39088.

Kay, D. (2011). *Fairness in a car-dependent society*. Sustainable Development Commission.

Li, J. (2015). *Statistics on child road casualities in Hong Kong*. Making Our Road Transport Safer for Children, Hong Kong.

McCahill, C., & Garrick, N. (2012). Automobile use and land consumption: Empirical evidence from 12 cities. *Urban Design International, 17*(3), 221–227.

Melia, S., & Shergold, I. (2016). *Pedestrianisation and politics: Evidence gaps and a case study of Brighton's Old Town*. file:///C:/Users/admin/AppData/Local/Temp/UTSG%202016%20-%20Melia%20and%20Shergold.pdf.

Merino, L., Caballero, F., Martinez-de Dios, J., & Ollero, A. (2005). Cooperative fire detection using unmanned aerial vehicles. *Proceedings of the 2005 IEEE international conference on robotics and automation*. 1884–1889. 10.1109/ROBOT.2005.1570338.

Murray, S. (2011). Liveanomics: Urban liveability and economic growth. *The Economist*. https://documents.pub/document/liveanomics-urban-liveability-and-economic-growth-iveanomics-urban-liveability.html.

National Highway Traffic Safety Administration. (2019). *2018 fatal motor vehicle crashes:Overview*.https://crashstats.nhtsa.dot.gov/Api/Public/ViewPublication/812826.

Niblett, R., & Palmer, D. (1993). Park and Ride in London and the south east. *Journal of the Institution of Highways & Transportation, 40*(2), 4–10.

O'Sullivan, F. (2021). *Make way for the "one-minute city"*. https://www.bloomberg.com/news/features/2021-01-05/a-tiny-twist-on-street-design-the-one-minute-city.

Parliament, House of Commons. (2002). *Transport, local government and the regions – Ninthreport*.https://publications.parliament.uk/pa/cm200102/cmselect/cmtlgr/557/55704.htm.

Pike, E. (2011). Opportunities to improve tire energy efficiency. *The International Council in Clean Transportation*. White Paper No. 13. https://theicct.org/sites/default/files/publications/ICCT_tireefficiency_jun2011.pdf.

Shaw, M., Thomas, B., & Smith, G. D. (2008). *The Grim Reaper's road map: An atlas of mortality in Britain*. Policy Press.

Shoup, D. (2014). The high cost of minimum parking requirements. In S. Ison & C. Mulley (Eds.), *Parking issues and policies* (pp. 87–113). Emerald Group Publishing.

Song, Z., He, Y., & Zhang, L. (2017). Integrated planning of Park-and-Ride facilities and transit service. *Transportation Research Part C: Emerging Technologies, 74*, 182–195.

Transport for London. (2003). *Review of 20 mph zones in London boroughs: Safety research report no. 2. Street Management*. http://content.tfl.gov.uk/research-summary-no2-20mph-zones.pdf.

Transport for London. (2020). *Annual Report and Statement of Accounts 2019/20*. http://content.tfl.gov.uk/tfl-annual-report-2019-20.pdf.

Wang, A., Liao, W., & Hein, A.-P. (2012). Bigger, better, broader: A perspective on China's auto market in 2020. *Automotive & Assembly Practice, 15*(10). https://www.mckinsey.com/~/media/mckinsey/dotcom/client_service/automotive%20and%20assembly/pdfs/mckinsey%20%20perspective%20on%20chinas%20auto%20market%20in%202020.ashx.

Wards Auto. (2017). *U.S. car and truck sales, 1931–2016*. https://wardsintelligence.informa.com/WI060798/US-Car-and-Truck-Sales-19312016.

Weitzman, M., Gortmaker, S. L., Sobol, A. M., & Perrin, J. M. (1992). Recent trends in the prevalence and severity of childhood asthma. *Jama, 268*(19), 2673–2677.

WHO. (2018). *Global status report on road safety 2018: Summary*. https://apps.who.int/iris/bitstream/handle/10665/277370/WHO-NMH-NVI-18.20-eng.pdf?ua=1.

WHO. (2020). *Road traffic injuries: Key facts.* https://www.who.int/news-room/fact-sheets/detail/road-traffic-injuries.

WHO. (n.d.). *Ambient air pollution.* https://www.who.int/health-topics/air-pollution#tab=tab_2

World Cities Culture Forum. (n.d.). *Bilfritt byliv – Car free city life.* Greater London Authority (GLA). http://www.worldcitiescultureforum.com/case_studies/bilfritt-byliv-car-free-city-life.

Wright, R. J., Hsu, H.-H. L., Chiu, Y.-H. M., Coull, B. A., Simon, M. C., Hudda, N., Schwartz, J., Kloog, I., & Durant, J. L. (2021). Prenatal ambient ultrafine particle exposure and childhood asthma in the northeastern United States. *American Journal of Respiratory and Critical Care Medicine.* https://www.atsjournals.org/doi/10.1164/rccm.202010-3743OC.

Zart, N. (2017). The Ehang 184 passenger drone wants to take you into the air. *Clean Technica.* https://cleantechnica.com/2017/12/29/ehang-184-passenger-drone-wants-take-air.

Prosperity through Density

Accommodating Burgeoning Urban Populations

There are 7.8 billion people on the planet and this is projected to rise rapidly to 10 billion by 2056 with population explosions in Africa and Asia. Where will all these people live? Probably in cities both new and evolved, but just how big should a city be? Trends towards forming mega-urban clusters of 50 million people have been initiated to meet China's rapid urbanisation, yet the inhabitants of most developed countries prefer small city life. Regardless of the pros and cons of each, new urban development is necessarily going to have to be dense, and dense cities actually have a large number of benefits in terms of supporting social and community vibrancy, high-quality yet cheap public transport services, and high provision and efficient use of shared facilities. New data demonstrates that dense cities can actually be more healthy as well, whilst compact housing and prefabricated development models being trialled globally can prioritise shared convenience with community wellness that makes more efficient use of precious inner-city space.

164 Prosperity through Density

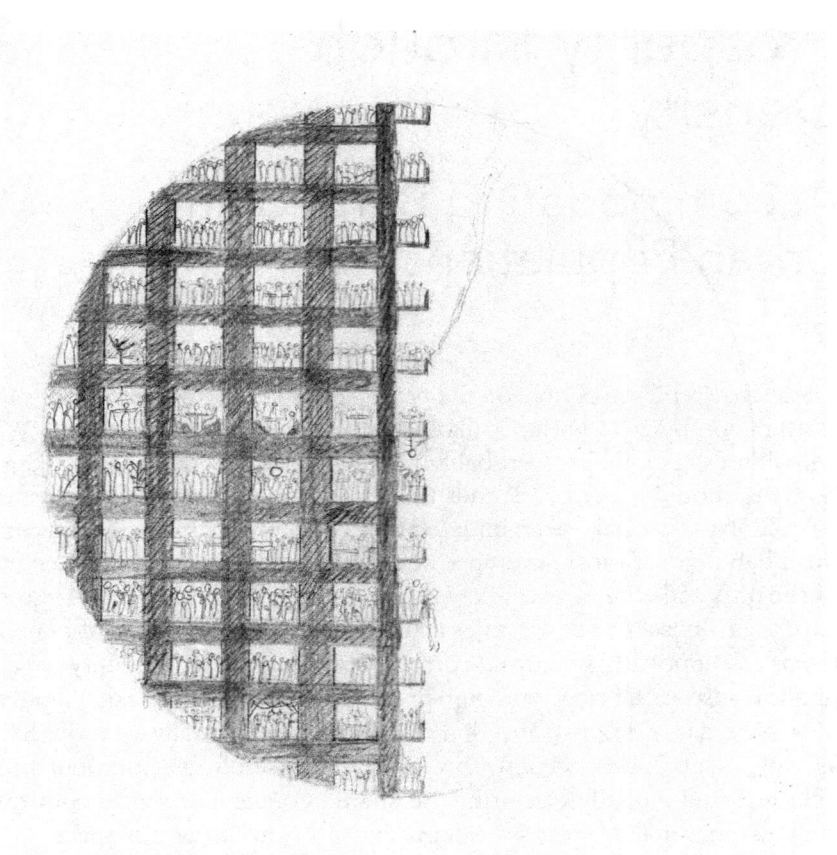

Ecumenopolis

"Make no little plans; they have no magic to stir men's blood"

Daniel Burnham, *Chicago Record-Herald*, 1910

Really Big Thinking

Currently about 55% of the world's population live in urban areas, a proportion that is expected to increase to 66% by 2050. Most developed countries have urban populations above 75% and when excluding city states, Belgium is the most urbanised OECD country at 98%. Therefore, most of this urban growth is going to be happening in developing regions where cities in Africa and Asia have populations growing at more than 6% (United Nations Department of Economic and Social Affairs, 2018). Currently, just over 60% of the total population in China live in urban areas, yet the urban population is forecast to reach 76% by 2050 (United Nations Department of Economic and Social Affairs, 2019), bringing it closer to level of more developed nations. It is estimated that 300 million Chinese living in rural areas in 2010 will have already moved into cities by 2025 (UNDP China, 2013), which is equivalent to more than half of the current rural population. Where will all these people go? This is a similar problem for other urbanising nations, including India, Pakistan, Indonesia, and Nigeria in particular, which will also need to absorb the biggest urban population expansion in terms of absolute numbers. Nigeria is urbanising faster than any other nation as the population grows by 2.6% per year and is set to expand from 206 million in 2020 by adding an extra 57 million people before 2030. Although India will record the second-biggest absolute increase in urban population after China, it will remain predominantly rural, with only 41.8% of the population being projected to live in cities in 2030 (United Nations Department of Economic and Social Affairs, 2019). Rapid urbanisation is said to boost economic development and consumer spending, and is often accompanied by the transition to smaller households and new consumption habits, which in turn can generate new business opportunities. However, the challenges that urbanisation brings can be significant and include housing shortages, worsening inequalities, pauperisation, infrastructure deficit, rising pollution, and sprawling urban agglomerations.

The success of China's urbanisation model will be hugely influential as it tries to avoid both the middle-income and urbanisation traps. A 2009 influential report by McKinsey, "Preparing for China's urban billion", suggested that China should tailor policies towards a more concentrated form of urbanisation, producing super-cities with average populations of 25 million people, and the development of city clusters, each with strong economic networks and combined populations of more than 60 million (Woetzel et al., 2009). This research suggested that concentrated urban growth scenarios could produce 20% higher per capita GDP than that yielded by dispersed growth scenarios. They would unfortunately have higher energy consumption, but also higher energy efficiency and would restrict the loss of arable land. The report also outlined that concentrating urbanisation would have the advantage of clustering the most skilled workers into urban centres that would be engines of economic growth, enabling China to move more rapidly to higher-value-added activities. Whilst extremely detailed, the report was unashamedly economically focused, based on standard economic approaches under GDP measurements of progress, and was not able to incorporate the impacts of global externalities, including the financial meltdown, climate change, or world pandemic, and also insufficiently analysed internalities, including the shadow of the slowdown in economic growth in China, reform in land policy, or hukou reform. The recent incredible pace of change of technology, the ease of communication and sharing, and the greater importance placed on quality-of-life issues mean that predicting the future based predominantly on past economic models has become increasingly unsustainable. Social and environmental issues in China and other fast-developing nations must increasingly come to shape decision-making; the need to keep the family together, reduce stress, maintain healthy lifestyles, enjoy more living space, and retain and pass on traditional culture and values. Research carried out by Yaohui Zhao at Peking University indicates that while economic theory demonstrates labour migration to the big cities increases efficiency due to the allocation of labour where it is most needed, the social cost of migration itself actually outweighs those gains economically. Migration is not a default situation; in general, people would rather stay where they are than uproot themselves with the inherent insecurity that this entails. There are both push and pull factors. Younger migrants are more influenced by "pull" factors, such as "expected earning opportunities", "personal development aspirations", and "urban lifestyle", where older migrants are more driven by "push" factors, including labour surplus or "difficult living conditions'.

Creating Urban Agglomerations

Following the McKinsey report, a 2013 Report by the United Nations Development Programme (UNDP China) with the Institute for Urban and Environmental Studies at the Chinese Academy of Social Sciences highlighted the importance of ten economic clusters and coined terms such as "ecological civilisation" to describe the urbanisation process (UNDP

China, 2013). In 2014, the central government announced a National New Urbanisation Plan (China, National Bureau of Statistics, 2012) whereby the population would be seen to peak at approximately 1.445 billion and its urbanisation rate would reach 70% and by that time, the population living in cities and towns would be over one billion (Yang & Shi, 2014). Officials of China's National Development and Reform Commission (NDRC) (China, NDRC, 2016) stated in 2015 that urban planning at multi-city level was now being prepared nationally, with more than 20 urban agglomerations around the country being established to create mega-city-regions, each containing over 50 million inhabitants, such as the Yangtze River Basin and Pearl River Delta. These would benefit from strategic-level co-operation in order to clearly differentiate urban development goals for cities within an agglomeration areas and "primarily acting to emphasize inter-operability and collaborative development". The concept of undertaking large-scale regional planning at a co-ordinated level seems to be just good old common sense, especially in view of the fact that data from the State Council shows that more than 3,500 new development areas had already been independently allocated in the country, creating residential capacity for 3.4 billion people – about 2.5 times the current population (Huang, 2016). The country has become world famous for the huge amount of empty housing stock and ghost cities (Shepard, 2015) created during the recent years of the economic boom.

It is obvious that transport and resource infrastructure needs to be considered on as wide a platform as possible and that specialisation and economies of scale are necessarily considered. It's upon further consideration of what this might actually mean at the requisite physical scales that it becomes rather more alarming. These "agglomeration zones" are the first step towards the actuality of creating 20 mega-mega-cities. Is that a bad thing? Both yes and no. In 2010, the rural population was almost 700 million people; 300 million of those moving to cities over two decades will have significant impacts on rural towns and economies. With just 20 agglomerations targeted to host the urban populations of 50–60 million each, these will account for nearly all of the one billion urban population in China, meaning that existing small rural towns and cities outside the agglomerations, predominantly in the more rural west, will face a mass exodus of populations with potentially disastrous effects. Some will be decimated, many will disappear completely. People will either live in a huge agglomeration or remain on the empty rural land.

High levels of urbanisation, at or above 75%, characterise developed nations in Europe and North America. However, a big difference here is that the percentage of big cities in these nations is relatively low compared to China. Close to half of global urban dwellers are more content to reside in relatively small settlements of fewer than 500,000 inhabitants, while only around one in eight live in mega-cities with more than 10 million inhabitants. The fastest growing urban agglomerations in these countries are medium-sized cities and those cities with fewer than one million inhabitants. This contrasts strongly with China's urbanisation model, where by 2025, the country will already have 221 cities with more than one million inhabitants compared to 35 cities of this size in Europe today. A total of 23 cities will have more than five million people and of the 31 mega-cities worldwide in 2016, six were in China. In recent years, a growing number of countries have been favouring strategies towards supporting rural rather than urban development, such as allocating land rights, actively managing land use and land redistribution, creating regional development zones, and promoting economic diversification and competitiveness in rural areas through the mobilisation of investment and the improvement of rural livelihoods (UN Secretary-General, 2008). Such initiatives can actively assist in maintaining healthy rural economies by reducing push and pull factors. The Chinese government has influenced the pattern of urbanisation through a number of mechanisms, including the "hukou" permanent residence registration system, land-sale policies, infrastructure investment, and incentives offered to local government officials. The most influential of these is the unique "hukou" system, which significantly distinguishes Chinese internal migration from migration in other developing countries. Urban–rural class inequality is typically reflected globally through income differentials, whereas Chinese migrant workers have also suffered from being excluded from basic urban social services, including housing, social security, and education for their children. The Chinese government has already committed to eliminating discrimination against rural workers through the hukou, with reforms starting in 2014 and the system being extended to cover pensions, education, and healthcare services. In 2019, the National Development and Reform Commission announced a plan to cancel hukou requirements for cities with populations of between one and three million. The objective of the reform is to finally merge urban and rural hukou systems into one in which migrant workers can have equal access to public resources as urban residents do in smaller cities. This opens the door for rural urbanisation where urban benefits could be adopted in rural towns.

Can Small Cities Thrive?

So could small Chinese cities that are urban in status but rurally located provide other sufficient attractions to outweigh the push and pull factors of big city migration? Could the 300 million migrants currently projected to head to 20 new mega-agglomerations be encouraged to urbanise into say 300 rural cities of fewer than one million people, or even into 1,000 expanded towns of 300,000 people? Could the city size balance exhibited by developed nations be appropriate to China? What does a town of this size look like and what might be the sustainable opportunities that scale affords? It will be essential to develop facilities, currently missing in rural areas, appropriate to a desirable development level in terms of transport, health, education, leisure, and culture. A city of one million people must in particular focus on providing a full range of education opportunities, especially in the tertiary sector to avoid brain drain. Rural city colleges and universities could be locally focused in terms of preparing specialised and vocational training and retraining directed at local economies. Trends indicate that businesses are increasingly moving towards apprenticeships, internships and part-time training. New education opportunities exist in collaborative, technical, and flexible learning areas. Youths with potential need to see that high-quality personal and economic growth opportunities are available locally and not just in the mega-mega cities.

As the world converts to renewable energy production and the associated technology innovation, new production models using individual and community co-operative energy generation could offer wonderful opportunities to invigorate rural global communities being left behind in the race to urbanisation. Local development banks that support farmers and businesses with financing could be assisted to facilitate the decentralisation of power production to local micro-production (solar/wind/energy storage). The creation of bottom-up wealth through local renewable power production and onward sales to the grid could significantly reduce the costs of agricultural mechanisation and boost rural economies at all scales. Energy and food could be exported to the mega-regions, whilst the benefits of the new rural cities could encourage labour to remain at home. Information and communications technology is rapidly fostering economies of footloose, independent business. In China, rural urbanisation could be further boosted through enhanced connectivity via the impressive and expanding high-speed rail network, which means that all rural towns and cities could be quickly and efficiently connected. Rural new towns and medium-sized cities could have a sustainable vision of economic self-containment, generated through energy export; this could be enhanced by attractive social and environmental life quality benefits brought about through the IT revolution. Bottom-up wealth-creation opportunities, particularly through power production, modernised agriculture, and cultural tourism, could provide huge opportunities for small rural cities, especially when supported by investment structures that promote sustainable local industry, targeted education, and cultural quality. Might this be a more solid alternative to the identified concerns associated with endless urban migration and city agglomeration?

Thinking Big

Whilst close to one half of the world's urban population lived in settlements of fewer than 500,000 inhabitants in 2014, this proportion is in fact projected to shrink slightly with continued population and urbanisation growth. Yet by 2030, these small cities and towns will still be home to around 45% of urban dwellers who enjoy the benefits of urban facilities coupled with access to countryside. This proportion of the urban population in small cities varies considerably across regions, with close to two-thirds of Europe's urban dwellers residing in small urban places, as do more than half of Africa's urban dwellers. In contrast, only one-third of urban residents in North America live in settlements with fewer than 500,000 people. Regional differences also reflect the contrasts in settlement patterns as well as variations in the official definition of urban areas across countries and regions. With population expansion set to snowball in Africa and Asia in particular in the next few decades, the coming decisions and approaches adopted in these specific regions towards the scale of planning of cities will have far-reaching implications.

Big cities offer undeniable opportunities to expand access to the key services of education and healthcare for large numbers of people in an economically efficient manner. They are also typically able to provide public transportation, housing, electricity, water, and sanitation for a densely settled population in a cheaper and less environmentally damaging manner than providing a similar level of services to a predominantly rural household. Importantly, urban dwellers also have access to larger and more diversified labour markets, can widen their marriage prospects, are able to sample a wider variety of leisure and entertainment opportunities, and generally enjoy more choices overall. However, there are also drawbacks. Chief amongst these are the detachment from family and friends, an initial sense of alienation, the high cost of living, pollution, and stress. Significantly, urban areas are seen as potentially high-risk hotspots in relation to epidemics, natural disasters, and social disruption given their concentrations of population and infrastructure, their key roles for larger economic, political and social processes, and their inherent instabilities and vulnerabilities. In addition, urban migration is a chief factor in the loss of local cultural traditions and the safeguarding of the collective memory, where native languages and customs are often lost as they fail to be passed on to younger generations.

In summary, scaling up cities to form large urban agglomerations would seem to run the risk of generating a number of problems, amongst them the following:

- reduced opportunities for local decision-making;
- the increased likelihood of standardisation and generic planning;
- loss of distinct local characteristics;
- requirements for costly underground infrastructure systems;
- space pressures on waste disposal;
- the increased incidence of environmental pollution;
- reduction in diversity;
- reduction of food resources close to urban centres;
- increased pressure on natural systems, including water, green space, and ecology;
- reduced access to the countryside and a disassociation from nature; and
- the utilisation of premium-quality agricultural land for development.

So at what stage does a city become too big? Is it possible to find a balance between the opportunities of the super-city and the benefits of segregation and decentralisation? Just how big should a city be?

The 3Ds

Theory has it that when you improve a product, you create increased demand for it. Similarly, improving the efficiency and liveability of a city will create increased inward migration, exacerbating the pressure on problems that still need to be solved. As a result, "the chief cause of problems are solutions" (Sevareid, 1970). History has shown that policies that aim to restrict rural–urban migration are ineffective at forestalling city growth and can even produce economic, social, and environmental harms. Moreover, places do well when they promote transformations by following the concepts of economic geography. Research carried out by the World Bank found that the 3Ds – higher "density", shorter "distance", and fewer "divisions" – are essential for economic development and should be encouraged (World Bank, 2009), yet at the same time, it recognised that growth will be spatially unbalanced and that to try to spread it out is to discourage it and to fight prosperity, not poverty. Slum-dwellers now number a billion, but the rush to cities continues. As countries continue to urbanise, sustainable development challenges will need to be increasingly concentrated in cities, particularly in the lower middle-income brackets where the pace of urbanisation is fastest; however, policies aimed at a balanced distribution of urban growth, avoiding excessive migration to very large urban agglomerations, may best support such sustainable development. Improving the facilities and opportunities to 100 dispersed rural towns to produce "rural urbanity" and increase their size to 500,000 people may well prove a far more satisfactory solution in the long run than agglomerating cities into concentrations of 50 million people. Balanced distribution and promoting the growth of small and medium-sized cities, which is common in Latin America as a means to avoid further migration to the big cities, where there has been a relatively unsuccessful track record of containing urban migration, can help to address the problems resulting from excessive centralisation of economic and administrative functions, while also responding to the challenges of providing educational and life-quality opportunities for the urban poor, and mitigating the negative environmental impacts often associated with large and rapidly growing urban agglomerations.

Tall or Wide?

With more and more people moving to cities, regardless of the size, there is always the danger of them sprawling out of control. Low-density suburban sprawl creates its own problems, in that it is very land-inefficient, leads to increased infrastructure costs, does not promote efficient transport solutions, and can be socially derelict (Mtantato, 2012). As the global population increases, cities must necessarily become more compact, with high-density neighbourhoods being created to support social and community vibrancy, high-quality yet cheap public transport services, and a movement to the use of shared facilities and their upkeep. Processes of sharing, matching, and learning allow industries to flourish in higher-density populations that would not be as efficient at a smaller scale (Deichmann, 2017). Compact and tall building types also have the greatest heat energy-efficiency at the neighbourhood scale (Rode et al., 2014). Tomorrow's cities are going to have to keep getting more dense and potentially taller, but they can also be greener, more healthy, and great living places.

Figures vary depending on the administrative boundaries adopted, but the world's densest cities are typically old and typically low to mid-rise. Paris is well known as being Europe's densest city with over 20,000 population per square kilometre, but Athens, Barcelona, Lyon and Monaco are all more dense than New York City, and dozens of major European centres have more compact populations than San Francisco, the next major US city on the list at roughly 6,600 people per square kilometre. European cities developed in ancient times around walking and the horse, and distances needed to be convenient. New world development was shaped around the railroad, streetcars, and then the private vehicle, all promoting a less compact form and facilitating sprawl and suburban living around landmark high-rise centres. Central Paris is distinctly different from other major Western cities in terms of population density, with strict planning rules and limits on building height creating long avenues of consistent height, typically at six floors. Baron Georges-Eugène Haussmann reformed 75% of the central city between 1853 and 1870, ignoring the historical Roman street form in much the same way as if he were building a new town and evicting vast numbers of the poor. Central Paris features high levels of ground occupancy, a large percentage of shared walls, narrow streets, and private courtyards with carefully considered relationships between the height of buildings and the width of streets. But even those German cities rebuilt after the Second World War in the latter half of the twentieth century follow similar traits; Berlin, Frankfurt, Dresden, Leipzig, and Warsaw chose to rebuild their urban centres based on the traditional forms of the dense, low-rise city where almost all of the streets are dominated by rows of multi-storey buildings.

The Dense Suburbs

Contrastingly, Asia's newly expanded cities are generally tall. Whilst Mumbai, Karachi, Dhaka, Manila, and Tokyo have all exhibited compact mid-rise development, with their traditionally narrow streets and low-rise buildings being reshaped rapidly to accommodate expanding populations, they have still used building regulations to contain development height and maintain some of the densest populations in the world. Yet other Asian cities have been free to develop without significant height restrictions. Singapore and Hong Kong, limited by land, have had to go upwards, and the Chinese model has been to create extensive vertical neighbourhoods, including significant areas of related open space. The opening of the Petronas Twin Towers in 1998 as the tallest buildings in the world put Kuala Lumpur on the high-rise development map and similar new developments since then have completely transformed the city. In 1950, the population was around 260,000, while today it is approximately 1.4 million (United Nations Department of Economic and Social Affairs, 2019); however, that core has not actually grown nearly as fast as intended under various strategic plans during the last century. With an ageing population and growth rates continually declining from a high in the 1980s, significant outward migration from the "City" has been a clear trend, having been witnessed first-hand by well-known local entrepreneur Andrew Lee, founder of the Kuala Lumpur City Gallery. Lee suggests that this trend has not resulted from any lack of employment opportunities, instead being primarily due to a chronic shortage of affordable housing at the urban centre, causing a strong movement of young people who have been forced to move to small, outlying towns, but who nonetheless commute daily back into the city to work. Thus, a metropolitan area of "Greater KL" (Klang Valley) has been created and developed rapidly since the millennium, generating a booming suburban population that today means Greater KL boasts a city of over 7.5 million people, combined with an urban agglomeration policy intended to further spur the country's economic growth to reach almost 10 million by 2030 (United Nations Department of Economic and Social Affairs, 2019). The newly developed suburbs are high-density and affordable, connected by metro lines and are within a commuting time of 45 minutes to an hour. However, Lee has noticed a new trend of young professionals coming back to live in the city centre as the quality of the environment is significantly improving. Back in 1972, Queen Elizabeth II visited Kuala Lumpur for the first time, and Lee remembers the event and the period well: "We lived in flats nearby Chinatown, my father was a chef at a big hotel and in those days we walked everywhere; it was very green, shaded and tree covered and we had a close-knit community. Nowadays most of the trees have been lost and there are too many large roads to make walking convenient. It's difficult to move around the streets and the city feels "hot'." Yet he notes that changes are afoot. The completion of the Metro, LRT and Monorail projects are encouraging more people to walk again: "The city has been adding both trees and a network of pedestrian connections to major buildings. There are covered walkways and air-conditioned skybridges." There are now 11 parks within the city and requirements for significant green coverage in development, even resulting in shopping malls being connected to green space and thus becoming more attractive to visit. Lee relates how city trees were frequently removed for development until about ten years ago, when there was a growing realisation of the importance of trees in the city, particularly on the part of developers. Many of the large trees were originally planted during the 1950s using adaptable species from the British colonies in India and South America. "They are impressive, but not easy to maintain and the roots are disruptive. Today's plantings are local, native species, better adapted to both the environment and ecology" (Wilson, 2019).

Yet Kuala Lumpur is still a baby compared to Shanghai, with its rapidly growing population currently at 22 million (Worldometer, 2020), set to boast the largest metropolitan area in the world when overtaking Tokyo sometime before 2025. Statistics show that the population density of Shanghai's downtown district is also much higher than that of central Tokyo, although lower than that of Seoul and Beijing, yet the density of the outer area may already have surpassed that of all other metropolitan areas. Its eight main inner districts – Huangpu, Xuhui, Changning, Jingan, Putuo, Zhabei, Hongkou, and Yangpu – were already supporting over 24,000 people per square kilometre in 2013, much higher than in the city centres of Shenzhen, Guangzhou or inner London. Shanghai plans to cap its population at 25 million and Beijing at 23 million, diverting further inward migration to the wider agglomeration areas whilst systematically making room only for a "new very high-income middle class", and pushing the lower-earning middle classes out to beyond the edges of the city limits (Sassen, 2014).

How Big Should a City Be?

Whilst urbanisation is strongly promoted through migration to urban areas, there still appears to be a massive mismatch in terms of supply and demand. Furthermore, whilst it is well established that dense populations are more efficient in terms of wealth creation and cost-benefit ratios, it would seem that there comes a time when a city is just too big and the economies of scale become affected by the law of diminishing returns. Mega-cities may in fact become increasingly less efficient the more they continue to grow. Louis Bettencourt provides mathematic evidence of this in Chinese and Asian cities, pointing out that cities reach a "G" spot where their size is optimised; increasing city size beyond that point reduces "connectivity efficiency" and they become destabilised, since physical and social connections become unwieldy and difficult to maintain (Bettencourt, 2013). So what is the "optimal" size for a city, especially for the intended cities needing to support the huge urbanisations taking place in Africa and Asia? Should urbanisation follow the conventional economic wisdom and follow the latest China urbanisation experiment of creating massive mega-cities and mega agglomerations with newly created "under-connected" development areas to be filled. Or should there perhaps be a place for investing in existing small towns and cities in rural areas to generate "urbanisation in-place" that reaches more efficient urban sizes and meets the density, distance, and division requirements of geographical economics, encouraging localised and district-level rather than national-scale migration? Opportunity generation and social mobility, the fundamentals of migration pressure, can be alleviated without the need for huge population displacement and a plethora of cities can grow over time towards reaching their optimal "G" spot rather than continually moving away from it. Perhaps there is a case for integrating both, providing mega-cities together with greater investment across smaller cities.

As countries urbanise, incomes go up and dense cities can actually become more healthy as well. New data demonstrates that housing densities of fewer than 1,800 units per square kilometre, including those in suburbia, increase the chances of someone being obese by about 10% (Sarkar et al., 2017). Lower-density development encourages sedentary behaviour, including driving to stores and work, and less cycling and walking. By contrast, living in areas above the 1,800 units per square kilometre density threshold can have a 10% lower chance of becoming obese, even in inner cities where people are more likely to live in apartment blocks and smaller homes (Sarkar et al., 2017). The benefits don't stop there. Many assumed that dense cities were more conducive to the spread of COVID-19, yet studies have shown no link to higher infection rates and in fact the contrary – that dense areas were associated with lower COVID-19 death rates, usually due to the close proximity of better health and support infrastructure, and where the coverage of high-speed internet and door-to-door delivery services are conveniently available at competitive prices, making it easier for residents to stay at home and avoid unnecessary contact with others (Hamidi et al., 2020). However, higher COVID-19 infection and mortality rates do in fact correlate to the wider context of metropolitan areas with a higher vulnerability to pandemic outbreaks where there are a number of tightly linked economic, social, and commuting relationships, making urban agglomerations especially vulnerable.

Thinking Smaller

Trends have been rapidly and necessarily moving towards smaller living spaces in dense cities, with rental and purchase costs shooting up globally. Further influences are the restrictions put in place during the COVID-19 pandemic, together with the growth of the sharing economy that had already started to create new ways of thinking about many basic features of life, including ownership, transport, and accommodation. The Airbnb phenomenon showed new ways of thinking about utilising housing resources (Wachsmuth et al., 2017) and a renaissance in utilising prefabricated housing has been coupled with a societal willingness to live more "spartan" lifestyles (Nguyen, 2018). "Manufactured" housing, utilising both modular and panel systems, is starting to provide wider housing opportunities due to recent technological advances in construction quality. Micro-houses, including mobile homes that can be fully constructed off-site and moved into place on wheels, can act as a source of temporary or long-term affordable housing, utilising private urban land such as garden space, and are becoming popular with first-time residents wanting to find a home. No land ownership is required and building codes do not necessarily apply (Modulartoday, 2018), whilst their standardised manufacture means that costs are minimised (Homes Direct, 2018). "Manufactured" construction is completely assembled off site and transported into place intact, while "Modular" construction is formed from separate box-like modules which are then secured together to form a whole. "Panel" building is accomplished by laying down the floor and then lowering each section of wall into place one at a time. The post-war housing shortage in the UK was dealt with using "temporary manufactured housing" based on American principles of prefabricated construction. "Prefab" is a broad term that encompasses several different types of prefabricated building. Technically, any building that has sections of the structure built in a factory and then assembled on site can fall under the "prefab" designation, including both "modular" and "panel" built as well as fully "manufactured" construction. Considered to be the world's tallest "modular" tower, "461 Dean" in central Brooklyn, New York at 32 storeys high is billed as a new solution to meet the high demand for urban housing. Its 930 steel modules were fabricated off site at a factory in the nearby Brooklyn Navy Yard and shipped to the site by truck. Half of the apartments have been set aside for low and middle-income residents. The eight-storey Carbon 12 building in Portland, Oregon is the tallest commercial structure in the US to be built from mass timber, laminated structural support elements that are extremely strong, durable, and able to be grown sustainably. Timber buildings have the ability to sequester massive amounts of carbon by tying up the wood in buildings for decades or even longer. Currently recognised as the world's tallest timber building at 85 metres the 18-storey Mjösa Tower opened in Norway in 2019 as did the 53 metre Tallwood House in Vancouver, Canada. The buildings are getting taller, with the HoHo in Vienna being 24 storeys and the Baobab in Paris being proposed at 35 storeys. There are new commercial mass timber buildings in Amsterdam, Atlanta, London, and Lagos, with some 21 timber buildings already over 50 metres (CTBUH Journal, 2017). Mass timber can be cheaper than concrete and steel, depending on where it is sourced, but costs are tumbling as the technique becomes more mainstream. Once production is scaled up across the globe, mass timber should be considerably cheaper. Researchers at Australia's University of New South Wales (UNSW) comparing a tall timber building with a concrete and steel equivalent in 2020 showed that the timber building remained marginally more expensive to produce in terms of material costs. However, savings could be found in other ways, in particular the ability to prefabricate wooden components, meaning that other construction costs may fall as well as the potential for shorter construction periods requiring shorter financing periods (Oldfield, 2019).

Embracing Density

The Futureproof City will thus need to be one of both density and intensity. The mega-city agglomerations of China aim to concentrate the resources and consumption of its population, but the resiliency of these in terms of homogenisation and their ability to spread risk becomes questionable, along with the fundamentals of whether such large agglomerations are actually beneficial in terms of both economic and societal progress. Insufficient and insubstantial research seems to have been undertaken before reaching the enormous decision of placing one billion people in 20 huge urban areas, and this is perhaps one of the biggest socio-economic experiments in the course of humanity. The Chinese economic advance and urbanisation appears to have come several decades too early for the greater good, being based on twentieth-century principles of consumption growth, road-based planning, and petro-carbon production, meaning these new cities are already out of date even before they are off the drawing board. Regrettably, the great urbanisation has occurred before the knowledge-based revolution that the Big Data Digital Decade that is imminent will hopefully bring, providing smart, integrated, and holistic solutions based on complex system data analysis that are really necessary for such huge development decisions. Being able to "Think Fast, Think Smart" may mean that the same huge environmental costs that China's development has witnessed can be avoided, whilst the social and economic costs remain to be seen; however, the next decade of urbanisation and population growth must be based on sounder footings in the growth points of Africa and South Asia.

So as cities get larger, they must also get denser, regardless of their size, in order to avoid the perils of sprawl and the impact on land that this entails. Within that dynamic, "space" will be at an absolute premium, yet "Prosperity through Density" can be realised through a belated modernisation in the planning and construction industries towards high-technology design and sustainable, flexible, modular building systems that facilitate the efficient and ever-adaptive reuse of structures rather than their replacement, along with minimised waste and carbon impacts.

The transition of the space between buildings away from road-dominated uses to more productive societal benefits in terms of "Unleashing Urban Potential" will further improve the quality, vitality, and liveability of dense urban living. Thinking "compact" and thinking "shared" will assist in adopting smarter solutions towards the safe and dependable housing provision necessary for more people within less space, yet at the same time creating a more efficient, more resilient, and more prosperous urban realm.

References

Bettencourt, L. M. (2013). The origins of scaling in cities. *science, 340*(6139), 1438–1441.
China, National Bureau of Statistics. (2012). *Statistical communiqué on the 2011 national economic and social development*. http://www.stats.gov.cn/english/PressRelease/201202/t20120222_72118.html.
China, NDRC. (2016). *China's policies and actions for addressing climate change*. https://www.ndrc.gov.cn/gzdt/201611/t20161102_825493.html.
CTBUH Journal. (2017). Tall timber: A global audit. *The Council on Tall Buildings and Urban Habitat, 2*, 47–49. https://global.ctbuh.org/resources/papers/3350-TBIN.pdf.
Deichmann, U. (2017). *High-density cities hold the key to transforming economic geography*. http://www.worldbank.org/en/news/feature/2017/01/26/high-density-cities-hold-the-key-to-transforming-economic-geography.
Hamidi, S., Sabouri, S., & Ewing, R. (2020). Does density aggravate the COVID-19 pandemic? Early findings and lessons for planners. *Journal of the American Planning Association, 86*(4), 495–509.
Homes Direct. (2018). *Average cost of a manufactured home in 2018*. https://www.thehomesdirect.com/blog/average-cost-of-a-manufactured-home.
Huang, J. (2016, 14 July). Plan to build 3,500 new urban areas criticized as "unrealistic". *People's Daily*. https://www.chinadaily.com.cn/china/2016-07/14/content_26090290.htm.
McMahon, E. T., & Benedict, M. (2000). Green infrastructure. *Planning Commissioners Journal, 37*(4), 4–7.
Modulartoday. (2018). *Modular homes, mobile homes & traditional homes compared*. https://www.modulartoday.com/comparison.html.
Mtantato, S. (2012). *Impact of current land-use patterns on public transport and human settlements*. Submission for the 2012/13 Division of Revenue – Technical Report.
Nguyen H. N., Rintamäki T., & Saarijärvi H. (2018). Customer value in sharing economy: The Airbnb case. In A., Smedlund, A. Lindblom, & L. Mitronen

(Eds.), *Collaborative value co-creation in the platform economy*. Springer. https://doi.org/10.1007/978-981-10-8956-5_12.

Oldfield, P. (2019). *The sustainable tall building: A design primer*. Routledge.

Rode, P., Keim, C., Robazza, G., Viejo, P., & Schofield, J. (2014). Cities and energy: Urban morphology and residential heat-energy demand. *Environment and Planning B: Planning and Design, 41*(1), 138–162.

Sarkar, C., Webster, C., & Gallacher, J. (2017). Association between adiposity outcomes and residential density: A full-data, cross-sectional analysis of 419 562 UK Biobank adult participants. *The Lancet Planetary Health, 1*(7), e277–e288. https://doi.org/https://doi.org/10.1016/S2542-5196(17)30119-5.

Sassen, S. (2014). *Expulsions: Brutality and complexity in the global economy*. Belknap Press of Harvard University Press.

Sevareid, E. (1970, 29 December). Sevareid's law. *CBS News*.

Shepard, W. (2015). *Ghost cities of China: The story of cities without people in the world's most populated country*. Zed Books.

United Nations Department of Economic and Social Affairs. (2018). *The world's cities in 2018: Data booklet (ST/ESA/ SER.A/417)*.

United Nations Department of Economic and Social Affairs. (2019). *World urbanization prospects: The 2018 revision, highlights (ST/ESA/SER.A/423)*. Population Division.

UN Secretary-General. (2008). *World population monitoring, focusing on population distribution, urbanization, internal migration and development. Report of the Secretary-General to the forty-first session of the Commission on Population and Development, E/CN.9/2008/3*. United Nations Economic and Social Council. https://documents-dds-ny.un.org/doc/UNDOC/GEN/N08/205/14/PDF/N0820514.pdf?OpenElement.

UNDP China. (2013). *China human development report. 2013: Sustainable and liveable cities: Toward ecological civilisation* (G. Luchsinger, Ed. Vol. D668 Archival Library of Chinese Publications CIP Data H.Z. (2013) No.122691). China Translation and Publishing Corporation.

Wachsmuth, D., Kerrigan, D., Chaney, D., & Shillolo, A. (2017). Short-term cities: Airbnb's impact on Canadian housing markets. *Policy report. Urban Politics and Governance research group, School of Urban Planning, McGill University*.

Wilson, B. D. (2019). Community the heart of heritage: Barry Wilson interviews Andrea Bruciati. *The Magazine of Urbanisation, 115*, 52–59. http://www.ciudsrc.com/new_zazhi/fengmian/yijiuwuliuqizazhi/2019-07-24/143871.html.

Woetzel, J., Mendonca, L., Devan, J., Negri, S., Hu, Y., Jordan, L., Li, X., Maasry, A., Tsen, G., & Yu, F. (2009). *Preparing for China's urban billion*. https://www.mckinsey.com/~/media/mckinsey/featured%20insights/urbanization/preparing%20for%20urban%20billion%20in%20china/mgi_preparing_for_chinas_urban_billion_full_report.ashx.

World Bank. (2009). *World development report 2009: Reshaping economic geography*. https://openknowledge.worldbank.org/handle/10986/5991.

Worldometer. (2020). *China demographics*. https://www.worldometers.info/demographics/china-demographics.

Yang, Z. H., & Shi, L. (2014). The strategy prepare of Chinese new urbanization. *Journal of Management*, 27(2), 28–34 (in Chinese),.

Both Safe and Dependable

10

Providing New Means to Quality Shelter for All

Providing people with shelter is a basic human need and yet the global housing crisis is set to intensify as wealth distribution narrows, climate disasters intensify, and cross-border migration extends, leaving demographic groups that were once secure now vulnerable. That being the case, should housing be a commodity used for speculation and does everyone need to own a house? Different governments take different approaches to social equity and yet something needs to radically change if UN Sustainable Development Goal 11 is to be met in ensuring "access for all to adequate, safe and affordable housing". New models are not only going to have to primarily address the affordability element in order to maintain social stability and urban cohesion, but also to understand that low-tech, localised, and sustainable models are essential, especially in newly urbanising, developing countries where the quality of housing provision and not just the quantity is of equal importance.

184 Both Safe and Dependable

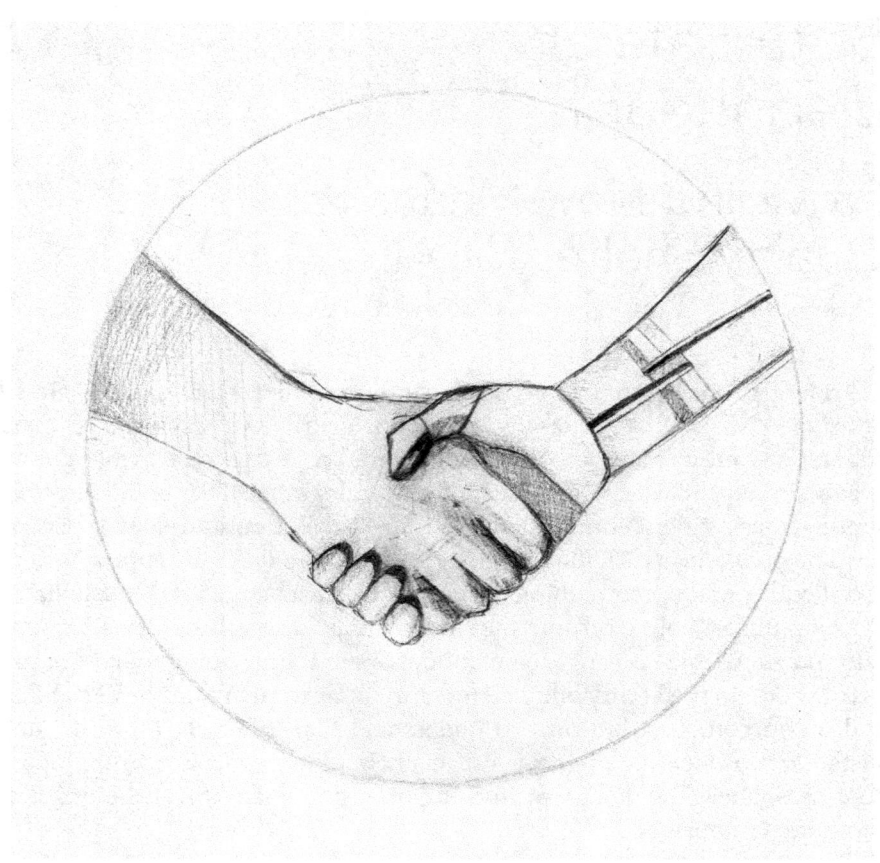

Safe and Dependable

*"What needs a man that I have not
Within my own four walls?"*

Thomas Carlyle, *My Own Four Walls*, c.1825

Towers in the Park

It was at the end of the second great period of industrial revolution and mass urbanisation in the late nineteenth century that the idea that the state might provide people with secure and dependable places to live steadily gained ground. Initially in the UK, philanthropists had started to provide housing in city tenement blocks to house the huge influx of urban manual workers, whilst some factory owners built entire villages for their workers, such as Saltaire in 1853 and Port Sunlight in 1888. These philanthropists saw creating social housing as the surest way to improve the health and welfare of others, whilst satisfying their own needs through giving (Dreier, 1997; Kottke et al., 2018); meanwhile, the greatest thinkers and academics put their energies into creating new towns, types of housing, and fairer social systems. George Peabody founded the Peabody Trust to build better and stable housing for London's poor in 1862 (George Peabody (1795–1869), founder of modern philanthropy, 1994). The "Garden City Movement" initiated by Sir Ebenezer Howard in 1898 shared the idea that the working class deserved better and more affordable housing (Booth, 2014).

To meet the needs of newly urbanised workers, tenement buildings emerged in Glasgow between 1850 and 1900, built using locally sourced materials and typically four storeys in height, but never taller than the width of the street; the regular blocks created the city's distinctive "grid" pattern. Most apartments had just one or two rooms and were normally built in working-class areas like the East End, although middle-class areas had three-room flats and some were even larger. Although tenements were initially successful in housing large numbers of families, this later led to problems such as poor sanitation, disease, and overcrowding, where between 30 and 50 people were often sharing one outdoor toilet and water tap in the backyard (Ball, 2017; McKean, 2004). The origins of French social housing also lie in the private sector, with the first state aid provided to limited profit companies by the "Loi Siegfried" in 1894. In the US, early tenement reform was also primarily a philanthropic venture, with model tenements built as early as the 1870s, which attempted to use new architectural and management models to address the physical and social problems of the slums.

However, the origins of state-provisioned social housing lie in the UK and its "Housing of the Working Classes Act" of 1890, which resulted in the first council estate, "Boundary Street", built three years later on the border of Shoreditch and Bethnal Green in east London. By 1919, local authorities were required by law to provide "council housing" and after the Second World War, the government was building such dwellings in huge numbers in order to replace homes destroyed in the war, peaking at 220,000 in 1953. In France, the post-war governments had launched major construction initiatives, including the creation of new towns ("villes nouvelles") and new city suburbs, including low-rent housing known as "Habitation à Loyer Modéré" (HLM). This housing is now generally referred to as "l'habitat social" to include a slightly wider remit than just housing. The state acquired land and then advantageously funded companies to build its huge housing complexes.

The 1960s and 1970s in Glasgow saw poorer families no longer able to keep up with the cost of tenement maintenance, and some areas of the city like Gorbals and Anderston became slums (Douglas, 2007). Across Britain, slum clearance became typical across industrial towns of the UK, as millions were uprooted from cramped, rundown inner-city terraces and rehoused in purpose-built new towns or more fashionable high-rise blocks. A whole generation was introduced to the new pleasures of indoor toilets, front and rear gardens, or landscaped housing estates. However, the cheap, poorly designed and built tower blocks started to cause their own problems; not only was the build quality lost, but more importantly the day-to-day management was far from a priority for the local governments building them. The "tower in the park" aspiration of the influential architect Le Corbusier, featuring concrete walkways and "streets in the sky" that had once seemed so pristine and futuristic, were becoming grim havens of decay and lawlessness, not just in Britain but also across Europe and the US. Whilst they did succeed in providing lower-income families with a place to live through the mission to provide popular housing, this system also led to the creation of suburban ghettos, with the distinct problems of neglect and disrepair. By contrast, the old stone tenements in Glasgow that managed to survive demolition in the twentieth century have now been refurbished and have become fashionable places to live, having long been a key part of the fabric and character of the city; around 73% of Glaswegians live in these mid-rise apartments today, compared with just under 25% living "off the ground" in comparable cities in the south of Britain (Williams, 2019).

Urban renewal had become a way to eliminate blight, but was not in fact a solution for constructing new housing. For instance, in the ten years after the US Housing Act of 1949 was passed, 425,000 units were erased under its directives, yet only 125,000 units were constructed (Biles, 2000).

Entire communities in poorer, urban neighbourhoods were demolished to make way for modern developments. Activist and author Jane Jacobs would famously describe the new housing as: "Low-income projects that become worse centres of delinquency, vandalism, and general social hopelessness than the slums they were supposed to replace. Middle-income housing projects which are truly marvels of dullness and regimentation, sealed against any buoyancy or vitality of city life. Luxury housing projects that mitigate their inanity, or try to, with vapid vulgarity ... This is not the rebuilding of cities. This is the sacking of cities" (Jacobs, 1961).

In 1979, 42% of Britons lived in council homes. Today that figure is just under 8%. Things began to change when the government of Margaret Thatcher introduced "right to buy", allowing state-owned housing to be sold to tenants with the idea that councils should use the funds to pay down their debts rather than build new houses. The mission was not to ensure affordable rents for working people, but to help them to get a foot on the property ownership ladder and 1.6 million council homes were sold between 1979 and 2013 (Harris, 2016). However, lessons had not been learnt and the numbers of new council homes being built plummeted. Council housing went from being a cornerstone of national social development to that of a marginalised and stigmatised consideration during an unprecedented boom in house prices, fuelled by cheap credit and the now shortage of affordable rented accommodation.

In the US, rents have been rising for more than a decade, as have the numbers of renters. According to analysis by the Urban Institute, there are only 28 affordable units for every 100 renting households with lower incomes. Between 2001 and 2013, the US housing market saw the disappearance of 2.4 million affordable units, both subsidised and market-rate, for the lower half of income earners. The loss is seen as most severe in primary housing markets such as New York City, but is also apparent across the country, where neglect and deterioration also impact affordability (Getsinger et al., 2017).

One of the "Targets" of UN Sustainable Development Goal 11 is to "ensure access for all to adequate, safe and affordable housing and basic services and upgrade slums by 2030" (UN Agenda 2030, 2015). However, as politicians the world over try to draw in the growing middle classes, housing policies are shifting and the benchmark for affordability is continually being raised. Meeting poorer people's housing needs is requiring larger and larger subsidies, at a time when most countries are in actual fact cutting back on public spending or even pulling out of state-subsidised housing altogether. If this is happening in rich countries such as Britain and the US, it is even more likely in poorer countries with tighter budgets and limited tax bases.

People are stuck in inadequate homes or pay so much of their incomes on housing that they are forced to forgo other necessities.

According to Numbeo, as of December 2020, the price to income ratio of the five Chinese cities of Shenzhen, Hong Kong, Beijing, Shanghai, and Guangzhou are five of the top ten most expensive in the world, along with Damascus, Tehran, Manila, Mumbai, and Phnom Penh. Both Shenzhen and Hong Kong require above 45 years of typical salary earnings to pay back the costs of buying an average property, up from 40 years in 2017, whilst the China national average remained stable at around 28 years. In 2017 China was by some way the most unaffordable residential ownership market globally; however, during that time, it has been caught up and overtaken by Cambodia, Kenya, Sri Lanka, the Philippines, and Iran, where housing affordability is worryingly spiralling out of control. To put this into context, the US continues to prop up the list with a national average payback period of just 3.7 years (Numbeo, 2020). Rental yields in the US are some of the world's best, whereas the rental market in China is still some way behind rising house prices, making buy-to-rent unattractive for homeowners and so leaving newly purchased property deliberately empty, typically for years.

Lack of access to decent affordable housing has become an issue in both rich and poor economies. Even in developed markets, low-income families in inadequate housing have higher levels of unemployment, and their children are more likely to do poorly in school and quit sooner than other students. High housing costs squeeze middle-income families, and in the costliest cities, even households earning far more than the median income can be financially stretched by rent or mortgage payments, limiting the growth of the local economy (Woetzel et al., 2014).

Does Everyone Need to Own a House?

Not everyone can own property and not everyone wants to own property. Germany, for instance, has some of the lowest property ownership levels in the developed world, where about half of the population are living in rental accommodation (Eurostat, 2019). This is mostly an issue of choice, since arguably the "tenant is king", enjoying rights and being afforded strong protection against landlords. There exists the freedom to decorate properties in which tenants live, although there is the obligation to repaint walls to "neutral colours" before leaving, and so those who rent tend to treat the property as a real home, doing far more of the maintenance themselves than a tenant would be allowed to in, say, Hong Kong. On average, a tenant spends three to seven years in one property, much longer than in other countries. The negative equity that follows property booms has reinforced the beliefs of Germans in terms of their suspicion of rising house prices. They do not sit around the dinner table discussing how much their home has risen in value over the past month. According to the Paris-based OECD, house prices increased by an average of 83% between 1970 and 2008 in OECD countries, while in Germany, they fell by 17% (Kollewe & Elliott, 2011). It's also difficult for Germans to get mortgages, a large deposit is needed, and this is combined with a strong cultural reluctance towards risk and borrowing.

By contrast, for the Chinese, it seems that owning a home is one of the most important life aspirations. It represents security in a fragile existence and for young men, there even exists the cultural pressure of needing to secure a property prior to taking a wife. Lack of affordable first homes is causing stress in the younger population, which is being evidenced by couples marrying later in life, becoming older parents, or perhaps not even marrying at all. More recently with spiralling prices, purchasing property as a financial investment has appeared essential to younger generations who otherwise see their peers with money getting even richer through property speculation. It is clear that all of China's big cities have becoming overwhelmingly expensive for their citizens in terms of property ownership.

The German situation, where landlords have limited powers and lending is heavily restricted, provides a clear illustration of factors that do exist to make housing less attractive as a speculative investment tool. In France, after damage during the Second World War had reduced the number of houses in many cities, rental prices dramatically rose, and the government passed a law in 1948 to restrict rental charges, effectively ending the economic benefits of housing investment and helping to balance landlord and tenant relations (Loiseau & Bonvalet, 2005). In Singapore, over 80% of the population live in government-developed public housing estates where the Housing and Development Board (HDB) is hugely backed by state funding (Singapore, HDB, 2021). Laissez-faire economics in the housing markets only seems to lead in one direction – a further concentration of assets at the expense of those without. As a "basic human need", governments have a fundamental responsibility to ensure that housing is not treated as a luxury good and is both available and affordable. A diamond has value only due to its rarity of supply and it is a luxury; its demand has to be manufactured though marketing, having little intrinsic value. Nobody actually needs a diamond. But shelter is different. It is too important to be treated like a commodity, to be traded around in indifference to the plight of those without it. There are plenty of ways for human individuals to get rich without it being based on constraining the basic needs of food, water, or shelter. The lack of affordable housing has high costs in terms of health, environmental degradation, transportation, and homelessness. Strong, mixed-income, diverse communities are stable, healthy, and economically viable, and they support a variety of stores, services, and entertainment that make cities vibrant and interesting. Teachers, police, and health workers should be able to live in the communities in which they work. Without more affordability in housing supply, they will not be able to do so. As the global population rises and space becomes ever more precious, is it reasonable that people go homeless even when adequate nearby accommodation remains empty? Is it acceptable for property to be hoarded, controlled, and traded for the further benefit of those least in need? Civic unrest and social disruption repeatedly result from such desperate situations, and governments must take a strong hand in strengthening the supply side of housing provision in the public sector, whilst balancing the demand side against commodity speculation. They must come to see that provision of quality affordable housing for all is a community investment rather than a burden.

Are Houses for Living In?

"Houses are for living in, not for speculation" was President Xi's renewed clarion call at the 19th Party Congress in 2016 (Yang, 2016). It followed the continued tightening of housing measures across China up until that point, when Xiamen became the first city nationwide to introduce a complete sales ban. More than 40 cities followed suit, with Xi'an, Chongqing, Nanchang, Nanning, Changsha, Guiyang, Shijiazhuang, and Wuhan tightening housing controls, with most banning house sales within two or three years after purchase. The Ministry of Housing and Construction subsequently initiated housing rental trials in 12 cities, including Guangzhou, Shenzhen, Nanjing, Hangzhou, and Xiamen. In her first policy address, Hong Kong Chief Executive Carrie Lam focused on the housing crisis and suggested that extending homeownership was going to be at the core policy, whilst "housing is not a simple commodity". She pointed out that: "Our community has a rightful expectation towards the Government to provide adequate housing. This is also fundamental to social harmony and stability" (HKSAR, Information Services, 2017). This seems to just about toe-the-line of Beijing, where President Xi highlighted that authorities should put in place a housing system that ensures supply through multiple sources, provides housing support through multiple channels, and encourages both housing rental and purchase. Despite its long track record of social housing provision, where just under half of the population is in some form of assisted housing (HKSAR, Transport and Housing Bureau, 2020), there is an uncomfortable fit when considered with Hong Kong's otherwise vociferous laissez-faire approach in encouraging private-sector provision of most public services and facilities. The influential Our Hong Kong Foundation proposes a new and elaborate scheme to improve efficiencies in the housing market, but more importantly the overarching scope is to "inject wealth to households through the form of homeownership, encouraging households to satisfy their housing demand through the private market" (Wong & Tsang, 2017) – in other words, housing should be treated absolutely as a commodity and the main driver of wealth creation, and not as a basic human need. Does this kind of thinking not exemplify the priorities of cities like Hong Kong, where pure wealth creation is considered more important than quality-of-life issues?

Studies show people typically associate homeownership not with making money, but with putting down roots, starting a family, and gaining a measure of security and control over the place in which they live (McCabe, 2018). In other words, they want to feel like citizens, with a stake in their society. There is also evidence of a remarkable connection between homeownership and the cultivation of strong communities, where owning a home significantly increases a person's sense of belonging to their neighbourhood (Lindblad et al., 2013). Young people who want to own but don't yet do so talk about not really seeing the point of committing to the area in which they are living or getting to know the people with whom they share a street or building. These are the things that make a vital difference to whether we build a common life together or simply exist in a series of separate worlds. As such, homeownership is tremendously valuable as a social tool; however, such studies reinforce the concept that housing "is for living in and not speculation". If citizens feel they need to own a house primarily as a means to survive economically, then something is very wrong, and ownership can also be a financial albatross in a depressed sales market or when interest rates are rising. It may also be considered that though the provision of quality rental housing, balanced landlord/tenant rights, and well-considered urban design, vibrant, safe, and secure communities can also be built without the requirement of homeownership. Creating communities where non-owners are still able to be stakeholders and take pride in their community may become more of an aspirational housing approach than that of simply creating ownership.

A New Hope

It can be argued that income rather than either price or availability is the primary factor that determines housing affordability (Tilly, 2006). Therefore, understanding affordable housing challenges requires understanding trends and disparities in income and wealth. Housing is often the single biggest expenditure of low and middle-income families. Furthermore, it seems clear that, regardless of whether for rental or purchase, housing needs not only to be affordable, but also affordable in all locations, whether in the central city or the outskirts of town. In many places nowadays, it is not affordable in itself and especially not affordable in critical downtown areas. This has a number of implications for society. As older neighbourhoods are redeveloped or gentrified, rental prices increase rapidly as landlords find new tenants willing to pay higher market rates for housing. Lower-income families, many of whom have been living in such neighbourhoods all their lives, are left without affordable rental units. Finding local accommodation matched to their income level means smaller spaces and poorer quality, culminating in those living at the bottom of the income bracket finding themselves in completely unacceptable private rental housing conditions such as subdivided apartments or even caged spaces, as can be found in Hong Kong. As an alternative, moving to cheaper districts has other implications, with the upheaval of a family causing trauma in terms of the ability of finding new schools or work, or of the greater travel distances required to maintain established life. Living close to work saves time, reduces costs, and reduces the impact on city services. Most importantly, people choose to maintain their social cohesion and are generally reticent to leave behind friends and life habits. Ageing in place can only be effective if housing provision affords it. In addition to the distress it causes families who cannot find a place to live, lack of affordable housing is considered by many urban planners to have negative effects on a community's overall health (Bhatta, 2010). The availability of affordable housing in close proximity to mass transit systems and linked to job distribution has become severely imbalanced in this era of rapid regional urbanisation and growing city density. Cities require a full range of workers, from bankers to street cleaners. Each needs local housing, preferably close to their work, which is affordable for their income bracket. As street cleaners sweep the roads of the bankers, this implies that both should live close together. Affordable housing shortages in inner cities might lead to the deprivation of vital workers like police officers, fire-fighters, teachers, and nurses, who would be unable to find affordable accommodation near their place of work. Low-income renters are typically service workers whose jobs are also essential to the community. These include restaurant staff, retail clerks, cashiers, daycare workers, hairdressers, maintenance technicians, and security guards, as well as disabled and retired people living on Social Security. In a time of mass rural-urban migration, the overall desirability of moving to a city must become influenced by its housing costs, particularly if this concerns a low-paid worker. Without affordable housing, in diverse, mixed downtown neighbourhoods, where will all the workers live and who will do their jobs?

The current situation, created by planners and endorsed by governments in the last millennium, focused on generating segregated, income-specific communities located out of town where jobs are scarce and long distances of commuting are required. This should have run its course in the developed world, where every city has well-documented problems associated with low-income, edge-of-town, mass-housing schemes. Yet, over the past decade, *mixed-income housing*, a relatively new concept in affordable housing development, has been rising in popularity across the US, with progressive cities providing inner-city housing for lower-income and more affluent residents together. Local governments appear to prefer mixed-income housing to segregation of low-income residents in 100% affordable projects because again policy lessons have taught them that poverty concentration is not ideal. The City of Austin's SMART (Safe, Mixed-income, Accessible, Reasonably priced, Transit-oriented) Housing Program offers developers a schedule of incentives based on the level of affordable housing provided. The city provides additional density and height variance, or floor/area ratio, to encourage provision of affordable housing and other community benefits, such as open space and streetscape. Developers are expected to set aside 25% of units as affordable or pay an in-lieu fee into the city's housing fund (Kirk, 2012).

Hong Kong continues to push quick-fix, tired but trusted, public, peri-urban housing projects, providing few local jobs whilst creating pressure on the existing transport system. At the same time, it promotes out-of-town, central business district clusters without facilitating residential mixes to develop within them. Meanwhile in China, centuries-old communities in urban villages are being swept away daily by the pen of a young city planner, to be replaced by new international-style development with sky-high rents and empty units. Once rural collectives, "urban villages or chengzhongcun" have become swallowed up by ever-expanding city development, with increasing flows of migrants looking for work in labour-intensive industries and the service sector. Those villages located at the heart of the cities, which are the main focus of attention, have an important function in Chinese urbanisation in terms of acting as a first point of arrival for migrant labour. Low-cost accommodation and an instant network of social connections make them an obvious draw to newcomers. Guangzhou and Shenzhen are supposedly home to 139 and 241 "chengzhongcun" respectively according to many articles, and in Shenzhen approximately half of the population of 10 million live in the "chengzhongcun". The villages therefore provide a hugely important role in affordable housing and as a transient community focus. There have been numerous redevelopments of urban villages in the last few decades. Typical examples have been the wholesale redevelopment of villages whereby the "stakeholders" are able to partner with government and/or developers, and obtain property and ownership rights within the new development or ownership company. Different economic models have been applied; however, the motivations are always the same in terms of fully realising land values for both villagers and developers, whilst government considers standardised and gentrifying redevelopment as a city improvement. Some redevelopments, such as Huanggang village in Shenzhen, which was one of the first to organise itself into an urban administrative structure, have capitalised incredibly on their positioning. In 1992, Shenzhen let its villages set up their own village joint-stock companies. In 1994, villages were moved from rural to urban land classification and therefore became administered by the government (Wang et al., 2009). The Shenzhen Huanggang Real Estate Holding Ltd., a joint-stock company set up by villagers in 1992 with a fund of 200 million yuan, was 20 years later conservatively worth over six billion yuan. The village company owns two large hotels, a department store, office buildings, restaurants, and rental properties and in 2009, the company erected its first skyscraper, the "Huanggang Business Centre", a 62-floor office building in the centre of Shenzhen (Wang, 2013).

New Ideas Emerging

Such gentrification sees the complete loss of large-scale affordable migrant housing, which has to move elsewhere and put pressure on other villages. The biggest challenge emerging is the need for recognition of migrants as stakeholders in negotiations; they are still the main losers, while villagers make further gains. It can be argued that redevelopment projects for informal settlements around the world have been most successful when conducted by three categories of stakeholder – the state, the market, and the public (UN-Habitat, 2004). Migrants need to have a bigger role with those who have been living in urban villages for several years, being allowed to take part in planning processes. Dharavi, a large "slum" area in the centre of Mumbai, India, gives a parallel example of approaches to redevelopment. Under the government-led Dharavi Redevelopment Project (DRP), developers offer to provide the people living there who are able to prove their residence since 2000 with a new, 300-square-foot house for free. In return, the authorities have allowed the builders to go higher (increasing the floor space index from

1.33 to 4), thereby concentrating residents into tower blocks and freeing up space for luxury high rises that will reap huge returns. According to the government's plan, residents and occupants should be moved into 43% of the land they currently occupy, freeing up 57% for other development (*The Hindu*, 2017). The plan has created a storm of controversy. The clash of opinions on Dharavi's future triggered a decade-long stalemate, culminating in Mumbai's Urban Design Research Institute (UDRI), an independent organisation advocating for more equitable development in its home city, launching an international competition entitled "Re-inventing Dharavi" as a challenge for fresh thinking and to solicit the best ideas for this endless issue. The focus aimed at advocating for more equitable development outcomes that particularly took into account the needs of those residing there presently. This aimed to address not only the need for increased housing provision and amenities, but also to appreciate the fabric of the community and the need for incorporating micro-entrepreneurship and social interaction. Strategies considered over a range of time periods and disciplines envisaged that a larger group of people would need to be involved in the process, including government, civil society, NGOs, and, most importantly, the people of Dharavi (UDRI, 2016). "How would residents envision their future if they had their rights?" argued Plural, winners of the competition. The rights being denied to them, include "the right to entitlement", "the right to participate", and "the right to livelihood" (Carr, 2015). The proposed solution aimed to eliminate profiteering opportunities from the land commodity itself, calling for the current landowners in Dharavi – the biggest of which is the government – to release all ownership rights to a Dharavi Community Land Trust which would then redistribute the ownership rights among the 850,000 community, inspired by Gandhi's notion of land as a community inheritance. The not-for-profit Trust, governed by former landowners, community members, and neighbourhood associations, would first task itself with fully understanding the multiple and divergent needs of each of the existing 156 neighbourhoods before considering how to incrementally develop accordingly. Up to this point, the major hindrances to the DRP have been the incredible complexities of land ownership, from the various government agencies to private owners, along with the array of residential inhabitants and their own claims. The Land Trust concept attempts to solve such a problem at a stroke, but remains ignored. The incoming government chose to further incentivise the DRP to get over the line in 2018 by offering up five sectors together for single consortium development, yet this drew only two bidders and was subsequently scrapped in 2020 (Deshpande, 2020). As the project drags on, people's requirements will keep changing and 16 years after its inception, it remains far from settled.

When undertaking city development, not only is delay due to the many political and administrative factors, but it is also linked to the way that the socio-economic and socio-cultural environment is continuously changing. The requirement suddenly now is to imagine and prepare for a post-COVID world.

We are about to see a plethora of new global models for home part-purchase or fractional home purchase. New hybrid homeownership and land rental models, utilising shared or fractional ownership and usage rights, are becoming increasingly common (*Mortgage Finance Gazette*, 2018). Platforms such as "resident-owned communities" (ROC) provide flexibility for owners to share the management and control of infrastructure, operations, parking, and common areas, and are suggestive of a return to traditional concepts of sharing in land assets and the wealth they can create as the benefits of "the commons" enjoy a renaissance (Brown, 2012). ROC USA is a not-for-profit venture formed from a collaboration of regional organisations that have helped thousands of members in 270 communities across 18 states join together to buy and run their communities (ROC USA, 2021). Facilitated by digital technology and the internet, such models can provide more affordable housing ownership, increased community use of facilities, and opportunities to shape specific services that respond to local aspirations and needs through stakeholder involvement and the sense of ownership that this delivers. Responsible, shared land management can also improve community cohesion where projects help to build a stronger sense of local identity, pride, confidence, achievement, and belonging (French et al., 2008). Members may own their homes and rent empty spaces to generate revenue that covers the servicing of debts and operating expenses. Could the state also be encouraged to provide and manage such facilities, even in terms of utilising land temporarily?

The city of Beijing has developed a scheme to introduce homes with property rights to be shared by the government and buyers. Individual buyers are able to buy a share in such homes and will still have the full right of use (*China Daily*, 2017). This appears similar to the Shared Ownership Schemes of the Western Australia government. Alipay, Alibaba's third-party online payment platform, has launched a credit database for all rental homes, tenants, and landlords registered with the Alipay platform, whilst market disruptor Airbnb has developed a new platform to provide mortgage deposits in exchange for rental access.

Meanwhile, typical suburban-style family houses have become unsuited to the new demographic, with the need for more dense individual apartment living resulting in a large amount of stranded assets in the housing market. New platforms, with shared or fractional ownership and usage rights, are likely to develop in the coming years. Platform cooperatives, which share the value they create with the users they depend on, are on the rise. We can hope and possibly expect such platforms to heavily influence the supply of housing in the next few years, making ownership as we know it a thing of the past.

An insufficient supply of affordable housing seems then to have become a common crisis worldwide for both rich and poor economies. Yet, as the main urbanising regions, Asia and Africa have the most important parts to play in housing expanding populations. Affordable housing is an essential component, but is one that will need to be market-driven as well as government-supported. Affordable "green building" can be provided at essentially very low cost and according to Sundaresan Raghupathy, Executive Director of the Confederation of Indian Industry, the building sector in India has embraced sustainable design and construction practices in the past decade, so much so that the green building movement is leading the way in terms of addressing low-cost housing strategies in India. The incremental cost in affordable "green housing" has decreased to less than 2% and the Indian Green Building Council (IGBC) in partnership with the Ministry of Housing and Urban Poverty Alleviation (MOHUPA) is working to ensure that the cost of green affordable homes is equal to or less than that of a conventional home within the next five years. Such green solutions are predominantly low-tech and are often based on traditional local building techniques coupled with contemporary knowledge application, which is transferable worldwide (Raghupathy, 2015).

Given that it is not possible or necessarily desirable to increase homeownership rapidly, aims should focus on increasing quality, stability, and control in the rental sector (both public and private). This will mean developing tenure that offers greater security and perhaps also the chance to take steps towards ownership. There is also a need for more and much better-quality public housing. A worldwide housing revolution appears to be about to break, with micro, mobile and temporary manufactured housing appealing to the younger generation. A more visionary approach to what is really important in housing is essential. Building more homeownership may seem economically vital; however, it's more the quality of the living community that makes the real difference to the sort of society being built together.

Quality Ingredients for Quality Cities

Whilst the increasingly insufficient supply of basic shelter seems to have become a leading trigger for a global crisis that is rapidly growing out of control in the face of population explosion and economic injustice, the origins are more complex than just being a housing issue. Traditional societal values and infrastructure, particularly in the developed world, are on the verge of complete collapse and torn communities featuring homelessness, repossession and unaffordable costs are looking towards populist leadership in applying band-aid fixes to deep-seated structural failures. One new development model being prototyped is aimed at an over 35-year-old demographic, a group not traditionally targeted as being in need of housing support, but one that is now finding itself increasingly impacted by a housing landscape characterised by investment speculation, short-term rental profits, and austerity measures of governments that are unable to borrow money cheaply to provide necessary social or affordable housing. With so much of "everything" having become privatised in developed economies with the sole intent of creating profit, there has been a huge surge in the "hidden homeless" worldwide, who are sleeping on people's sofas, living in cars, or caught in a rental trap where they are unable to find the security bond to get into rental accommodation. Women over the age of 50 form a particularly significant part of the growing problem.

According to Margaret Mee, Social Enterprise & Impact Investment Director at Connect Invest Global (UK), "the cost of meeting the basic human need for shelter has now become too great for many in the face of technological change, loss of job security, freelancing and disappearance of traditional workplace jobs, whereby there has being insufficient re-education and re-skilling for the mid to older generation" (Mee, 2018). According to Mee, affordable housing doesn't address the "home security" issues concerning older generations: "When I am an old lady, I don't want to be having to worry about losing the place I live in. I want to know I am secure in my home until I die. It goes well beyond affordability." This is where her new model comes in – a localised development community with motivations beyond the norm; one that integrates government, industry, utility companies, and communications providers to work together to provide not only affordable housing but also whole new ecosystems creating a social impact which includes generating and supporting small local enterprise, social connectivity, and skills training. Governments can no longer fulfil these roles – according to Mee, they don't have the finance. She considers that new models will have to be based on public-private not-for-profit partnerships (PPNFP) with funding that creates social impact. Tomorrow's investment sectors will need to focus not just on "financial return" but just as importantly on "social return", with projects and enterprises where returns are linked to positive social impact & stability in local communities rather than in taking out short term profits. Whilst they will still need to be "for profit", believes Mee, their return on investment ethos will have to change. These new development communities will need to target the key service providers at the heart of our cities where transit is also key; the teachers, medics, careworkers, firefighters, and cleaners, providing mid-rise and fairly dense, eco-friendly units with one or two rooms. Such a type of accommodation doesn't need to target the nuclear family in Mee's mind, since it is "the diverse community that forms the beating heart". Such a community must be flexible and allow "ageing-in-place", where residents can scale up or scale down within the development depending on their needs, yet remain socially invested in the community. "They just provide that 'great place to live', says Mee, which is a 'secure place', with lots of light to guard against depression and access to a shared garden. They include medical centres with a focus on ageing well, locally produced food markets, service providers and places to hang out and create social interaction. A place 'to know', 'be known' and 'to grow'. Business doesn't need bricks and mortar homogeneity, it needs local, social entrepreneurship models which are part of the community and local money stays local. The letting model is predominantly socially driven, not just economically. It needs kickstart support, with such things as tax breaks and small business rates and shared connectivity. Mee considers that the costs of being a small business are just too prohibitive nowadays

A critical factor in communities moving forward is the need to have flexibility. The need to be working in adaptable space, positioning development for today that can easily be adapted for tomorrow is essential. The only certainty for the future is change, but anticipating the nature of that change is quite uncertain. How is it possible to see where change might start to come – can regulation keep up with innovation? Regulation has always been on the backfoot, but now more than ever, local government needs to become more driven by social change and quicker to respond. The current dynamic isn't working; it leads to dissent and frustration. This is a well-documented narrative it seems. "First technology changes, which lead to large scale social disruption; the result being that governments don't have the tools to govern the system. So how can they then plan for the future when they can't even be effective in the now? Social policy is in disarray globally, particularly in developed countries and nobody has answers", explains Mee.

It seems that the new models that Mee and others are looking at in fact take over much of the old role of local government and empower the community in terms of health, education, housing, welfare, training, and food supply. Throw into the mix the possibilities of decentralised energy production, storage, and both the savings and revenue stream potential of smart-grid connection that can be anticipated with the rapid transition to renewables and advanced battery development, build in green and smart building advances, and add managed, shared transport solutions through pooled, fleet provision rather than individual ownership, and the resulting models start to become more like business opportunities in themselves, enabled by Big Data technology solutions that can further drive opportunity and shared responsibility rather than being just housing solutions alone. This goes back to self-supporting private initiatives whereby charities, government, and social enterprises can partner to create, support, and empower new "social ecosystems". Such a shift seems difficult to administer at a national scale and in order for such transitions to happen, they would need to start within the auspices of the town or city. The "Futureproof City" will in fact necessarily develop organically in this direction, through its own vision, flexibility, and localised policy, in order to meet resiliency needs and maintain social stability focused on "Putting Wellness First". It will actively seek and trial new innovations across all areas in order to address continued inadequacies, particularly in housing and social inequality, with the clear understanding that inclusive, bottom-up planning and decision-making achieves longer-term beneficial outcomes. It will be *reconsidering* business-as-usual approaches, *rethinking* business-as-usual values, and *redirecting* business-as-usual resources in order to attract and retain the best brainpower and quality labour supply from across the globe. "Those local governments that don't grasp the seriousness of what is happening and are not able to rapidly innovate will get left behind", suggests Mee, "with the massive implication of spiralling budgets, and health and welfare costs. Technology can provide tools to help manage change, but its community that is the core ingredient of cities. People are gregarious, social animals with basic needs. Develop quality ingredients and you develop quality cities."

References

Ball, C. (2017). *A history of Glasgow tenements*. https://cairnestateagency.com/history-glasgow-tenements.

Bhatta, B. (2010). *Analysis of urban growth and sprawl from remote sensing data*. Springer.

Biles, R. (2000). Public housing and the postwar urban renaissance, 1949–1973. In R. Biles, J. F. Bauman, & K. M. Szylvian (Eds.), *From tenements to the Taylor homes* (pp. 143–162). Penn State University Press. https://doi.org/10.5325/j.ctv14gpbjz.15.

Booth, R. (2014, 22 April). New garden cities must offer genuinely affordable homes, says charity. *The Guardian*. https://www.theguardian.com/politics/2014/apr/22/garden-cities-affordable-homes-tcpa-ebbsfleet-howard-letchworth.

Brown, R. (2012, 11 October). How trailer park cooperatives could benefit Maine. http://bangordailynews.com/2012/10/11/opinion/how-trailer-park-cooperatives-could-benefit-maine.

Carr, C. (2015, 18 February). The best idea to redevelop Dharavi slum? Scrap the plans and start again. *The Guardian*. https://www.theguardian.com/cities/2015/feb/18/best-ideas-redevelop-dharavi-slum-developers-india.

China Daily. (2017, 21 September). Beijing unveils joint ownership housing scheme. http://www.chinadaily.com.cn/china/2017-09/21/content_32292967.htm

Deshpande, A. (2020, 30 October). More delays to redevelopment of Dharavi slums in Mumbai. *The Hindu*. https://www.thehindu.com/news/cities/mumbai/more-delays-to-redevelopment-of-dharavi-slums-in-mumbai/article32976544.ece.

Douglas, P. (2007). *The evolution of the Glasgow tenement*. https://dennistoun.co.uk/digest/37.the-evolution-of-the-glasgow-tenement.

Dreier, P. (1997). Philanthropy and the housing crisis: The dilemmas of private charity and public policy. *Housing Policy Debate, 8*, 235–293.

Eurostat, E. (2019). *Distribution of population by tenure status, type of household and income group*. https://ec.europa.eu/eurostat/web/products-datasets/-/ilc_lvho02.

French, C. A., Giraud, K., & Ward, S. K. (2008). Building wealth through ownership: Resident-owned manufactured housing communities in New Hampshire. *Journal of Extension, 46*(2), 127–128. https://scholars.unh.edu/nren_facpub/8.

George Peabody (1795–1869), founder of modern philanthropy. (1994). *Peabody Journal of Education, 70*(1), 17–32. https://doi.org/10.1080/01619569409538797.

Getsinger, L., Posey, L., MacDonald, G., & Leopold, J. (2017). *The housing affordability gap for extremely low-income renters in 2014*. https://www.urban.org/sites/default/files/publication/89921/gap_map_report.pdf.

Harris, J. (2016, 4 January). The end of council housing. *The Guardian*. https://www.theguardian.com/society/2016/jan/04/end-of-council-housing-bill-secure-tenancies-pay-to-stay.

The Hindu. (2017, 16 September). Community land trust model best suited to reinvent Dharavi. https://www.thehindu.com/news/cities/mumbai/community-land-trust-model-best-suited-to-reinvent-dharavi/article19700938.ece.

HKSAR, Information Services. (2017). *The Chief Executive's 2017 policy address*. Information Services Department (ISD), the Hong Kong Special Administrative Region of the People's Republic of China. https://www.policyaddress.gov.hk/2017/eng/pdf/PA2017.pdf.

HKSAR, Transport and Housing Bureau. (2020). *Hong Kong: The facts – Housing*. Information Services Department, Hong Kong Special Administrative Region of the People's Republic of China. https://www.thb.gov.hk/eng/psp/publications/housing/hongkongthefacts/index.htm.

Jacobs, J. (1961). *The death and life of great American cities*. Random House.

Kirk, P. (2012, 19 June). Making mixed-income housing work. *Urban Land Magazine*. https://urbanland.uli.org/economy-markets-trends/making-mixed-income-housing-work.

Kollewe, J., & Elliott, L. (2011, 16 March). Home sweet home is a rented property for many Germans. *The Guardian*. https://www.theguardian.com/world/2011/mar/16/new-europe-germany-property.

Kottke, T., Abariotes, A., & Spoonheim, J. B. (2018). Access to affordable housing promotes health and well-being and reduces hospital visits. *The Permanente Journal, 22*. https://doi.org/10.7812/tpp/17-079.

Lindblad, M. R., Manturuk, K. R., & Quercia, R. G. (2013). Sense of community and informal social control among lower income households: The role of homeownership and collective efficacy in reducing subjective neighborhood crime and disorder. *American Journal of Community Psychology, 51*(1), 123–139. https://doi.org/10.1007/s10464-012-9507-9.

Loiseau, M., & Bonvalet, C. (2005). L'impact de la loi de 1948 sur les trajectoires résidentielles en Île-de-France [The impact of the 1948 Housing Law on residential trajectories in the Paris region]. *Population, 60*(3), 351–366. https://doi.org/10.3917/popu.503.0351.

McCabe, B. J. (2018). Why buy a home? Race, ethnicity, and homeownership preferences in the United States. *Sociology of Race and Ethnicity, 4*(4), 452–472. https://doi.org/10.1177/2332649217753648.

McKean, C. (2004). *1770s to 1830s – Buildings and cityscape: Tenements*. https://www.theglasgowstory.com/story/?id=TGSDF10.

Mee, M. (2018, 30 August). *New social ecosystems germinating as old orders collapse: Barry Wilson interviews Margaret Mee* [Interview]. London;

Mortgage Finance Gazette. (2018, 14 February). Shared ownership: Perceived risks and potential rewards for lenders. https://www.mortgagefinancegazette.com/features/shared-ownership-perceived-risks-potential-rewards-lenders-14-02-2018.

Numbeo. (2020). *Property Prices Index by city 2020*. https://www.numbeo.com/property-investment/rankings.jsp.

Raghupathy, S. (2015, 30 October). *Green affordable houses – Indian experience*. World GBC Congress 2015, Hong Kong. https://worldgbc2015.hkgbc.org.hk/upload/presentationfiles/Day2/PlenarySession/Panel2/Green-Affordable-Houses-Indian-Experience_Mr-Sundaresan-RAGHUPATHY.pdf.

ROC USA. (2021). *ROC USA resident owned communities*. https://rocusa.org/about-roc-usa.

Singapore, HDB. (2021). *Public housing – A Singapore icon*. https://www.hdb.gov.sg/about-us/our-role/public-housing-a-singapore-icon.

Tilly, C. (2006). The economic environment of housing: Income inequality and insecurity. In R.G. Bratt, M.E. Stone, and C. Hartman (Eds.), *The economic environment of housing: Income inequality and insecurity* (pp. 20–37). Temple University Press.

UDRI. (2016) *Reinventing Dharavi: An ideas competition*. Urban Design Research Institute, Mumbai. http://www.udri.org/projects/reinventing-dharavi-ideas-competition.

UN, Agenda 2030. (2015). *Transforming our world: The 2030 Agenda for Sustainable Development*. https://sustainabledevelopment.un.org/content/documents/21252030%20Agenda%20for%20Sustainable%20Development%20web.pdf.

UN-Habitat. (2004). The challenge of slums: Global report on human settlements *Management of Environmental Quality, 15*(3), 337–338. https://doi.org/10.1108/meq.2004.15.3.337.3.

Wang, Y. P., Wang, Y., & Wu, J. (2009). Urbanization and informal development in China: Urban villages in Shenzhen. *International Journal of Urban and Regional Research, 33*(4), 957–973.

Wang, D. W. D. (2013). Continuity and change in the urban villages of shenzhen. *International Journal of China Studies, 4*(2), 233-VI. http://eproxy.lib.hku.hk/login?url=https://www-proquest-com.eproxy.lib.hku.hk/scholarly-journals/continuity-change-urban-villages-shenzhen/docview/1449791462/se-2?accountid=14548.

Williams, C. (2019, 15 January). The story of Glasgow's oldest tenements *Glasgow Live*. https://www.glasgowlive.co.uk/news/history/look-glasgows-oldest-tenements-history-15044421.

Woetzel, J., Mischke, J., & Ram, S. (2014, 25 December). The world's housing crisis doesn't need a revolutionary solution. *Harvard Business Review*. https://hbr.org/2014/12/the-worlds-housing-crisis-doesnt-need-a-revolutionary-solution.

Wong, Y., & Tsang, W. (2017). *Housing policy reform to narrow wealth gap, urgent formation of land to improve people's livelihood*. Land and Housing Policy Research Series Issue. Our Hong Kong Foundation. https://www.ourhkfoundation.org.hk/sites/default/files/media/pdf/ohkf_land_and_housing_2017_en_17102017.pdf.

Yang, Y. (2016, 19 December). China house price growth slows as lending curbs take hold. *Financial Times*.

Conclusion: Towards a New Mindset
Meeting the Needs of the Coming Urban Revolution

The city and urban society have continually advanced and stepped backward over the preceding century. Little has fundamentally changed as a result – but it is about to. Spurred on by the exponential divergence of the coming Digital Decade, a new urban revolution is manifest, whereby disruption and radical change will be facilitated by access to better information, meaningful civic involvement in decision-making, and a critical understanding of the urgency for change. New approaches to property and land holding, and the processes of conceiving, funding and managing development must change completely wherein the benefits of the commons can see a renaissance in a world of ever more limited resources. The Futureproof City will meet these challenges and will create meaningful progress in the lives of its inhabitants; however, all societies will need to adapt rapidly to a new mindset, rejecting long-accepted norms in the face of the unknown.

206 Conclusion: Towards a New Mindset

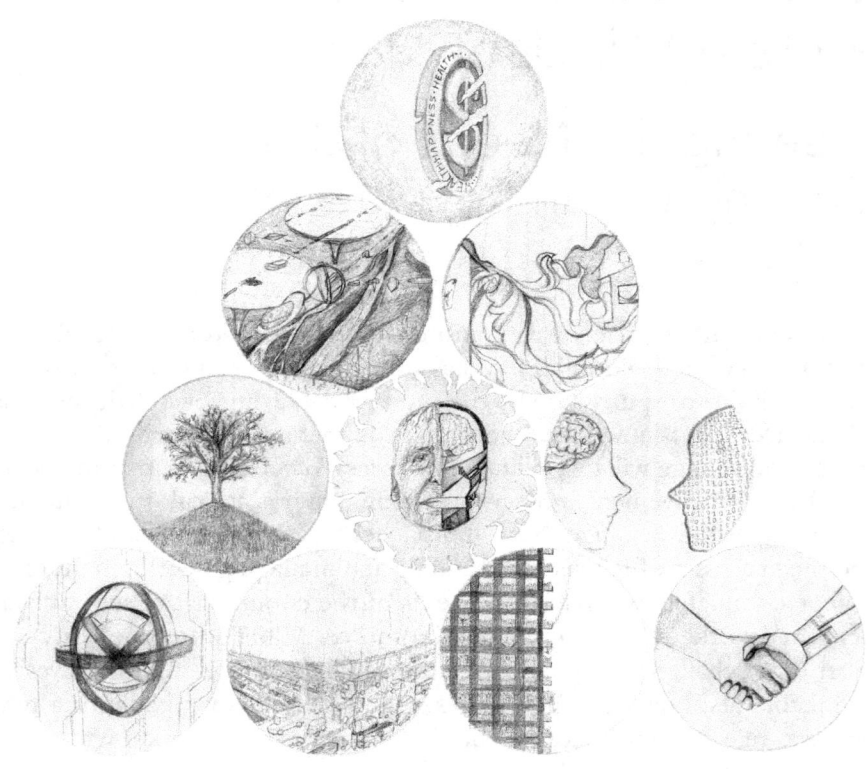

The Futureproof City

Ecumenopolis

Visionaries of literature and the silver screen have accurately predicted the future changes in our world, from robots to the mobile phone. Back in 1997, the special edition of the Star Wars film *Return of the Jedi* introduced the planet "Coruscant" to the masses, but it was in fact first mentioned in Timothy Zahn's 1991 novel *Heir to the Empire* as being an "ecumenopolis", or rather a "city occupying an entire planet". The word was invented in 1967 by the Greek city planner Constantinos Doxiadis to represent the idea that in the future, urban areas and megalopolises would eventually fuse, and there would be a single continuous worldwide city as a progression from the current unstoppable urbanisation and population growth trends. This concept had already been current in science fiction since Isaac Asimov imagined the planet Trantor in 1942 (Reiss, 1942). With a land surface of 194 million km² (Clarke, 2017) roughly 130% of the Earth's surface area (Asimov, 1951), Trantor was entirely enclosed in artificial domes. Development stretched deep underground and it was home to a population of 45 billion human inhabitants and a population density of 232 people per km² (600 per square mile), similar to the current population density of Germany or Connecticut, but well below that of Shanghai at 3800 per km² (Textor, 2020). The city's population was devoted almost entirely to either administration or maintenance of the planet itself, including energy provided by "heatsinks" (geothermal core taps) and production of food via underground farming and yeasts, produced entirely with care provided by robots called tik-toks, whilst nearby planets supplied food which the world-city could not grow for itself.

Doxiadis also created a scenario based on the traditions and trends of urban development of his time, predicting at first a European "eperopolis" (continent city) which would be based on the area between London, Paris, the Rhine-Ruhr region, and Amsterdam. With today's Earth heading towards 11 billion people by the end of the century, adding 50% to the existing population, will Earth be covered by endless emergent development and who will own all these resources and the land that they are built on? Can highly contained metropolitan densities preclude cities in developing countries from sprawling into one great eperopolis, as that presaged by Doxiadis or perhaps the vision of Azimov will prove amazingly prescient.

The Common Ownership

The short period of just a few hundred recent years has seen most of the world's land privatised, insomuch as it has been taken out of some form of collective ownership and management, and handed over to individuals. The idea that one man could possess all rights to one stretch of land to the exclusion of everybody else was outside the comprehension of most tribespeople or, indeed, of medieval peasants.

Land reform started slowly, in Britain, about 500 years ago, with the "enclosure" of agricultural lands – the subdivision and fencing of common land into individual plots which were allocated to those people "deemed to have rights to the land enclosed". The king, or local lord, might have claimed ownership of an estate in one sense of the word, but until enclosure, the peasant enjoyed all sorts of so-called "usufructuary" rights which enabled him or her to graze livestock, cut wood or peat, draw water, or grow crops on various plots of land at specific times of the year (Fairlie, 2009).

The idea of divine rights of land ownership, "god given" to a human representative on Earth, became all-pervasive following the invasion of England by the Duke of Normandy in 1066, having been first introduced by the Romans for their deified emperors, from whom all land in the Empire was held. In 1795, the US and Spain signed the Treaty of San Lorenzo, carving up much of the North American continent between them. What followed was a century of catastrophes for the indigenous populations globally as their land was taken from them piece by piece. In less than 100 years, with the Dawes Act of 1887 effectively abolishing tribal self-governance and forcing assimilation, there was very little left to Native Americans, whilst the expansion of the British Empire in the nineteenth century saw its version of the feudal land system imposed on about a quarter of the world. The subsequent period of New Imperialism between the 1880s and the start of the First World War saw the scramble for Africa as global politics and struggles for power and resources played out with the European nations of Britain, France, Germany, Portugal, Belgium, and Italy adding almost 23 million km² (9 million square miles) to their self-proclaimed possessions; a further fifth of the world's land (*New World Encyclopedia*, 2019). Africa, the Americas, much of Asia, Australasia, and remote islands everywhere were all carved up and claimed by outside authorities drawing arbitrary lines across swathes of land, abusing and displacing the inhabitants in the process. The relationship between humans and land begins with a fundamental claim by people or countries to "own" land. On that basis, the world divides into two simple categories: those countries that allow citizens to own the land to which they hold legal title; and those that grant only tenancies, permitting the state to claim a total prior right to the use of all land within its borders.

In Imperial China, communal and customary rights were, as in Britain, invested in landlords, nobles, religious institutions, and village communities, whereby landlords traditionally paid taxes in return for debatable "land-owning" rights, known as subsoil (田骨) rights, but did not have the right to actively use the land which was rented by the peasantry for agricultural purposes, the so-called topsoil (田皮) rights. The socialist revolution saw dramatic changes in ownership and control over land in China. Regarding rural land, these changes began with the establishment of the Higher Agricultural Production Cooperatives in 1956; thereafter, rural private land ownership was effectively abolished through land reform, which left land in the hands of the state or the collective. In the cities, whist residential property was initially left untouched, policies chipped away at the rights of landowners until private ownership existed in name only. Since 1982, state ownership of urban land has been considered a pillar of Chinese socialism (Clarke, 2017).

The Grab for Land

Communal farming of open land, which dominated the central counties of England throughout the late medieval period and continued into the late modern period, is a classic common property system that can still be seen in many parts of the world because it affords large economies of scale to small farmers. However, as England progressed towards modernity, communal land use came under attack from the wealthy gentry who wanted to privatise its use and used their power and influence to benefit directly from this. English history is a succession of rural uprisings and depopulated villages as the peasantry responded with a series of ill-fated revolts, starting with the 1381 Peasants' Revolt and Jack Cade's Rebellion of 1450, in which land rights were a prominent demand of the rebels (Collings, 1906). By the time of Kett's Rebellion of 1549, enclosure was the main issue, as it was in the Captain Pouch revolts of 1604–1607 (Tate, 1967). Between 1760 and 1870, about 7 million acres (about one-sixth of the area of England) were changed, by some 4,000 Acts of Parliament, from common land to enclosed land, whereby the beneficiaries were frequently the very Members of Parliament enacting the legislation (Slater, 1913). The people not only had their customary and legal access to lands snatched away from them, but also the very basis of their livelihoods. The Return of Owners of Land, 1873 census, or "Modern Doomsday" as it is known, exposed the inequity of land ownership in Victorian Britain: all land in the then United Kingdom of Britain and Ireland was "owned" by just 4.5% of the population (Bateman, 1883; Lindert, 1986). Most land was by then the property of a very small network of aristocratic families, most of which had dual links to the House of Commons and the House of Lords. Those who owned everything also had political control over everything (Rubinstein, 1981; Krein, 2013; Brown, 2015).

Britain set out, more or less deliberately, to become a highly urbanised economy with a large urban proletariat dispossessed from the countryside. It was characterised by highly concentrated landownership, including farms that were far larger than in any other country in Europe. Industrialisation and urbanisation tripled the population of cities in just 50 years between 1851 and 1901. At the same time, the rural population declined by 1.4 million people, whilst the total population of England and Wales rose by 14.5 million (Fairlie, 2009). By 1935, the rural population was spread remarkably thinly, with one worker for every 12 hectares in the UK compared with one for every 3.4 hectares across Europe (Warriner, 1939). Enclosure of the commons and the privatisation of land use, which was more advanced in the UK than anywhere else in Europe, played a key role in Britain's urbanisation at the time and was consciously seen as a main driver of transformation. The aristocratic families and traditional landed gentry, having withheld the longstanding common land usage rights from the peasantry, were able to sell long leases given by the Crown for building development. Today just 36,000 people (0.06% of the population) have the rights to more than half of the rural land in England and Wales (*Country Life*, 2010).

As China rapidly industrialises and urbanises, it has also had to develop ways to marketise land use and raise money. It addressed this in urban areas in a similar way to Britain by selling long-term leases on urban land, known as land-use rights (LURs), for an upfront payment whereby the land will theoretically revert to the state at the end of the term. These rights are currently set at 70 years for residential land and 40 years for commercial property and are tradeable, subject to basic planning restrictions, and may be compensated if expropriated by the state before term. Initially, LURs were issued without any clarity on what would happen at the end of the leases until in 2017, when Premier Li Keqiang suggested Beijing will permit perpetual free renewals and that the government is in the process of drafting the relevant legislation (*Sina News*, 2017). Perpetual free renewals could mean that people who paid for a 70-year use right now find themselves with what could be otherwise simply called "private land ownership". Rural land is different from state-owned urban land and is ostensibly owned by village collectives set up in the 1950s during the Great Leap Forward. At the beginning of 2020, a newly revised Land Administration Law came into effect allowing "collective land for 'for-profit' construction in a rural area to be transferred to others or leased out by landowners" and "after obtaining the 'land-use right' for such land … the user can further transfer the right" (Zhang, 2020). This has effectively added rural land into the private ownership stockpile and into the hands of the few once again.

Disappearing Public Spaces

A total of just 1% of the world's population now owns over 50% of the world's wealth (Credit Suisse, 2017). In London, large swathes of the capital are owned by six "great estates" such as the Grosvenor Estate, which dates back to 1677. England's old aristocratic fiefdoms have now rebranded themselves as large corporate enterprises and are in competition with global players to gain further control of public space in cities. Appearing in London in the 1980s, privately owned public spaces (POPS) emerged providing spaces that are seemingly accessible to members of the public and have the look and feel of public land. First appearing in New York in 1961 where the city initiated the use of density bonuses and other mechanisms to actively engage the private sector in providing publicly accessible spaces, these large squares, parks and thoroughfares are actually owned and controlled by developers and their private backers, and their use has been spreading significantly beyond the US and the UK, now being found in Auckland, Hong Kong, Toronto, and Pretoria (Schmidt et al., 2011). Examples include the Queen Elizabeth Olympic Park, which is managed as a private site by the London Legacy Development Corporation, King's Cross Estate, one of the largest redevelopment projects in London which includes more than four acres of open and publicly accessible space, as well as Birmingham's canalside development Brindleyplace. As local governments look to make cost savings and relieve their management burden, they allocate such responsibilities to developers, but such sites are not subject to ordinary government bye-laws, but rather are governed by restrictions drawn up by the "landowner" and usually enforced by private security companies.

Private control over large open spaces in London is not in fact unusual. The new developments of the nineteenth century, including those of the "great estates", saw many areas effectively created as gated communities, sealed off from the general public and policed by private entities. It was subsequently only through long public struggles, waged to force open land and ensure that streets, squares, and parks were adopted by local government, that enabled the public to exert any measure of control. Under today's laws, public access to pseudo-public spaces remains at the discretion of landowners who are allowed to draw up their own rules for "acceptable behaviour" on their sites and alter them at will. They are not obliged to make these rules public and unless landowners choose to volunteer such information, the public have no way of knowing what regulations they are bound by or enjoy a legal right to, be it taking photos, having a picnic, or even simply sitting down and having a rest, without resulting in removal by security guards. Whilst often successfully increasing the total quantity of publicly accessible space, the benefits to government are in the reduced need for public space maintenance, whilst the quality of the resulting spaces has been called into question, as managers of POPS are often concerned more with ease of management and less with providing a public good. In Hong Kong, for example, which still retains land lease arrangements based on the British system, POPS do not even have to be open to the public. Areas such as shopping mall plazas and private gardens in residential developments are counted as recreation open space and contribute to the key figure of two square metres of open space provision per person required in the planning guidelines, even if the public cannot access them. Only just over a quarter of open space provision in private development is publicly accessible. Essentially public space has become privatised.

Community-Managed City Space

The adoption of gated residential communities in China's development boom has been a standard model. The system has its roots in the country's ancient, medieval cities, but the idea really took off with the advent of the centrally planned work units of the communist economic system in the 1950s. These compounds are generally open to pedestrian access, but many forbid cars of non-residents, whilst others even prevent passers-by from entering. However, a 2016 urban planning directive issued by the China's Ministry of Housing and Urban Rural Development declared that internal roads in private housing estates should "gradually open up" to the public, primarily in order to ease traffic congestion, whilst "no new gated communities can in principle be built in the future". The directive does not go as far as suggesting "knocking down the walls" of existing private compounds, but merely containing "general guidelines" whereby local governments would be required to cautiously draw up plans to implement this with public consultation; however, it does underline the essential conviction of public over private access.

How far should public access go? The British public remains well used to "rights of way", a term used to describe "the legal right, established by usage or grant, to pass along a specific route through grounds or property belonging to another". In Northern Europe and the US under "freedom to roam", the general public's right to access public or privately owned land for recreation and exercise may not be restricted to specific paths or trails. The public typically expect to be able to walk their dog on a golf course or hike through a woodland. However, one cannot quite anticipate being granted the same access to roam unfettered across leased land in China, such as an exclusive city golf course – the public don't perhaps even consider that such rights could exist. But why should unfettered access to land not be a common right and essential to the new urban populations? Why should terms of use and behaviour agreeable to a majority not be clearly established? Why should the common land resource be available to just the few? As the cities have swollen through urbanisation, what was once cheap, accessible land outside the city has now become hugely valuable urban open space, forming land banks that are held by large corporations or developers for future benefit.

The idea that land and its resources should be owned or held by individuals, families, or companies is a relatively modern idea. Land was traditionally seen the world over as a common asset for use by everyone. However, as populations have increased, the grab for land and its control has become a primary generator of wealth. Private land ownership, coupled with its inheritance over generations, has exacerbated inequality. Once again, the global wealth divide has reached staggering proportions and inevitably social stability is threatened, meaning that changing land ownership and management solutions are once again inevitable. In 1677, the London heiress Mary Davies married Sir Thomas Grosvenor, bringing with her the ownership of 500 acres of swampland, pasture, and orchard, but more importantly it was unencumbered from common use by a public then disenfranchised from their historical land use rights. This today is some of the most expensive real estate on the planet, where more than half of that land in London's Mayfair and Belgravia is still "owned" by Mary and Sir Thomas's descendants as Grosvenor Estate.

A Common Renaissance

Community ownership and land management models are becoming increasingly utilised globally, and are suggestive of a return to the direction of sharing in land assets and the wealth they can create through the benefits of "the commons". Facilitated by digital technology, blockchain, and the internet, such models can provide more affordable housing ownership, increased community use of facilities, and opportunities to shape specific services that respond to local aspirations and needs. Such concepts could be invaluable to developing populations, especially where the recording of land interests is piecemeal or non-existent, and populations are frequently vulnerable to land grabbing by both the state and other such powerful interests. The UN "Continuum of Land Rights" aims "to guide policies and strategies to improve equity in land tenure and land transactions, and to increase official recognition of different tenure types that provide various levels of security" (UN-Habitat, 2016). The focus of the Continuum is to provide an alternative approach to the individual titling of property being seen as the ultimate form of tenure security. It recognises that interests may be documented as well as undocumented, formal as well as informal, legal or extra-legal, individualised or grouped, and may include herdsman, residents of slums, or informal settlements (Barry & Augustinus, 2016).

Stakeholder involvement and the sense of ownership that delivers responsible, shared land management can also improve community cohesion where projects help to build a stronger sense of local identity, pride, confidence, achievement, and belonging. Partial ownership or "Mutual Home Ownership" is a developing form of shared ownership that enables groups of people to club together to buy or build homes that they might not otherwise be able to afford. In return for their investment into a legal "Society", members obtain equity and rights of use to one of the society homes. Investment can comprise both capital and a collective mortgage (Chatterton, 2015). Costs can be spread across a group in society, with more affluent stakeholders being able to hold more equity shares than the value of their home, making other homes in the scheme more affordable for households on modest incomes. When a stakeholder leaves, they can sell their share, releasing the capital. A number of iterations could be formed around shared equity models depending on the location and potentially scaled out for greater economies.

The key to the success of the "commons" is, like all business, rooted in good management. It is essential to ensure that the governance of any community assets is transparent and accountable to the stakeholders, and that those managing assets on behalf of the group are supported to fulfil their role successfully. Expanding the model of land banks and community land trusts could help democratise economies. Land speculation would give way to a positive and structured incentive to invest in transparently productive businesses, to which the cost of urban land would prove less of a hurdle. By capturing rising property values and surpluses, community land banks would pool investment assets which could be applied to local transition challenges. Lithos Road Housing Co-op, which includes 13 rental units and nine shared equity units in London, follows the example of tenant ownership co-ops in Sweden where the tenant-members build equity through their monthly payments. This mixture of rental and shared equity is how Mutual Home Ownership Societies are likely to function in big cities. Nigerian co-operative societies have provided similar housing loans and micro-financing to a substantial number of members, enabling the purchase of land and housing construction. However, construction methods in developing countries continue to prohibit affordability, whilst bureaucracy in terms of accessing finance to land and construction remains a constraint. More committed government initiatives, support, and dedicated information platforms could alleviate these issues (Azeez & Mogaji-Allison, 2017).

The developed world seems to have come full circle in the last 100 years and we are back where we started, with the capital and the land back in the hands of the few. Today's youth, even those from the educated and professional classes, are not only growing up with a diminished hope of ever owning their own property, but are also increasingly unable to afford to rent suitable accommodation in the places where they need to live and work. A radical and significant shift in the attitudes towards housing needs to take place if the UN Sustainable Development Goals are going to be met by 2030, but this appears to be very unlikely. The philanthropists of the nineteenth century made the creation of social housing to alleviate the difficulties of the urban working classes as the greatest means to improving the lives of others, but eventually nations and proletariats rose up, realising that such philanthropy was a mere band-aid to hide the deep sickness at the heart of imbalanced society. A similar point has been reached once again today, where there needs to be a significant change in mindset brought about by establishing completely new ways to think and act concerning equity and ownership.

The Singapore Ethos

The Singapore ethos seems to form around the three distinct cores of "vision", "partnership", and "community" in order to achieve a greater sense of joint ownership, product, and empowerment through development. Increasing the emphasis on community solutions is a key factor in ensuring that no single perspective dominates whilst addressing problems. The Singapore government recognises the complexity surrounding all these issues and the need for greater interdependency of systems in land development, including infrastructure, housing, transport, community governance, and ageing – what Elaine Tan calls "Multi-dimensional issues requiring multidimensional approaches" – and Singapore is increasingly moving towards mass co-operation, not just of the public and private sectors, but also in ensuring that academia, NGOs, and non-profit organisations are collaborators in creating holistic, comprehensive, integrated solutions and are not just consulted for their opinion (Tan, 2018).

Mindsets globally process change, collaboration, and ownership in different ways. European principles will not always translate to Africa, and

US concepts don't necessarily fit the situation in Asia, yet these foreign ideas and ideals have often been thrust upon such populations or alternatively jumped upon as seemingly better scenarios than those currently seen. "The social component is different in Asia" suggests Marta Pozo Gil, former Director and Sustainability Leader at MVRDV (Asia) (Wilson, 2018). In the Netherlands, participation and social support is the norm and society is primarily "civic minded"; conversely, China is more heavily reliant on family networks for social inclusion and taking care of each other. For instance, when it comes to design for older people, "it is important to go beyond the standard urban design principles, which in many cases are technical solutions, and focus on the societal relations and how they can be developed in a wider way." Step by step, architects, urban planners, and designers in general can come together to change people's mindsets through such work. In this sense, the whole process can become a model that can shape the mindset and behaviour of the users, and hopefully a wider society. "This has tremendous potential but also big responsibility" says Pozo Gil.

Seeking Cultural Identity

Finding the right cultural solutions will be increasingly important and there is no one-size-fits-all solution, despite an increasingly globalised world. Colonialism may have destroyed indigenous cultures, but the new colonist today appears to be globalisation. Consider jumping out of a plane somewhere across the world in the middle of the night – once the parachute lands and the sun comes up, is it possible to know where you are? Countries like the US and China have become so generic across their vast landscapes with utilitarian, concrete-frame and sheet-glass building forms, grid planning, and standardised highway construction. Soulless, rootless internationalisation is creeping into the most far-flung corners of the globe, fast eroding local cultural identity. But does this actually matter? Andrew Lee believes that Kuala Lumpur is losing its unique character and that this is a problem: "Fast-track development has led to standardised processes and cheaper construction methods (Wilson, 2019a)." Lee feels that the Petronas (twin) Towers, the iconic landmarks of both Kuala Lumpur and even Malaysia itself, have that key quality of relating to the local culture and generating a strong identity. The design was inspired by characteristics of Islamic architecture such as repetitive geometries and arabesques, with the simple geometric plan of two interlocking squares that create an eight-pointed star and represent the Islamic principles of "unity within unity, harmony, stability and rationality". By contrast, much of the current crop of high-rise buildings, both recently and soon to be completed, really could be built to look the same anywhere in the world. "It's a problem globally, cities are becoming identical", Lee says.

An inner-city area called Pudu, an old and charming, low-rise district in something of a state of decay, full of shophouses, eateries, and local character, including Kuala Lumpur's oldest bus station (Pudu Sentral) and one of its largest wet markets, provides affordable housing at the centre of the city, but appears ripe for urban regeneration. Indeed, the old Pudu Jail site is currently being wholly redeveloped with a mixed development, including a retail mall, entertainment hub, offices, hotel, and serviced apartments. But the intended new buildings are all in that bland, international, "anyplace", glass-tower style (*Straits Times*, 2017). The Jail itself was built by the British in stages between 1891 and 1895, but was demolished without perhaps having first taken time to study, consider, and debate its historic value to society as an integral part of the nation's history, and identify whether there was value of its preservation for future generations. Redevelopment could have been implemented through adaptive reuse, where the structure could have been maintained and only its function changed, whilst additional floor space could have been provided through additional building. Seemingly positive "regeneration" in Pudu may end up being complete "redevelopment", and the special character and unique heritage of this old district will be quickly lost in the grab for cheap land, whilst longstanding communities can no longer afford to remain there as gentrification takes hold. The economic potential that could be realised through heritage appreciation and tourism cannot be understated, a great example being the recently restored and developed Victoria Prison in Hong Kong, stunningly restored and augmented with premium-quality, modern additions designed by renowned architects OMA, and reimagining itself as "The Tai Kwun Centre for Heritage and Arts". Older structures need large inputs of capital to maintain their condition as well as to adapt them to modern-day building and safety codes. However, maintaining and adapting older buildings sustains an important cultural link with the past, as they are living history, often utilising materials and craftsmanship that can no longer be found in the modern era. The preservation of historic urban development is a one-way street. There is no chance to renovate or to save a cultural site once it is gone and we can never be certain what will be valued in the future. This reality highlights the importance of locating and saving structures of cultural significance, because once a piece of history is destroyed, it is lost forever.

Cultural heritage is a broad concept, made up of both the large and the small, the tangible and the intangible. It may be evidenced in building form, townscape fabric, or archaeological remains. It may be perceived through human practices – the food prepared, the clothes styled, the religions followed, or the skills learnt – and further preserved through artefacts, structures, books, pictures, photographs, and art, but especially oral tradition. Importantly, it provides essential variety in an increasingly standardised world, and for the majority of communities, exploring cultural heritage and preserving traditions for the next generation offers an automatic sense of unity and belonging within a group, and provides a variety of benefits that allow for a better understanding of previous generations and of the history from which people both originate and identify themselves.

Andrea Bruciati, Director of the UNESCO World Heritage Sites Villa d'Este and Villa Adriana located in the town of Tivoli, a short distance from Rome, feels people become really appreciative of the beneficial economic and civic opportunities afforded to them once "the" heritage becomes "their" heritage. He states that his goal for the ancient sites is to both harness the cultural quality of existing heritage and then further invigorate it to become the pulsating heart of the communities who live and work there. He is clear that the successful preservation and integration of cultural assets is strongly dependent on whole communities becoming valued stakeholders and taking pride, gratification, and feelings of stewardship in their uniqueness. In the past at Tivoli, he suggests that the heritage sites had been considered distinct from the town and its people, and were protected and conserved as separate entities in a conservative management style, needing to actually be defended from the destructive actions of the townsfolk themselves. However, by seeking to create a more symbiotic relationship, raising awareness of the value of the heritage sites to the townsfolk, combined with activating their potential for community use and management, they became intrinsically part of the people's positive identity about themselves and their town (Wilson, 2019).

As long ago as 1972, UNESCO established the World Heritage Committee at its Convention Concerning the Protection of the World Cultural and Natural Heritage (UNESCO, 1972), noting that it was increasingly threatened with destruction not only by the traditional causes of decay, but also by changing social and economic conditions aggravating the situation, resulting in formidable damage and destruction. Today there are 1,031 World Heritage Sites (802 cultural, 197 natural and 32 mixed properties) in 163 countries (UNESCO, 1992). Each of these sites is considered important to the international community; however, these specific sites do not protect the overall character, traditions, or identity of a region. The pace of change of those conditions identified in 1972 is now lightning-fast since the advent of the internet era and threatens them in new ways. It is essential that development approaches for the planet focus on diversity rather than homogeneity and localisation over standardisation. Despite widespread assumptions to the contrary, there is no prescribed path for the development of a society and no single model on which development strategies should be based. The Western model of development, conceived as a linear process involving largely economic factors, is often incompatible with the complex social, cultural, and political dimensions of societies pursuing different goals that reflect their own values (UNESCO, 2009a). The important role of culture in development is increasingly being acknowledged and it is to be hoped that the focus being placed on diversification by the UN will reinforce this promising environment. Yet the difficulties encountered to date in quantifying the contribution of culture have contributed to its seeming unimportance and marginalisation in national and international development strategies. In the face of this challenge, UNESCO developed Culture for Development Indicators (CDIS) as an advocacy and policy tool that assesses the multi-dimensional role of culture in development processes through facts and figures. The Indicators demonstrate through data how culture and development interact and enrich one another, assess the environment in place for sustaining and enhancing cultural assets and processes for development, and offer a global overview of national challenges and opportunities, informing cultural policies and development strategies to fully profit from culture's potential (UNESCO, 2009b). The CDIS has been conceived as a pragmatic and effective tool that guides the construction and analysis of indicators for policy purposes in low and middle-income countries. It offers an opportunity to strengthen the case for the inclusion of culture in development strategies and agendas as it provides an empirical demonstration of the contribution of culture to sustainable development, economic growth, and social progress. After all, many cities are being transformed and developed based on concepts with little scientific data collection or deep analysis, but rather on the look of a designer's overseas reference photographs or impressive artistic rendering.

Doing Things Differently

The Dutch have been world innovators in "changing mindset". There are more bicycles than residents in the Netherlands, and in cities like Amsterdam and The Hague, up to 70% of all journeys are made by bike. In the 1950s and 1960s, as car ownership rocketed, and much as in China today, roads became increasingly congested and cyclists were squeezed off the road. The jump in car numbers caused a huge rise in the number of deaths. In response to this, a social movement "Stop de Kindermoord" (Stop the Child Murder) arose, demanding safer cycling conditions for children. The oil crisis of the 1970s put further pressure on the Dutch government to restrict motor vehicles in its towns and cities, and to invest in improved cycling infrastructure and other forms of transport that would make Dutch streets safer, and towns and cities more people-friendly and liveable. Has the same collision point not been reached once again on a global scale? The power of social movements cannot be underestimated. Dutch urban planners smartly diverged from the car-centric road-building policies being pursued throughout the urbanising West and street signs accompanied by the words "Bike Street: Cars are guests" reinforces that those using pedal power have priority and cars (almost always) wait patiently, the idea being that "the bike is right". The development of "woonerf" (living yard), abundantly applied throughout the 1970s and 1980s and still prevalent today, legally and officially recognises and prioritises the traditional living functions of the street – walking, talking, and playing – over and above the traffic function, using the full width of the street space to walk and play. Traffic in a "woonerf" is restricted to "walking pace" at 15 km/h and parking is also restricted. Streets were adapted further with the work of Hans Monderman, who continued to "change mindset" with his pioneering of "Shared Space". Doing things differently implies extended effort, research, and detailed work to demonstrate that innovative plans can work; nevertheless, progress only comes by challenging the status quo. In China, there is a strong willingness to try new approaches rather than the resistance to change that is typical of Western culture; however, Pozo Gil states that "where policies, social behaviour and support systems are different, just copying or transferring overseas solutions can't work ... There need to be local solutions to local problems, but bringing in thinkers from different backgrounds is crucial to generate new perspectives and to view things through a different lens. Only then, can change truly come, it's the process that's important" (Wilson, 2018). Pozo Gil believes that there needs to be an understanding from all parties that any project or initiative will always need to be adapted. There are always local ingredients of lifestyle, needs, and aesthetics that are different, and even if you try to strictly follow an overseas example, there are codes, laws, systems, and guidelines that will adjust the project and localise it: "The process shapes the outcome." So development must address the identified needs of the people who will use it. Therefore, it's essential to engage all the stakeholders early on in the development process, including the urban neighbourhood, and not just carry out physical mapping alone. Success cannot be judged on the quality of the materials used, the way it looks, or compliance with technical guidelines or ratings. The programmes delivered must be "relevant" rather than the guesses or instincts of the designer, government, or officials; the project must function primarily for the end users. In the Netherlands, it's the "community" that are primarily the neighbourhood managers and not the "government", which fundamentally alters the end-use objectives of a project. "We must also be guided by density however, where there is more concentration, outcomes resonate more", suggests Pozo Gil.

Amid all these significant issues is the fact that streets traditionally acted as places of mixed-use function. A variety of events existing in the public realm beyond merely travelling, including trading, eating, playing, watching, resting, and chatting. Communities are built up via the interaction of people on the streets, giving cities a sense of vibrancy and place. The current means by which developing countries are adopting road orientated urban planning policy is rapidly creating large no-go areas for citizens. The road kerb defines an area of streets where pedestrians are not welcome and empowers motorists to behave autonomously. Cities are severed by wide roads with fast-moving traffic, with citizens hemmed in behind railings and barriers, and cordoned into crossing areas like livestock. Modern roads prohibit the flexible movement of pedestrians through the community and dominate the use of public space solely for vehicle travel. The traditional functions of streets are lost and the diversity of use and unique local context are replaced by standardised road engineering solutions across a country, resulting in soulless, carbon-copy, unsophisticated urban areas. These streets are part of the public realm, yet the majority of urban populations are excluded from the use of vast areas of cities, which are dedicated almost exclusively to the minority who own and use private vehicles.

Yet if the car is really going to have less influence on lives in future and urban streets in newly developing towns are really going to be dedicated to a variety of public transport uses rather than for private vehicles, ever more emerging solutions in urban transport need to be developed quickly that can suit different situations at the local scale. Road building has become the first tool of both new development planning and urban redevelopment. Lines have been plotted across acres of countryside, hills, and settlements. But other solutions already exist. The world's first integrated urban gondola and ever-expanding Metrocable system in Medellín, Colombia is a multi-line system that connects the city centre with outlying, less affluent areas on the hillsides. Opened in 2004, the gondola system has been credited with reducing poverty and violent crime (Cerdá et al., 2012). Mi Teleférico in La Paz, Bolivia has transported 50 million passengers in two years of operations and was so successful that the city is now planning to extend the system by 20 km. Caracas Metrocable, Venezuela, MIOCable in Cali, Colombia, Constantine Telepherique in Constantine, Algeria, and the Yenimahalle Teleferik gondola in Ankara, Turkey are all considered to be successful urban transport systems developed in the last decade. The potential to expand the hierarchy of such systems in much the same way as ski resorts, with chair lifts and moving walkways, to deal with narrow and dense urban environments both on even ground as well as on hilly sites remains little explored. The opportunities to utilise existing urban corridors between buildings and above street level offer new lateral urban transitions, effectively putting "trams in the air". In combination with emerging automated carrier units and aerial vehicles, urban cars as we know them could effectively disappear from urban cities. Studying photographs on 5th Avenue in New York at the turn of the twentieth century, it is impossible to see a car, dominated as it was by the congested sidewalks and endless streams of horses and carriages. However, by 1913, not a single horse or carriage can be seen. The car had gone into mass production with Henry Ford's Model T in 1908 and cars were no longer the preserve of the privileged. This transition occurred in just five years.

Measuring Diversity

It's fascinating today to see the multiplicity of things that can change all at the same time, together, in the same place – a moment of historic transformation. Technology and energy supply will soon further contribute to change the whole fabric of urbanity and the way in which people are going to live. As mobility and infrastructure re-invents itself, there will be massive transitions coming in terms of how the city may be experienced, including underground hypersonic transportation, urban air transportation, and new ride-sharing apps. Cities are moving forward at high speed and change is all around us. The built environment has a huge influence on how people act out their daily lives, even more so than the influence of other people. One important technology that will radically accelerate change in cities is Big Data analytics. With the ability to collect, organise, and rapidly analyse large amounts of data, it will be possible to obtain a much more accurate understanding of how people use the city and how they would like to use it, enabling better thinking and better solutions for communities at both the individual and collective levels. Sustainable technologies are commonplace and inexpensive, and will standardise rapidly. Creating and measuring raised thresholds for all buildings, neighbourhood developments, and decoration to meet increasing carbon-neutrality standards will soon be a basic requirement. Monitoring standards for building performance and urban public space in terms of heat gain, energy and water use, air quality, and health are urgently needed and must be introduced in order to learn how to continue to create better urban places to live. Nevertheless, Big Data comes with big challenges in order to create positive changes. Saskia Sassen highlights how people not contributing to economic data no longer seem to really exist and are excluded from planning and progress, and how this can be understood as a type of "expulsion" of people from professional livelihoods, from living space, and even from the very data of existence. People are either born lucky or not lucky (Sassen, 2014). Older people are a group that have all too often been categorised in the non-productive demographic, leading them to be "expelled", and more data should help to bring them back to the fore of citizenship. Nobody can escape the age trap; nobody gets lucky in an ageing population, not even the wealthy. Everyone can relate to the older members of their family and can understand that they themselves will be in the same position one day. The importance of building inclusive city spaces that don't marginalise older people will be increasingly normalised. Pozo Gil notes that: "In any change there will always be people who complain, because it requires people to stop doing things that are familiar and start doing things that are new. People need time to adjust. But humans are incredibly adaptable and very soon they will have forgotten how things were before; sometimes just very simple changes can make a huge difference for the better" (Wilson, 2018).

With little existing data and local experience to follow, the Chinese economic revolution has been built on the back of "copy and adapt" tactics, initially resulting in huge wastefulness and inefficiency, but now also leading to a new spirit of real-time trial and error in development and to rapid change in thinking and execution. Bold leadership and envisioning, coupled with a strong tendency towards regulation and adaption only after implementation, has seen China's development model demonstrate that change can be effected very rapidly. It is not linear, as in the West, but a far more "iterative" or circular process of repeated improvement. Every project is a pilot project, a first phase, to be improved upon by being a test bed for real-time learning. There is no time to plan too carefully or in too much detail, as the pace of change is too fast; spend a long thinking and the baseline will have changed and the market will have already moved on. According to Pozo Gil: "Speed is good, it promotes change and change is generally a good thing. What's more, good changes promote further better changes. However, speed definitely affects people, it puts them under pressure, makes them nervous and less reliable. The pressure of speed can lead to chaos and this to a breakdown in communication. It's then that the quality of expectations aren't delivered. Problems don't come from speed, problems come from poor communication" (Wilson, 2018). So high speed can lead to fast learning, but also to poor communication, and China has shown that this can be a problem for all developing economies.

Enforcing Change

We know that the climate emergency requires the inevitable move to renewable power sources. We know that information and communications technology (ICT) advances mean that behaviour patterns are rapidly shifting. We know that artificial intelligence (AI) and automation will erode traditional jobs and services at a time when the population is constantly increasing. We know that rising sea levels will lead to repeated and massive coastal flooding globally, with famine and refugee crises, and an overwhelming loss of productivity. We know these things are happening quickly, very quickly. We could and perhaps should be radically and urgently aligning our lifestyles and redesigning our cities based on these inevitabilities. But are we? The COVID-19 pandemic has proven that extensive and extremely rapid, galvanising change is possible given the necessary conviction and stimulus, and that populations are in fact both able and willing to accommodate significant change when necessary, whether that's change of work modes with staff working from home, closing down streets to create safer, more liveable places, or adopting new technologies to communicate and interact. It may be that history will show that the COVID-19 pandemic was the vital destabiliser and trigger that led to the moment when new politics, visions, and leadership could be employed, harnessing the long-understood solutions of balanced modes of production, social equity, and environmental understanding. If there is a return to the old normal and the business-as-usual model continues to prevail over the next decade, particularly in terms of how to plan and shape the next generation of cities, then there can be no future for most. The year 2020 may prove to be the start of the most rapid decade of transformation ever experienced. The EU finally started initiating new global standards with its European Green Deal landmark strategy that puts sustainable development as the policy driver to address climate change and environmental degradation through a decoupling of economic growth from resource use. A change in the US political situation should see a similarly profound and necessary adjustment to match and exceed the ambitions of the EU, where knowledge leadership again becomes valued. Meanwhile, growth in Environmental, Social, and Corporate Governance (ESG) financing pushes traditional investment choices to the wall and the values of global multi-nationals can plummet overnight. Once coveted fossil fuels begin being divested on an unprecedented scale and consumer uptake of new life modes can be anticipated to swing heavily following mass tipping points in energy, transport, and food production.

Since 1990, more than 1,500 climate-related lawsuits have been instigated across six continents in 37 countries, according to a 2020 report published by the London School of Economics' Grantham Research Institute on Climate

Change, and climate change litigation has been growing in importance as a way of either advancing or delaying effective action on the climate emergency (Setzer & Byrnes, 2020). Cases are increasingly being brought as more strategic ways to hold governments and companies to account for damaging climate impacts, and this kind of litigation against national governments and against fossil fuel companies may be expected to become unrelenting as plaintiffs become increasingly experienced in utilising the law. Indeed, also in 2020, the International Bar Association released a model for how to more effectively litigate in relation to climate change, outlining arguments and legal precedents that might assist future plaintiffs since the requirements for successful litigation vary significantly around the world and tactics need be adjusted according to experiences and precedent (International Bar Association, 2020). Environmental lawyers ClientEarth continue to win cases against the UK government over the country's illegal and harmful levels of air pollution (Judiciary UK, 2018), and the UK government's plans for a third runway at Heathrow Airport were put on hold after being ruled illegal in early 2020 by the Court of Appeal because ministers did not adequately take into account the government's commitments to tackle the climate crisis (Judiciary UK, 2020). The Heathrow case was the first major ruling based on the Paris Agreement and although it was later overturned in the Supreme Court, it could be expected to spur more global suits based on those obligations. In December 2020, the European Court of Justice ordered 33 European governments to respond to a landmark climate lawsuit lodged by six youth campaigners from Portugal who say that governments are moving too slowly to reduce the greenhouse gas emissions that are destabilising the climate. Meanwhile, in February 2021, the Paris Administrative Court ruled in favour of the plaintiffs in a landmark case acknowledging the responsibility of the French state for the climate crisis, and in so doing taking a crucial step towards obtaining a court order that will force the state to act (Tribunal Administratif de Paris, 2021). Over the months leading up to the Paris judgement, the highest courts in the Netherlands, Ireland, Switzerland, and Norway all had to deal with rights-based climate cases (Varvastian, 2020). The impact of the Strasbourg Court in particular could be profound, since it will set legal standards and the case crosses multiple international boundaries. Change has arrived.

Faster Than You Imagine

The twentieth century was about "command and control", but this century has already shifted to "suggest and select". The population has become hardwired to being instantly informed about all and any matter and can subsequently evaluate these through social media, ultimately mandating an action or product with transparent and real-time reaction. This is the future of urban governance and decision-making as citizens increasingly shape the civic process with a new focus on "Putting Wellness First" and collaborating over changes, becoming scientifically informed over equity, inclusivity, ageing, housing, and services rather than economics alone. As algorithms become more sophisticated and deep learning systems analyse ever-growing datasets, the Digital Decade has the capacity to enable humanity to do things much better. Market forecasts have assumed business-as-usual or traditional usage patterns, without anticipating shifts to be as fast or disruptive as they continue to be, where the acceleration of change is increasing exponentially. So change will be fast – faster than you imagine. The removal from urban centres first of the combustion engine and then of the private vehicle altogether will precede the arrival of automated transport and servicing on the back of faster, smarter information systems. Parking can be removed and this should mean safer streets along with less roadside pollution for pedestrians, cyclists, and micro-vehicles. Shared and autonomous vehicles will soon be part of an ecosystem of intelligent communications systems and built-fabric agents that act as personal data vendors. The information they use to select a route will be based on all the data they have about a customer's lifestyle preferences, contacts, and needs. Moving forward, every part of our cities will be alive, responsive, and evaluated. Adapted and reimagined roads should mean the creation of more interesting spaces that are less standardised, include more greenery, and feature fewer obstructions. This should mean that our city streets in the near future will not need traffic lights, road signs, kerbs, railings, or protective barriers. These changes are ready to happen, but our leaders are not prepared for them and nor do they have the regulatory mechanisms to adjust quickly enough to meet these changes. The planning and construction industries and their processes remain in the analogue age, but cannot remain so, and thus the "Futureproof City" is any city on the verge of a necessary urban revolution, one which will increasingly reject simplistic business-as-usual approaches to address complex and interrelated urban systems, adopting experimentation and iteration under a new "digi-civic" renaissance as a mandate for change. At its core are concepts of shared use, a resurrection of the commons, and new discourse on the nature of ownership itself, supported by the blockchain, as a means of rebalancing social equity and avoiding environmental catastrophe.

As Shai Agassi, founder of Better Place, states: "Every social transformation requires... the bravery of Churchill, the vision of JFK, the determination of Reagan, the rare ability to galvanise a country or the world to take the right step for a greater cause. We are standing on the verge of such an event" (Agassi & Zarur, 2008).

References

Agassi, S., & Zarur, A. (2008). *Transforming global transportation, fuel independence at country level as a business opportunity*. White Paper.
Asimov, I. (1951). *Foundation*. Gnome.
Azeez, T., & Mogaji-Allison, B. (2017). Constraints of affordable housing through cooperative societies in tertiary institutions in Lagos State, Nigeria. *Journal of Geography and Regional Planning, 10*(3), 39–46.
Barry, M., & Augustinus, C. (2016). *Framework for evaluating continuum of land rights scenarios*. https://unhabitat.org/sites/default/files/download-manager-files/Framework%20for%20Evaluating%20Continuum%20of%20Land%20Rights%20Scenarios_English_2016.pdf.
Bateman, J. (1883). *The Great Landowners of Great Britain and Ireland: A List of All Owners of Three Thousand Acres and Upwards, Worth Ł3, 000 a Year; Also, One Thousand Three Hundred Owners of Two Thousand Acres and Upwards, in England, Scotland, Ireland & Wales, Their Acreage, and Income from Land, Culled from the Modern Domesday Book; Also Their Colleges, Clubs, and Services. Corrected in the Vast Majority of Cases by the Owners Themselves*. Harrison & Sons.
Brown, D. (2015). New men of wealth and the purchase of land in Great Britain and Ireland, 1780 to 1879. *Agricultural History Review, 63*(2), 286–310.
Cerdá, M., Morenoff, J. D., Hansen, B. B., Tessari Hicks, K. J., Duque, L. F., Restrepo, A., & Diez-Roux, A. V. (2012). Reducing violence by transforming neighborhoods: A Natural experiment in Medellín, Colombia. *American Journal of Epidemiology, 175*(10), 1045–1053. https://doi.org/10.1093/aje/kwr428.
Chatterton, P. (2015). *Low impact living: A field guide to ecological, affordable community building*. Routledge.
Clarke, D. (2017, 16 May). Has China restored private land ownership? The implications of Beijing's new policy. *Foreign Affairs Magazine*. https://www.foreignaffairs.com/articles/china/2017-05-16/has-china-restored-private-land-ownership.
Collings, J. (1906). *Land reform: Occupying ownership, peasant proprietary, and rural education*. Longmans, Green, & Co.
Country Life. (2010, 16 November). Who really owns Britain? https://www.countrylife.co.uk/articles/who-really-owns-britain-20219.
Credit Suisse. (2017). *2017 Global Wealth Report*. https://www.credit-suisse.com/media/assets/corporate/docs/about-us/research/publications/global-wealth-report-2017-en.pdf.

Fairlie, S. (2009). A short history of enclosure in Britain. *The Land* https://www.academia.edu/6873388/A_Short_History_of_Enclosure_in_Britain. .

International Bar Association. (2020). *Model statute for proceedings challenging government failure to act on climate change.* https://www.ibanet.org/Climate-Change-Model-Statute.

Judiciary UK. (2018). *The Queen (on the application of ClientEarth) No.3 v. Secretary of State for Environment, Food and Rural Affairs, Secretary of State for Transport, Welsh Ministers and Mayor of London.* Royal Courts of Justice, Case No: CO/4922/2017. https://www.judiciary.uk/wp-content/uploads/2018/02/clientearth-no3-final-judgmentdocx.pdf.

Judiciary UK. (2020). *R. (on the application of Plan B Earth) and Secretary of State for Transport and (1)Heathrow Airport Ltd. (2) Arora Holdings Ltd. and WWF-UK* . Royal Courts of Justice. Case Nos: C1/2019/1053, C1/2019/1056 and C1/2019/1145. https://www.judiciary.uk/wp-content/uploads/2020/02/Heathrow-judgment-on-planning-issues-27-February-2020.pdf.

Krein, D. F. (2013). The great landowners in the House of Commons, 1833–85. *Parliamentary History, 32*(3), 460–476.

Lindert, P. H. (1986). Unequal English wealth since 1670. *Journal of Political Economy, 94*(6), 1127–1162.

New World Encyclopedia. (2019). Scramble for Africahttps://www.newworldencyclopedia.org/p/index.php?title=Scramble_for_Africa&oldid=1026554.

Reiss, M. (Ed.). (1942). *Black Friar of the flame* (Vol. 1). Love Romances Publishing Co., Inc.

Rubinstein, W. (1981). New men of wealth and the purchase of land in nineteenth-century Britain. *Past & Present, 92,* 125–147. http://www.jstor.org/stable/650752.

Sassen, S. (2014). *Expulsions: Brutality and complexity in the global economy.* Belknap Press of Harvard University Press.

Schmidt, S., Nemeth, J., & Botsford, E. (2011). The evolution of privately owned public spaces in New York City. *Urban Design International, 16*(4), 270–284. https://doi.org/10.1057/udi.2011.12.

Setzer, J., & Byrnes, R. (2020). *Global trends in climate change litigation: 2020 snapshot.* Grantham Research Institute on Climate Change and the Environment and Centre for Climate Change Economics and Policy.

Sina News. (2017, 15 March). Seventeen year leases renewable. http://finance.sina.com.cn/china/2017-03-15/doc-ifychhuq4651990.shtml.

Slater, G. (1913). *The Land: The report of the Land Enquiry Committee* (Vol. 2). Hodder & Stoughton.

Straits Times. (2017, 21 June). Swanky township coming up on Pudu Jail site. https://www.straitstimes.com/asia/se-asia/swanky-township-coming-up-on-pudu-jail-site.

Tan, S. H. E. (2018, 22 June 2018). *Designing for an age-enabled and inclusive community*. HKIUD Conference 2018 – Actions for Active Ageing – Urban Design for All, Hong Kong. https://www.hkiud.org/actions/aa/aa_180622.php

Tate, W. E. (1967). *The English village community and the enclosure movements*. Gollancz.

Textor, C. (2020, 12/11/2020). *Population density in Shanghai, China 2008–2018*. https://www.statista.com/statistics/1081928/china-population-density-in-shanghai.

Tribunal Administratif de Paris. (2021). N°1904967, 1904968, 1904972, 1904976/4–1. https://laffairedusiecle.net/wp-content/uploads/2021/02/20210203-Jugement-Affaire-du-Sie%CC%80cle.pdf.

UN-Habitat. (2016). *Framework for evaluating continuum of land rights scenarios*. https://unhabitat.org/framework-for-evaluating-continuum-of-land-rights-scenarios.

UNESCO. (1972). Convention Concerning the Protection of the World Cultural and Natural Heritage. https://www.refworld.org/docid/4042287a4.html.

UNESCO. (1992). *World Heritage List*. http://whc.unesco.org/en/list.

UNESCO. (2009a). *Investing in cultural diversity and intercultural dialogue*. http://unesdoc.unesco.org/images/0018/001852/185202e.pdf Connect to online resource.

UNESCO. (2009b). *Culture for Development Indicators (CDIS)*. https://en.unesco.org/creativity/activities/cdis.

Varvastian, S. (2020). *Children's climate change case at the European Court of Human Rights: What's at stake?* https://theconversation.com/childrens-climate-change-case-at-the-european-court-of-human-rights-whats-at-stake-151417. Warriner, D. (1939). Review: Economics of peasant farming. 102, 464–465. https://doi.org/10.2307/2980081.

Wilson, B. D. (2018). Mindset the key to changing cities: Barry Wilson interviews Marta Pozo. *The Magazine of Urbanisation*, 111, 84–91. http://www.ciudsrc.com/new_zazhi/fengmian/erlingyibajiushiqi/2018-11-15/136085.html.

Wilson, B. D. (2019a). Back to the future: Barry Wilson interviews Andrew Lee. *The Magazine of Urbanisation*, 113, 64–71. http://www.ciudsrc.com/new_zazhi/fengmian/yijiuwuliuqizazhi/2019-07-24/143871.html.

Wilson, B. D. (2019b). Community the heart of heritage: Barry Wilson interviews Andrea Bruciati. *The Magazine of Urbanisation*, 115, 52–59. http://www.ciudsrc.com/new_zazhi/fengmian/yijiuwuliuqizazhi/2019-07-24/143871.html.

Zhang, L. (2020, 20 February). *China: Revised Land Administration Law takes effect*. https://www.loc.gov/law/foreign-news/article/china-revised-land-administration-law-takes-effect.

Index

15 Minute City 44; *see also* Hidalgo, Anne
20's Plenty for Us 148; *see also* Transport Research Laboratory
2030 Agenda 6–7, 31, 40, 126, 129, 132; *see also* Habitat III
5G 32, 108–16, 155; *see also* Internet of Things (IoT)
9064 framework 89; *see also* care in the community

Accelerating National Low-Carbon City (Town) Pilots 42; *see also* China's New Urbanisation Plan 2014–2020
affordable housing 16, 185, 190, 192–4, 196–8; location 174, 193, 217; ownership 196, 213 *(see also* Mutual Home Ownership); provision 187, 189, 192–3, 197; quality 188, 190; safety 187; green housing 197 *(see also* Indian Green Building Council); and migrant housing 193–4
Agassi, Shai 226–7
age-friendly development 86–7, 93, 113
aged society 85–6; *see also* ageing society; super-aged society
ageing society, 85; *see also* aged society; super-aged society
ageing-actively 86, 91, 93, 95; *see also* Smart Ageing
ageing-friendly 87, 98, 157; *see also* Murata, Hiroyuki
ageing-in-place 86–7, 91, 95–7, 192, 199
air pollution 16, 23, 32, 144–6, 148, 155, 225; *see also* noise pollution
air quality 23, 41, 59, 75, 109, 132, 145, 149–50, 222
airborne particulate matter (APM) 32, 144
American Energy Innovation Act (2020) 126
Amsterdam 177, 207, 219
Ankara: Yenimahalle Teleferik 221; *see also* Cali MIOCable; Caracas Metrocable; Constantine Telepherique; La Paz Mi Teleférico; and Medellín Metrocable
Anthropocene 1–2
artificial intelligence (AI) 96, 104, 106–7, 109–10, 113, 115, 224
asthma 144
Athens 172
Atlanta (GA) 177
Auckland 44, 152, 211
augmented reality (AR) 104
Austin (TX) 193

automated aerial vehicles (AAVs) 156; *see also* autonomous vehicles (AVs)
automated parking 152, 157
automated people-movers 157, 221; *see also* smart transportation
autonomous vehicles (AVs) 108, 147, 155–6, 226; *see also* automated aerial vehicles (AAVs)
Azimov, Isaac 207

Bangkok 51
Barcelona 43, 152, 172; Eixample 43
barrier effect 104, 145
barrier-free access 93
batteries 126–33, 135, 200; blade battery 133; bromine-based batteries 128; flow batteries 128; fuel cells 126; LFP 128, 133; and Lithium-ion (Li-ion) 127–30, 133
battery storage 126–7, 129–31, 135
Beijing 56, 58, 89, 166, 175, 188, 196; Haidian district 108
Berlin 152, 173
Better Life Initiative 17
Bhutan 18; *see also* Gross National Happiness (GNH)
Big Data 25, 96, 107, 109, 178, 200, 223; analysis 43, 112, 222; sharing platforms 73; and data-sharing 105–6, 157
Big Spatial Data (BSD) 104; *see also* spatial data; and European Strategy for Data
Bilfritt Byliv 154
biocapacity 17; *see also* Ecological Footprint; Environmental Protection Index; Gini coefficient; Index of Economic Freedom; Life Satisfaction Index; and Ecological Footprint
biomass power 124; *see also* renewable energy
bioretention 56, 75
Birmingham: Brindleyplace 211; *see also* privately owned public spaces (POPS)
blockchain 226
Blumenthal, Richard 95, 111

Bogotá 44, 152
Bohmte 148; *see also* Shared Space
Boston 20, 53, 110, 152; Back Bay Fens 53; and Emerald Necklace 20, 53 (*see also* Olmsted, Frederick Law)
Brillianto 73; *see also* Green Infrastructure Partnership; Green Infrastructure Resource Library (GIRL); and Schüder, Ingo
Bruciati, Andrea 218; *see also* Tivoli, Villa Adriana; and Tivoli, Villa d'Este
Building Back Better 6
Building with Nature Standards 71; *see also* green and blue infrastructure, delivery
BYD 133; *see also* batteries; Contemporary Amperex Technology (CATL); electric vehicles (EVs); and Tesla

C40 Cities 31
Cali: MIOCable 221; *see also* Ankara Yenimahalle Teleferik; Caracas Metrocable; Constantine Telepherique; La Paz Mi Teleférico; and Medellín Metrocable
Captain Pouch revolts (1604–1607) 209
car-free zones 149
car-sharing 157; *see also* shared vehicles
Caracas: Metrocable 221; *see also* Ankara Yenimahalle Teleferik; Cali MIOCable; Constantine Telepherique; La Paz Mi Teleférico; and Medellín Metrocable
Cardiff 143
care in the community 86; *see also* 9064 framework
Changsha 190
chengzhongcun 193; *see also* Shenzhen, Huanggang village; and urban villages
China Ministry of Housing and Urban-Rural Development (MOHURD) 43
China National Development and Reform Commission (NDRC) 42–3, 110, 167

Index 233

China National Energy Administration 43, 124
China's New Urbanisation Plan (2014–2020) 42; *see also* Accelerating National Low-Carbon City (Town) Pilots
Chinese University of Hong Kong 93
Chongqing 58, 190
cisterns 56; *see also* Sustainable Urban Drainage Systems (SuDs)
City Prosperity Initiative 7, 154
City Sandbox 38
ClientEarth 225
Climate Bonds Initiative 31; *see also* Kidney, Sean
Coalition of Services of the Elderly (COSE) 95
Cohesion Fund 71; *see also* Trans-European Green Infrastructure Network (TEN-G)
Colau, Ada 43
Colbeck, Patrick 111
collective memory 171
collective ownership 208; *see also* community ownership; fractional ownership; Shared Ownership Schemes; community ownership; fractional ownership; Mutual Home Ownership; and ownership rights
Common Lens 39
common property system 209
commons 44, 131, 143, 196, 209–10, 213–14, 226
communal land 208–10, 213; *see also* shared land management
community co-operative energy generation, 124
community ownership 213; *see also* collective ownership; fractional ownership; Shared Ownership Schemes; fractional ownership; Mutual Home Ownership; ownership rights; shared home ownership; and resident-owned communities
community severance 145
complexity science 112

Conference of the Parties (COP23) 5
congestion charging 148–50; *see also* Healthy Streets
Constantine: Telepherique 221; *see also* Ankara: Yenimahalle Teleferik; Cali MIOCable; Caracas Metrocable; La Paz Mi Teleférico; and Medellín Metrocable
Contemporary Amperex Technology (CATL) 133; *see also* batteries; BYD; and Tesla
Contextualised Case Studies 39
continuing care retirement communities (CCRCs) 90
coronapistes 43; *see also* ephemeral terraces; and Hidalgo, Anne
council housing 186–7; *see also* l'habitat social
cultural heritage 217–18
culture 3, 18, 91, 124, 166, 169, 216, 219–20
Culture for Development Indicators (CDIS) 219
Cupertino (CA) 126
Cycling & Health Technology Industry R&D Center (CHC) 92

Dalian 58
Damascus 188
Dawes Act (1887) 208
density 172–3, 176, 192; *see also* high-density
Design with Nature 53; *see also* McHarg, Ian
Detroit 150
Dhaka 51, 173
Digital Brain 113
Digital Decade 98, 106–7, 113, 178, 226; *see also* European Strategy for Data
digital economy 3, 107–10, 112–13, 226
digitization index 3
disaster risk assessment 55; *see also* risk assessment
Doxiadis, Constantinos 207
Dresden 173
Dubai 36–7

ecological civilisation 166
Ecological Footprint 17; *see also* biocapacity; Environmental

Protection Index; Gini coefficient; Global Competitiveness Index; Global Peace Index; Human Development Index; Index of Economic Freedom; and Life Satisfaction Index
ecological planning approach 53
Edinburgh: 2050 City Vision 41
Ejby 148; *see also* Shared Space
elderly simulation suit 92; *see also* HKIUD Conference (2018) "Actions for Active Ageing - Urban Design for All"
electric micro-vehicles (MVs) 44, 151–2, 155–6, 226; *see also* autonomous vehicles (AVs)
electric vehicles (EVs) 128, 132–4, 144, 147; *see also* autonomous vehicles (AVs)
emissions: carbon 31, 43, 154; diesel 125, 132, 144; gas 41, 145, 225; regulations 132; targets 124; types 143; and vehicle 70, 76, 143–5, 149, 151
Emmen 148; *see also* Shared Space
Energy Innovation Action Plan (2016–2030) 43; *see also* Energy Technology Revolution Key Innovation Action Roadmap
energy storage 126–31, 133, 135, 169
Energy Technology Revolution Key Innovation Action Roadmap 43; *see also* China National Energy Administration; Energy Innovation Action Plan (2016–2030); and Energy Innovation Action Plan (2016–2030)
Environmental Protection Agency (EPA) 126; *see also* Green Power Partnership; and Green Infrastructure Modeling Toolkit
Environmental Protection Index 17; *see also* biocapacity; Ecological Footprint; Gini coefficient; Global Competitiveness Index; Global Peace Index; Index of Economic Freedom; biocapacity; and Ecological Footprint
Environmental, Social and Corporate Governance (ESG) 72, 224

ephemeral terraces 43; *see also* coronapistes; and Hidalgo, Anne
equitable development 195; *see also* Dharavi; and ownership rights
EU Green Infrastructure Strategy 71; *see also* Trans-European Green Infrastructure Network (TEN-G)
EU Strategy on Adaptation to Climate Change 78; *see also* European Green Deal
European Agricultural Fund for Rural Development (EAFRD) 71
European Court of Justice *see* Strasbourg Court
European Fisheries Fund (EFF) 71; *see also* Trans-European Green Infrastructure Network (TEN-G)
European Green Deal 6, 31, 224; *see also* EU Strategy on Adaptation to Climate Change
European Regional Development Fund (ERDF) 71; *see also* Trans-European Green Infrastructure Network (TEN-G)
European Social Fund (ESF) 71; *see also* Trans-European Green Infrastructure Network (TEN-G)
European Strategy for Data 106; *see also* Big Spatial Data (BSD); and Digital Decade

facial recognition 107–8
Fairlie, Simon, 55–6, 208, 210; *see also* Low-Impact Development (LID)
Farmer Review 3
Ford, Henry 222
Formative Position Studies 40
Fourth Industrial Revolution 1, 3, 37
fractional ownership 196; *see also* collective ownership; community ownership; Mutual Home Ownership; Shared Ownership Schemes; Mutual Home Ownership; ownership rights; and shared home ownership
Frankfurt 173
freedom to roam 212; *see also* rights of way
Fryslân 148; *see also* Shared Space

Future Smart Strategies 32; *see also* Wills, Ray
Future Streets 153; *see also* Street Moves

Gallup World Poll 18, 59
garden city 41, 185
gated residential communities 211–12
Genuine Progress Indicator 17; *see also* Human Development Index; and gross domestic product (GDP)
geothermal power 126
Gini coefficient 17; *see also* Environmental Protection Index; biocapacity; and Ecological Footprint
Glasgow 185–186; Anderston 186; and Gorbals 186
Global Competitiveness Index 17; *see also* Environmental Protection Index; and Ecological Footprint
Global Peace Index 17; *see also* Environmental Protection Index; and Ecological Footprint
Goldberg, Sharon 111
Grand Canal 56
Grantham Research Institute on Climate Change 224
Great Acceleration 2
Great Reset 1, 5–6
Greater Bay Area Urban Design Conference (2020) 60; *see also* Hong Kong Institute of Urban Design
green and blue infrastructure (GBI) 53, 68–81, 90, 96–8, 113, 152, 157; delivery 72; investment 68, 70, 72, 81; mainstreaming 71; planning 68, 70, 72, 76; resources, 68, 74, 76
Green Infrastructure Modeling Toolkit 71; *see also* Environmental Protection Agency (EPA)
Green Infrastructure Partnership 73; *see also* Brillianto; and Schüder, Ingo
Green Infrastructure Resource Library (GIRL) 73; *see also* Brillianto; and Schüder, Ingo
Green Power Partnership 125; *see also* Environmental Protection Agency (EPA); Renewable Energy Certificates (RECs); and solar power
green roofs 56; *see also* Sustainable Urban Drainage Systems (SuDs)
gross domestic product (GDP) 3, 15–18, 25, 31, 141, 166; *see also* Genuine Progress Indicator; Gross National Happiness (GNH); and System of National Accounts
Gross National Happiness (GNH) 17–18; *see also* Bhutan; gross domestic product (GDP); and Mansholt, Sicco
Grosvenor Estate 211, 213
Grosvenor, Thomas 213
Guangzhou 34, 51, 90, 175, 188, 190, 193
Guiyang 190
Guterres, António 6; *see also* New Global Deal; and New Social Contract

Habitat III 7; *see also* 2030 Agenda; New Urban Agenda; and Sustainable Development Goals (SDGs)
Habitation à Loyer Modéré (HLM) 186; *see also* social housing; l'habitat social
Hangzhou 56–7, 190
Haren 148; *see also* Shared Space
HDB Greenprint 42; *see also* Kampong Bugis; Marina South; Punggol Northshore; and Remaking Our Heartland
Healthy Cities Network 24
Healthy Streets 148; *see also* congestion charging
Heir to the Empire 207; *see also* Zhan, Timothy
HelpAge International 85–6, 95
heritage 54, 217–18
Hidalgo, Anne 43–4; *see also* 15 Minute City; coronapistes; and ephemeral terraces
hidden homeless 198; *see also* affordable housing; and Mee, Margaret
high-density 94, 144, 172, 174; *see also* density
Ho Chi Minh City 51

home ownership 188–91, 196–7; see also property ownership
home storage 129, 131, 133; see also energy storage
home zones 149; see also living streets; low-speed streets; Shared Space; and woonerf
Hong Kong 61, 114–16, 142–3, 173, 188–93, 211–12; Hong Kong International Airport 60; Hong Kong-Zhuhai-Macau Bridge (HZMB) 33–5; Lantau Tomorrow 60; Shenzhen Bay Crossing see Shenzhen Bay Bridge; and Tai Kwun Centre for Heritage and Arts 217
Hong Kong Institute of Urban Design 91; see also Greater Bay Area Urban Design Conference (2020); and HKIUD Conference (2018) "Actions for Active Ageing - Urban Design for All"
Hopewell Holdings 33; see also Wu, Gordon
Housing of the Working Classes Act (1890) 185
Howard, Ebenezer 185
Huawei 110, 113
hukou 88, 166, 168
Human Development Index 17; see also UN Human Development Report (UNHDR); Ecological Footprint; and Genuine Progress Indicator

Index of Economic Freedom 17; see also Environmental Protection Index; biocapacity; and Ecological Footprint
Indian Green Building Council (IGBC) 197; see also Ministry of Housing and Urban Poverty Alleviation (MOHUPA)
INSPIRE Directive 105; see also European Strategy for Data; and spatial data infrastructure (SDI)
intergenerational learning 95; see also age-friendly development; ageing-in-place; and Smart Ageing
International Agency for Research on Cancer (IARC) 111, 144; see also 5G; and International Commission on Non-Ionizing Radiation Protection (ICNIRP)
International Bar Association 225
International Commission on Non-Ionizing Radiation Protection (ICNIRP) 111–12; see also 5G; International Agency for Research on Cancer (IARC)
Internet of Things (IoT) 104; see also 5G
Ipswich 148; see also Shared Space

Jack Cade's Rebellion (1450) 209
Jacobs, Jane 187
Jakarta 51
Jobs, Steve 5

Kaplan, Anna 111
Kennedy, Robert 16
Kett's Rebellion (1549) 209
Khan, Sadiq 44; see also Streetspace
Kidney, Sean 31; see also Climate Bonds Initiative
Kolkata 51
Kuala Lumpur 173–4, 216–17; Klang Valley 174; and Pudu 217

l'habitat social 186; see also council housing; Habitation à Loyer Modéré (HLM); and social housing
La Paz: Mi Teleférico 221; see also Ankara Yenimahalle Teleferik; Cali MIOCable; Caracas Metrocable; Constantine Telepherique; and Medellín Metrocable
Lagos 177
Lam, Cheng Yuet-ngor - Carrie 190
land enclosure 21, 208–10
land ownership 21, 72, 81, 177, 195, 208–13; see also land rights; land-use rights (LURs); ownership rights; rights of way; UN Continuum of Land Rights; and usufructuary rights
land rights 168, 195, 209, 213; see also ownership rights; and shared land management
land trusts 195, 214; see also ownership rights; and shared land management

land-use rights (LURs) 210
Landscape Institute 22, 72
last mile problem 155, 157
Le Corbusier 186
Leipzig 173
Life Satisfaction Index 17; *see also* subjective well-being (SWB); biocapacity; and Ecological Footprint
LIFE+ 71; *see also* Trans-European Green Infrastructure Network (TEN-G)
liveable cities 22, 25, 41, 60, 147
living streets 149; *see also* home zones
Location-Based Services (LBS) 104; *see also* 5G; Big Spatial Data (BSD); and Internet of Things (IoT)
Loi Siegfried 185; *see also* social housing
London 21, 44, 85, 128, 143, 149, 175, 177, 185, 207, 213–14; Boundary Street 186 (*see also* council housing; and social housing); Exhibition Road 148 (*see also* Shared Space); Heathrow 225; Imperial College 128; King's Cross Estate 211; London School of Economics 224; Queen Elizabeth Olympic Park 211; Shard 152 (*see also* automated parking)
Loudon, John Claudius 21
Low-Impact Development (LID) 55–6, 58; *see also* Fairlie, Simon; and Sustainable Urban Drainage Systems (SuDs)
low-speed streets 149; *see also* road speeds; and home zones
lung cancer 23, 144; *see also* air pollution; and emissions, vehicle
Lutz, Robert 132–3
Lyon 172

Macau 33, 60
Manchester 143
Manila 51, 173, 188
Mansholt, Sicco 17; *see also* Gross National Happiness (GNH)
manufactured housing 176–7, 197
Maslow, Abraham 18, 113; *see also* Theory of Human Motivation

McHarg, Ian 53–4, 62; *see also Design with Nature*
Medellín: Metrocable 221; *see also* Ankara Yenimahalle Teleferik; Cali MIOCable; Caracas Metrocable; Constantine Telepherique; and La Paz Mi Teleférico
MedTech 87; *see also* Smart Ageing
Mee, Margaret 198–200
mega-agglomerations 167, 169; *see also* urban agglomerations
mega-cities 167–8, 175–6; *see also* urban agglomerations; and super-cities
metropolitan areas 8, 150, 174–6; *see also* mega-cities; and urban agglomerations
Mexico City 44, 152
micro-houses 177
micro-mobility 44, 157
micro-power 131
micro-production 169
migration 112, 124, 166, 168–72, 174–5, 192
Milan 44, 152
mini-grids 123, 126–7; *see also* off-grid power
Ministry of Housing and Urban Poverty Alleviation (MOHUPA) 197; *see also* Indian Green Building Council (IGBC)
mixed-income housing 193
mobile homes 177, 197
modular construction 153–4, 176–8; *see also* New York, 461 Dean
Monaco 172
Monderman, Hans 147, 220; *see also* road safety; and Shared Space
monitoring 7, 32, 96–7, 108–10, 115, 145, 222; *see also* 5G; spatial data; and spatial data infrastructure (SDI)
Mumbai 173, 188; Dharavi 194–5
Murata, Hiroyuki 87; *see also* Smart Ageing International Research Centre
Mutual Home Ownership 214; *see also* affordable housing, ownership; collective ownership; community ownership; fractional ownership; Shared Ownership Schemes; and shared home ownership

Nanchang 190
Nanjing 190
Nanning 190
National Health Service (NHS) 25
National Spatial Data Infrastructure (NSDI) 104–5; *see also* Big Data; and spatial data infrastructure (SDI)
New Economics Foundation 16–17
New Global Deal 6; *see also* Guterres, António
New Social Contract 6; *see also* Guterres, António
New Urban Agenda 7, 10, 60; *see also* Habitat III
New York 20, 111, 127, 172, 177, 187, 211, 222; 461 Dean 177 (*see also* modular construction); Brooklyn 20, 177; Central Park 20; and Prospect Park 20 (*see also* Olmsted, Frederick Law)
Newcastle 143
noise pollution 23, 104, 145; *see also* air pollution
Nuremberg 149

Oakland 153
off-grid power 123–5, 127; *see also* mini-grids
Office for Low Emission Vehicles (OLEV) 134; *see also* Road to Zero strategy; and vehicle charging infrastructure
Olmsted, Frederick Law 20, 53, 62; *see also* Boston, Back Bay Fens; Boston, Emerald Necklace; New York, Central Park; New York, Prospect Park; and Sustainable Urban Drainage Systems (SuDs)
Open Town Hall 37, 39
OPENspace 20, 22; *see also* Ward Thompson, Catharine
Organisation for Economic Co-operation and Development (OECD) 17, 85, 165, 189
Oslo 145, 154; *see also* Bilfritt Byliv; and parklet
Ostend 148; *see also* Shared Space

ownership rights 194–5; *see also* collective ownership; community ownership; fractional ownership; land rights; and land trusts
Oxford 149; *see also* Park and Ride

Paris 43–4, 152, 172–3, 177, 207, 225; The Baobab 177
Paris Administrative Court 225
Paris Climate Agreement 5, 126, 225
Park and Ride 149–50
parking 43, 134, 149–57, 196, 220, 226; costs 151; off-street 134, 150; on-street 149–52, 157; minimum requirements 151–2; *see also* automated parking
parklet 153–4
Peabody, George 185
Pearl River Delta 33, 60–1, 167
Peasants' Revolt (1381) 209
pedestrian and bicycle safety 143, 147–8; *see also* road accidents
pedestrianisation 147, 149
permeable surfaces 56; *see also* Sustainable Urban Drainage Systems (SuDs)
Perth 152; Hornsdale Power Reserve 127 (*see also* wind power); and Meadow Springs 130 (*see also* self supply power)
Philadelphia 20
Planning Playbook 37–8
Playbook Iteration 38
Port Sunlight 185
Portland 177
Pozo Gil, Marta 216, 220–1, 223
prefabricated housing 176; *see also* manufactured housing
Pretoria 211
privately owned public spaces (POPS) 211–12
property ownership 187–9; *see also* home ownership
public housing 189, 197; *see also* social housing; and council housing
public security management 108
public-private-not for profit partnerships (PPNFP) 198

Qingdao 58
Qiu, Baoxing 43, 57
Quality-Adjusted Life Year (QALY) 75
quality-of-life 166, 191

Raghupathy, Sundaresan 197
rail-less train 109
rain gardens 56; *see also* Sustainable Urban Drainage Systems (SuDs)
Rapid Pilots 37
Realm Trust 39
Reimer, Andrea 40–1
Remaking Our Heartland 42; *see also* HDB Greenprint
renewable energy 124–6, 128, 134–5, 169; *see also* biomass power; geothermal power; solar power; wind power
Renewable Energy Certificates (RECs) 126; *see also* Green Power Partnership
resident-owned communities 196; *see also* community ownership
ride-sharing 222; *see also* shared vehicles; and car sharing
right place development 52
rights of way 212; *see also* freedom to roam
risk assessment 37, 55, 60, 112; *see also* disaster risk assessment
road safety 141–2, 147; *see also* UN Global Road Safety Week; vehicle-safety technology; accidents 51, 53, 141–3, 145–6, 149 (*see also* pedestrian and bicycle safety); road design 142; speeds 143; controls 146; limits 44, 143, 148–9
Road to Zero strategy 134; *see also* Office for Low Emission Vehicles (OLEV)
Robertson, Gregor 40; *see also* Vancouver, World's Greenest City

Saltaire 185
Sampler, Jeffrey 36–9
San Francisco 153, 173
Sasaki, Hideo 61
Sassen, Saskia 175, 223
Schüder, Ingo 73; *see also* Green Infrastructure Partnership; and Green Infrastructure Resource Library (GIRL)
Schwartz, Martha 60
sea level rise 2, 59–62, 116, 224
Select Committee on Public Walks (1833) 20
self supply power 124–6, 129–30; *see also* mini-grids; off-grid power
Seoul 54–5, 57, 175; Cheonggyecheon 55 (*see also* green and blue infrastructure; and Sustainable Urban Drainage Systems)
Shanghai 58, 107, 133, 174–5, 188, 207
shared home ownership 196, 214–5; *see also* community ownership; fractional ownership; Mutual Home Ownership; and Shared Ownership Schemes
shared land management 196, 214; *see also* communal land; land rights; and land trusts
Shared Ownership Schemes 196; *see also* collective ownership; community ownership; fractional ownership; Mutual Home Ownership; and shared home ownership
Shared Space 148–9, 153, 220; *see also* Exhibition Road; home zones; and Monderman, Hans
shared transport 155, 200
shared vehicles 151, 154, 156; *see also* ride-sharing; and car-sharing
sharing economy 146, 155, 176
Shenzhen 58, 107–9, 113–16, 133, 175, 188, 190; Binhai New Area 61; Huanggang village 193–194 (*see also* chengzhongcun); Shenzhen International Airport 61; Shenzhen Bay Bridge 35 (*see also* Hong Kong, Shenzhen Bay Crossing); Shenzhen Zhongshan Link 33–34; and Shenzhen Metro 107
Shijiazhuang 190
Shoup, Donald 151
Singapore 41–2, 94–6, 105, 173, 189, 215; Kampong Bugis 42; Kampung

Admiralty 94; Marina South 42; and Punggol Northshore 42
Slaney Report (1833) 21
Smart Ageing 85, 87, 96; *see also* Murata, Hiroyuki
Smart Ageing International Research Centre 87; *see also* Murata, Hiroyuki
smart city 42, 103, 105, 109–16; smart agriculture 110; smart building 200; smart device 32, 107; smart transportation 110; and smart-grid 199
Smart Cushion 39
smog 23, 144
social housing 185, 190, 215; *see also* l'habitat social; and Loi Siegfried
social impact 96, 104, 198
solar integrated agriculture 124; *see also* Zhenfa New Energy
solar power 32, 123–30, 135, 169; *see also* Green Power Partnership; solar arrays 126; and solar panels; 123, 125–7, 129, 135
spatial data 104–5, 110, 146, 154; *see also* Big Spatial Data (BSD)
spatial data infrastructure (SDI) 104, 106; *see also* big data sharing platforms
sponge city 56–9, 61
sprawl 16, 87, 172–3, 178
Stockholm 153–4
Strasbourg Court 225
Street Moves 153; *see also* Future Streets
Streetspace 44; *see also* 15 Minute City; and Khan, Sadiq
Strutt, Joseph 21
subjective well-being (SWB) 17–19; *see also* Life Satisfaction Index
suburban 87, 150, 173–4, 186, 196
Sun City (AZ) 86, 90
super-aged society 85–6; *see also* aged society; and ageing society
super-cities 165, 171; *see also* mega-cities
surveillance systems 108
Sustainability Index 51
Sustainable Development Goals (SDGs) 6, 19, 187, 215; SDG Index and Dashboards 19; SDG Transformations 19; Sustainable Development Report 19
Sustainable Singapore Blueprint 41–2; *see also* HDB Greenprint; and Remaking Our Heartland
Sustainable Urban Drainage Systems (SuDs) 56, 58; *see also* Low-Impact Development (LID); and water-sensitive urban design (WSUD)
swales 56; *see also* Sustainable Urban Drainage Systems (SuDs)
System of National Accounts 15; *see also* gross domestic product (GDP)

Tan, Sze Hui - Elaine 215
Tehran 188
Tencent 107
tenements 185–186
Tesla 127, 129–31, 133–4; *see also* BYD; electric vehicles (EVs); and home storage
Thatcher, Margaret 187
The Hague 219
The National Accounts of Well-Being 16; *see also* gross domestic product (GDP); and New Economics Foundation
The Return of Owners of Land, census (1873) 209
The Villages (FL) 86, 193; *see also* age-friendly development
Theory of Human Motivation 18; *see also* Maslow, Abraham
Three Gorges Dam 51
Tianjin 58
timber building construction 177
Tivoli: Villa Adriana 218; and Villa d'Este 218; *see also* Bruciati, Andrea
Tokyo 87, 173, 175; Tama New Town 87
Toronto 211
Trans-European Green Infrastructure Network (TEN-G) 71; *see also* green and blue infrastructure (GBI); and EU Green Infrastructure Strategy
Transport Research Laboratory 148
tyre pressure monitoring systems (TPMS) 145

ultra-fine particles (UFPs) 144; *see also* air pollution
UN Continuum of Land Rights 213–14
UN Development Programme (UNDP) 124, 165–6
UN Educational, Scientific and Cultural Organization (UNESCO) 17, 218–19
UN Framework Convention on Climate Change (UNFCCC) 31
UN Global Road Safety Week 141; *see also* road safety
UN Human Development Report (UNHDR) 17; *see also* Human Development Index
UN Race to Zero 31
UN Safe System 141
UN- Committee of Experts on Global Geospatial Information Management (UN-GGIM) 105
UN-Habitat 7, 194, 214
urban agglomerations 165–72, 174–76, 178; *see also* mega-agglomerations; mega-cities; and metropolitan areas
Urban Concierge 38–9
urban villages 193–4; *see also* chengzhongcun
US Housing Act (1949) 186
usufructuary rights 208; *see also* land rights

Vancouver 40–41, 177; World's Greenest City 40; *see also* Robertson, Gregor
vehicle charging infrastructure 129, 131–2, 134, 146, 155; *see also* battery storage; and Office for Low Emission Vehicles (OLEV)
vehicle-safety technology 141, 143, 145; *see also* road safety
vehicles: sharing 154–5 (*see also* ride-sharing); and ownership 132–3, 142, 147, 151, 155, 219; *see also* autonomous vehicles (AVs); electric micro-vehicles (MVs); and electric vehicles (EVs)
Vienna 177
virtual reality (VR) 110
voice-interaction 107–8

Ward Thompson, Catharine 20, 22, 69–70, 75, 97; *see also* OPENspace
Warsaw 173
water harvesting 75; *see also* Sustainable Urban Drainage Systems (SuDs)
water-sensitive urban design (WSUD) 56; *see also* Sustainable Urban Drainage Systems (SuDs)
WHO Global Network for Age-Friendly Cities and Communities 86
WHO Healthy Cities Network 24
Wills, Ray 32–3; *see also* Future Smart Strategies
wind power 32, 103, 124–8, 135, 169; *see also* Perth, Hornsdale Power Reserve
woonerf 149, 220; *see also* home zones
World Bank 17, 171
World Green Building Council (WGBC) 40
World Happiness Report 18–19, 21, 166
World Health Organization (WHO) 17, 23–4, 85–6, 141, 144–5
World Sustainable Built Environment Conference (2017) 5; *see also* Hong Kong
Wu, Gordon 33; *see also* Hopewell Holdings
Wuhan 51, 190
Wyatt, Ben 130

Xi'an 190
Xiamen 190
Xixian New Area 58

Yangtze River 51, 57, 167
Yellow River 56
Yip, Stanley 42–3
Yu, Kongjian 61

Zhan, Timothy 207; *see also* Heir to the Empire
Zhenfa New Energy 124; *see also* renewable energy
Zhuzhou 109

For Product Safety Concerns and Information please contact our EU representative GPSR@taylorandfrancis.com
Taylor & Francis Verlag GmbH, Kaufingerstraße 24, 80331 München, Germany